# Making It Work

*Finding the Time
and Energy
for Your Career,
Marriage, Children,
and Self*

# VICTORIA HOUSTON

A FIRESIDE BOOK
PUBLISHED BY SIMON & SCHUSTER
NEW YORK  LONDON  TORONTO  SYDNEY  TOKYO  SINGAPORE

**Fireside**
Simon & Schuster Building
Rockefeller Center
1230 Avenue of the Americas
New York, New York 10020

First Fireside Edition 1991
Published by arrangement with Contemporary Books, Inc.
180 North Michigan, Chicago, IL 60601
FIRESIDE and colophon are registered trademarks
of Simon & Schuster Inc.
Manufactured in the United States of America

1 3 5 7 9 10 8 6 4 2 Pbk.

Library of Congress Cataloging in Publication Data

Houston, Victoria, date.
Making it work : finding the time and energy for your career,
marriage, children, and self / Victoria Houston.
p. cm.
Includes bibliographical references.
1. Dual-career families—United States.   2. Women in the
professions—United States—Life skills guides.   I. Title,
HQ536.H67 1991
306.87—dc20                                                    91-9156
                                                                    CIP
ISBN 0-671-73438-5 Pbk.

To my father and my grandfather,
who showed me daily that
the one you love can be
your best friend, too

# Contents

# Acknowledgments

As I conducted my interviews and wrote this book, I was inspired by the insights and experiences of the women and men who trusted me with the details of their most intimate struggles, joys, and fears. The stories of these pioneering people have changed my life, and I have done my best to see that they change yours. Their generosity in sharing their stories reflects their love and kindness toward each other and toward our changing world. To them I offer my deepest gratitude.

To my husband and "equal partner," Brant, I am deeply indebted for his help during the writing of this book—particularly for taking over all household responsibilities, including cooking, housecleaning, laundry, and child care—always with unflagging good humor. He is my inspiration.

I wish to thank my daughter, Nicole Melcher, and my father, Dr. John Kirsch, for providing me with some of my most valuable sources; and my good friends Judith Paine McBrien and Marlaine Selip for their insights and recommendations.

Dr. Sally H. Peterson deserves my special thanks, as her perceptive, supportive comments were the catalyst that led to this book. Stacy Prince, my editor, has brought extraordinary insight, guidance, and a sure feel for style and tone to the preparation of this manuscript. She is that rare editor who takes time with every detail, every nuance, and I know how fortunate I am to have had the opportunity to work with her. I want, too, to thank my agent, Martha Millard, for her enthusiastic support of this project from the very beginning—and all her faith in me, from the very first.

# Introduction

"Don't search for the answers. . . . Live the questions. . . .
[L]ive your way into the answer."

Rainer Maria Rilke

One day not long ago I was in Boston visiting with good friends, couples in their early thirties who have just had their first babies. One mother, who works full-time and is juggling her career with a marriage and raising a three-year-old, pulled me aside.

"Your kids are so successful," she said to me, referring to my two oldest children (my daughter, who graduated from Williams College in 1988, is teaching English in Japan, and my son just graduated from Brown). "How did you do it?"

"What?" I asked her, stunned. "Wait a minute. I don't know if my kids are successful."

"Of course they are," she said. "They made top grades all through high school and got into two of the most prestigious colleges in the country."

"That isn't success," I said. "I will know if I have raised my children successfully when I see them living balanced, full lives—happy with what they choose to do, happy with how they resolve their problems in their work, confident and secure with the people they love. When my kids are able to feel good about

1

how they balance their adult lives, then I will have succeeded as a parent. And they aren't there yet.

"Right now what they have is the *opportunity* to make their own choices. I will feel good when I see that they are strong and resourceful no matter what good and bad things happen, whatever they choose to do or be."

As I spoke, I realized how often we think of success in terms of definite things—the right school, the big raise, the elaborate wedding, the promotion to senior vice president. Maybe I was doing it myself when I spoke of "succeeding" as a parent. But life is what happens before and after each of those brief "markers." And success isn't the product; it's the process. Success is knowing that you have personal strength and skills to get through the hard times with your sense of self-worth and all your personal values intact.

Can you leave a job that isn't working out, yet protect your own sense of self-esteem and that of your former boss? Can you end a marriage without losing your own self-respect or damaging that of your partner? Can you live through a major life crisis with another person and come out on the other side still loving each other?

When I was doing the research for my last book, called *Loving a Younger Man*, I interviewed lots of women who had achieved this "success." It seems that women confident enough to risk loving a man society would not necessarily approve of were women who had their priorities in order, women confident of their own appeal and their own potential—in short, women who were happy with themselves and with their lives.

Time and again these women cited their partners as one of the main reasons for their satisfaction. At first I thought this was because the women had married sexy younger men, but the real reason went far beyond age. The wife would say, "Age isn't a problem for us. What makes him the right man for me is that he is the only man I've ever known who really treats me like an equal." Then the husband would say, "I never think of her as older. I'm just happy to be with a woman who knows what she wants and doesn't expect me to do it all."

Even more than their choice of mate, it seemed that the way

these women—and their partners—approached their lives was the key to their happiness. Later, when I began working on this book, I talked to women and men who were single, married, on the verge of divorce, or dedicated to staying single. And every time I interviewed a woman who seemed truly happy, I realized I was talking to a person who paid little attention to "the rules." Across the board the happy women I found had the ability to sort out their priorities, to deal with the crosscurrents of changing roles and changing expectations that keep hitting us over the head these days, and to approach all relationships as equal ones. They had minds open to all the possibilities of family and career and were willing to risk making revolutionary changes (at home, at work, or with the people they loved). In the process they invariably found themselves in partnerships that actually made working out the details of their complex lives easier.

In this book you'll meet a wide range of women* who have been able to put together the many pieces of the complex career-marriage-children-self puzzle in satisfying ways, albeit while constantly reevaluating their lives. Each has her own individual way of working things out. So while none of these women has "the answer," each of them provides reassuring proof that, if it is important to you, you *can* find a way to fit your puzzle pieces together.

---

*The names of these women and their families, as well as some details of their lives, have been changed to protect the privacy of all concerned.

# 1
# Tough Choices

These are amazing times. Opportunity is everywhere, choices abound, and never has it been more difficult to decide what to do, when, or with whom!

As exciting as all these options are, they are also scary. Along with options comes responsibility for our choices. And not only do we have to face the myriad decisions that come with these choices, but we have to do so in a world in which even the simplest things—going to the grocery store, setting up a business meeting, finding time to see a friend—are more complex than ever. Most perplexing of all is that many decisions necessitate secondary decisions; if you decide to work when your children are young, you must decide how your children will be looked after. Then you must decide the specifics—*which* day-care center, *which* baby-sitter. Choice begets decision begets choice. Complexity causes more complexity.

Many women I've spoken with feel they are living life on a moving escalator within a moving building. How can we make falling in love fit with everything else we want to do in life? What does it mean to be a woman today? What do we really want from our men? Should a woman work full-time throughout her life? Should a man take a great new job if it means his partner has to leave hers? Should a man accommodate a woman's career move if she's likely to take time off in a few years to be with her children?

Of course the ultimate challenge is trying to second-guess the future. "Will I always be single?" asks one woman. "Can I trust this marriage to last?" asks another. Is there anyone between eighteen and death who isn't confused?

It's tempting to avoid thinking about the meaning of recent societal changes, to feel overwhelmed by the sheer overload of choice. How does it help to know exactly how confused you are? Why not just stop worrying about it?

First, you aren't likely to "just stop worrying." Over half the women in America, married or single, lie awake at night trying to figure out how they'll make it if they end up on their own someday. I know because I did—and most of my friends tell me they do. They want to be career-oriented, but they want families too. Full-time mothers are envious of working moms, and vice versa. They want assurances about the future, and there aren't any.

Second, while worrying per se is not usually productive, making an effort to deal with your concerns is. Thinking over your options, rejecting one or two, and heading toward others is certainly better than staying confused. After all, it's unrealistic to expect to be able to "figure out" the situation entirely—no one has. But examining the issues can help you to plan, and to execute your plans as well. And it helps to know that you are not alone, as the women interviewed for this book will demonstrate.

For dynamic, smart women trying to have it all, just asking questions is a step in the right direction. Knowing what you don't know is the first step toward finding out who you are, what stage you are at, and where you think you want to go. We must look inside our own hearts and minds in order to examine from all sides what we think we want out of life. After all, you can't know what you want from another person unless you know what you want from yourself first.

Some questions you might ask yourself:

- What matters to you more—your career or your personal life or an even balance between the two? Should you consider changing the way things are now?
- Do you really want an equal partnership with your lover? Are you ready to give up the fantasy of being taken care of?
- If you are currently unattached, how will you find a person who will love you as an equal?
- If you are already married or involved with someone, do you know how to change the relationship so you can both get what you want?
- If you could choose, what kind of couple would you like to try to be?
- Would you prefer to be on your own rather than try to balance your life with someone else's?
- Are you willing to make changes in work, love, or parenting that will enable you to derive more satisfaction from your life?

Third, it's silly *not* to deal with choice and get used to dealing with it. It is my firm opinion that life is like a house of cards. None of us can be sure that our everyday lives will remain the same from this hour to the next. Think about all the events that derail your most careful plans—a car accident, a move, an unplanned pregnancy, the death of a parent or a child, or a restructuring of your company that eliminates your job.

I know very few people who don't feel that the moment they get one side of their lives in place another part comes crashing down. I have yet to meet a person who can honestly say he or she is living "happily ever after." That's why I think it is so important to be ready for whatever may happen.

But being ready isn't being depressed about what the future may hold or living in a constant state of anxiety. Being ready is having a plan.

If you have ever played cards, you'll know what I mean when I encourage you to think of life as a house of cards—not one that's likely to cave in on you but a house of cards you observe, manipulate, and move about as part of a game you play. A house of cards over which you have some control because when one card fails you, you have others in your hand.

When we can look at our choices in life as part of a game, something terrific happens: suddenly our night terrors vanish. Our knowledge of ourselves—our worries, needs, and strengths—becomes the source of our power over the future. Knowing we have multiple options for resolving any dilemma infuses us with confidence.

Not one of us, no matter how young or how old, how wealthy or how secure we are today, has a guarantee that life will be the same tomorrow. Nor is any of us too poor to be able to take charge of her life.

The three women whose stories follow were derailed when they least expected to be. While you may not identify with their experiences, don't be too quick to think it couldn't happen to you.

## Three Who Lost . . . and Won
### *Spring 1989*

It's 5:30 in the morning. Forty-year-old Kate bends over the graph paper spread across the drafting table set up in a tiny office in her Beverly Hills home. Warm ocean air flows through an open window as she moves a series of cutout images across the page with painstaking precision.

"Kate!"

She jumps at the unexpected sound of her husband's voice behind her.

"My God, Peter, don't scare me like that. Now, shh!" She puts her finger to her lips, motioning the forty-three-year-old man to be quiet. "You'll wake the kids. I've got to get this done— it has to be dropped at the printer's this morning."

"Kate, dammit, I wish you'd stop this work," says Peter.

Kate's shoulders slump in resignation as she sets her ruler down, ready for the usual argument. "And don't look at me that way," Peter continues, whispering loudly. "I don't understand what you think you're doing. I'm a successful broker—I'll make over $3 million this year, we've got this incredible house, you've got everything you want. What's this all about?" He raises his arms in exasperation. "All it does is take you away from me and the kids."

Kate opens her mouth to speak, then changes her mind, shrugs, and turns back to the drafting table. Peter looks at her and shakes his head. "I dunno," he says, "I'm making all this money, and I still can't get my wife to stay in bed with me . . ."

He marches back to their bedroom with heavy, thudding steps. Within a few seconds Kate hears more footsteps, these a light patter that rush up to the door to her office and stop.

"Gillie? Is that you?" Kate holds her ruler poised over the graph paper and looks up. "What's the matter? It's too early to get up. Go back to bed."

"Are you and Daddy fighting again?" Her four-year-old daughter's question causes another slump of Kate's shoulders.

"Honey, fighting is just how grown-ups work things out," says Kate. "Now go back to bed!" She listens for another patter of feet, then, with a heavy sigh, tries to concentrate again on the work in front of her.

Thousands of miles away, thirty-two-year-old Meredith stands at her kitchen window watching the sun rise over her small Minnesota farm. Frost steams off the newly turned soil in the vegetable garden. It's nearly 6:00 A.M. as she folds the last piece of laundry and pours two steaming cups of coffee.

Her husband, Ted, rushes in from the garden where he has just finished planting the broccoli, which Meredith will harvest and can. They met in high school and have been together since they were fifteen years old. He is a carpenter, supporting their family of seven on an annual income of $19,000. Though finances are always tight, they are able to manage with the fresh produce from their large garden and what Ted brings home from his fishing and hunting expeditions.

"I want you to drive up to Duluth with me this afternoon," says Ted as he lifts his coffee cup. "Let Mom watch the kids."

"Oh, Ted, I can't." Meredith smiles. "You know this is the

afternoon I help out at Dr. Kyle's. Mom's already watching the kids so I can work."

"Forget it—they're paying you peanuts anyway," says Ted. "Come with me and I'll show you this new job site that I'll be working on. Then we'll get some dinner."

"Ted, I can't," said Meredith. "They may pay me peanuts, but they also pay our health benefits. I can't not show up today. I just can't. Besides, it's the only way I'll have enough cash to enroll in another class next semester. If I lose five hours today, I won't have enough—"

"Forget school!" Ted slams his cup down so hard that the coffee sloshes onto the table. "Jeez—" Ted stands up and grabs his jacket—"when will it ever sink in that I do just fine for this family? We don't need you working."

He walks quickly to the door, then stops. "I don't think it's so great for the kids to sit at my mother's all day watching TV. Maybe you should just give up on this school thing." He leaves, slamming the door.

Meredith, her chin cupped in one hand, sits silently at the table, stirring her coffee slowly as tears creep down her cheeks. A rustling noise behind her brings a smile to her face again as the youngest of her five children, one-year-old Sam, toddles down the stairs, his white-blond curls a sunny halo around his sleepy face. "C'mere, cutie." Meredith sighs deeply as she sweeps him up onto her lap.

Far from the cool breezes of Minnesota, Erica sits on her Palo Alto patio, the balmy California sun warming her face. She is wearing khaki shorts and an old T-shirt. The breezes ruffle her short brown hair as she relaxes under the sun's soft glow. It's her first day off in a year. In fact, this is the day after she quit her job. She reaches for her portable phone and punches in a familiar number.

"Hello, Brian?" She can tell from the voice of the man she thinks she loves that his East Coast day is well under way if not already mildly frantic. "I did it. It's nine o'clock in the morning, and I'm sitting on my patio doing absolutely nothing." She twirls the phone cord and laughs softly.

"It feels great," she says, and then a sob catches in the back of her throat. It surprises her. She starts to weep, and that too surprises her, but the tears roll down. She tells Brian she'll call back later.

"Take it easy," he tells her. "You'll be okay. You'll be just fine."

Will she? Erica is thirty-one years old and has just resigned her position as the design director for a very successful computer software firm. Erica has seen her paycheck increase steadily to well over $100,000 a year. But as the money has increased, her time has disappeared. Two weeks ago she realized that the $2,000 she spent on a new windsurfing rig had been wasted—in six months she has gone board-sailing only once!

What really caused her to rethink her life was meeting thirty-three-year-old Brian. He was a man who charmed her from the moment they met at a seminar. Since he worked in the same field, they shared a common language. Erica couldn't get over how spontaneous Brian was, setting aside work to catch a midnight flight to Oregon, where he would spend an intensive three days windsurfing on the Gorge, or taking a whole Sunday to do nothing but read the papers, eat Chinese food, and see movies. Yet he excelled in his work. Unfortunately, Brian also lived on the opposite coast.

Over the past year they had managed to get together three times at industry conventions and to send each other frequent computer messages. Do we have a future together? wondered Erica. How could we? We haven't even had the time to really get to know one another.

The pressures at work had mounted as the company promoted Erica to chief design director in charge of overseeing all new software development plus outside acquisitions. The prestige was significant, the pressure physically and psychologically painful. In order to keep on top of the production schedule, she was working six-and-a-half days a week, ten to twelve hours a day.

She began to lose weight. Her temper was short. When staff was added to her department, she viewed every new designer not as a fresh set of ideas but as another person destined to rob her of time. Meanwhile, her bank account grew healthier and healthier, but she didn't even have an hour in which to squeeze in the purchase of a desperately needed new pair of shoes.

Whenever she thought of changing jobs, however, she thought of her parents. They had scrimped and saved so she could go to college and graduate school. Now they were so proud of her career and the marvelous income she had. Erica worried that news of her leaving her job might upset her parents. Then something happened that made her think of herself first for a change.

At Christmastime, when she went in for her annual gynecological checkup, Erica learned that she had an ovarian cyst that had to be removed. With it the surgeon prudently took her right ovary. During her six weeks of forced recovery time, Erica had time to reflect on her life, particularly whether or not she hoped to use her remaining ovary to try to have children someday. And she also had time, at last, to chat at length with Brian.

"I want more out of life than this," she heard herself say to him one night. "What can I do with money if I have no family to spend it on? How can I have a family if I have no time to find a man?"

They talked about their jobs. Brian's firm encouraged his autonomy, so he was able to work a four-day week at the office and two half-days at home. He traveled frequently, for work and for pleasure, and was building a reputation for innovative design, an achievement he attributed to having a flexible routine that allowed him plenty of time for creative thinking. Erica was envious.

"I have stature in this industry, too," she said. "Our company revenues were up $5 million last year because of two design projects I acquired for us. . . ." The more she talked about what she had accomplished, the more she thought about Brian's position. He made less money then she did, but he had his freedom, his ease, a personal life, and time to windsurf!

Then, one day, her computer screen scrolled up a provocative message from Brian: he wanted her to go to France with him. "I can't," Erica typed. "I have two designers in that week, and we're behind on our fall products. Sorry."

Brian called on the phone. "Erica," he said, "if you won't go to France with me, will you fly out here over the Memorial Day weekend? I'd like to drive you up to my folks' place on Lake Champlain. We'll windsurf, and you can meet a few people. But bring a wet suit—the water's still cold!"

Erica checked her calendar and heard herself begin to decline the invitation. Then she stopped. Her bank account contained over $50,000. Her hair was stringy. She was exhausted.

"Cancel my cancellation on France," she said. "I'm going. And I'll be there for Memorial Day too."

Then she hung up, typed a quick message to her supervisor, and called her secretary into her office. When she left that day, she was no longer on the payroll—she was on her own. Scared, but happy.

As she wept after talking to Brian, she realized the source of her tears: she was afraid she was going to disappoint her parents and their expectations of her. Finally she called them. She spoke slowly, and when she was finished her father said, "Erica, you've made so many good decisions over the last ten years, I'm sure you're doing the right thing. Don't hesitate to call if you need any help from us."

Erica put the phone down, stunned. If she'd known that would happen, she'd have quit six months earlier! But now she had to reshape her new life, and she didn't know where to begin. How would Brian fit in?

## *Fall 1989*

Kate finishes putting away the pots and pans before rushing off to pick up her two young daughters at the day-care center. Their lives have changed drastically since the stock market crash of 1987.

Her husband has lost everything, including his job. Even the money for their daughters' educations is gone. The Beverly Hills home has been sold, the vacation place at Lake Arrowhead is on the market. Kate is frustrated and disappointed, but not for the reasons you might imagine.

"Our real tragedy is that I've learned that Peter cannot, will not, share the emotional side of what's happened to us. He refuses to talk about it. All I know is, if you can't share the hard times, then why the hell are you married?"

Her eyes fill with tears as she tells me how very angry she is that her husband did not tell her about his financial misfortune until weeks after he knew that he was in trouble.

"How can you not tell the person you think you love about the most important, the most terrible, thing happening to you?" Kate lamented. "Why couldn't he let me help?"

She did help. When Peter finally broke the news of his bankruptcy, she was able to land a job as an art director for a West Hollywood design studio within a week. The salary was $60,000, with full benefits. As we talked, she was very proud of the benefit package that paid for all their health insurance, including marriage counseling for her and Peter. "I have always wanted to work—and I'd be working today even if all this had not occurred," said Kate. "Now the financial end matters more, but I've always felt that I wanted to work—needed to work—in order to be the whole person I was meant to be.

"I'm forty and moving forward," she said. "Maybe this is the best thing that could have happened. I'm not sure if our marriage will survive—Peter has to realize that we're in this together. Just because he made some mistakes, that doesn't mean our whole future is down the tubes. But unless he can acknowledge that his attitude has been wrong—that he has to listen to me, to work with me to change our life—I don't know if we can stay together.

"I can't tell you how many of my friends have been stunned by this. I think they thought that, just because we were worth forty or fifty million dollars one day, every day for the rest of our lives was set. Uh-huh. You never know . . .

"But this isn't the end of the world. We lost our money. So what? Maybe it's my turn for a change. I think life is pretty damn exciting right now. If only Peter will open up . . ."

Meredith has packed and moved. It was a long, hot, unhappy summer for her family. Money pressures, Ted's father's death in a car accident, the continuing battle over her work and classes took their toll: Ted had slipped steadily into severe alcoholism. One day he just didn't come home.

"The smartest thing I ever did was keep working and saving and taking one course at a time," said Meredith. "At first, when Ted left, I panicked. I couldn't imagine how I would be able to support myself and all five of these kids. My oldest is twelve, and little Sam is only a year old.

"Then I found out that my grades, which are excellent, and my low income qualified me to enroll full-time at the university and receive enough grants and loans to rent a four-bedroom town house for me and the kids. Suddenly things started to work out even though I hated to leave the farm.

"The school offers day care during my classes. The kids' school is right in the neighborhood, and I have relatives who live nearby, so we have some continuity in our lives.

"I can't tell you how great it feels to do well in my courses and know that I'm really accomplishing something. My plan is to get my doctorate and teach on the college level—already the word is that there will be plenty of jobs!"

Meanwhile Meredith is in touch with Ted, who is in a treatment program. The children are able to visit him regularly, and he is slowly getting his life together.

"I don't think Ted and I will ever live together again," said Meredith. "This was his second bout with alcoholism after being on the wagon for five years. I refuse to put up with it or put my kids through that kind of hell.

"The shame is we started out as best buddies. Then he got into this whole macho act: 'I'm the boss. I do it all.' But I've never expected him to provide everything for us. I had five babies because I wanted five babies—and I expected to help raise these kids in every way, financially and otherwise. But I want to be someone else besides a mother. Am I wrong to want so much? I don't think so. I look at my kids' happy faces today, and I know I'm right."

Erica moved in with Brian. At first it was fun, but then her anxiety over finding a new job began to gnaw at her. Meanwhile, piling both sets of possessions into tight living quarters forced Erica and Brian to do some hard thinking about their future.

A month after she left her job, Erica got some amusing news: the company had hired two people to replace her. Her feeling that she had been working too hard had not been unfounded. She had, indeed, been under enormous pressure. With that in mind, she decided that she would never again work so hard. Her natural enthusiasm for life returned, and she happily agreed to look for a new and larger apartment to share with Brian. They would take a year to live together before deciding whether they would marry.

Now that she had freed herself from worry over her parents' expectations of her, Erica was hesitant to commit to another person who might restrict her hopes for the future. She confronted Brian with her worry.

"I hope you know that I want to find a full-time position even if we decide to get married next year," she said.

"You'd better," said Brian. "It'll be tough to go sailing in Aruba together if we don't have two incomes."

"But I'm not sure what I'm going to do yet," said Erica.

"You'll figure it out," Brian replied blithely. "But I really think you should consider consulting rather than a salaried position—it'll give you more flexibility and possibly more money."

Erica liked his advice. She arranged to meet with several consultants in the field of computer hardware and software design to see how they had set up their businesses. Although she had considered changing careers completely, she decided against that when she felt the old anticipation and excitement rise while talking with the other consultants. Then she met a packager, a person who served as the intermediary between independent consultants and designers and the different software firms looking for their expertise on a project basis. Suddenly a plan fell into place as Erica recognized a career possibility that fit her talents and experience.

An hour after she had had lunch with the packager, she placed a call to her former employer. When she hung up, she had her first client. Not wasting a moment, she picked up her phone again and punched in another number. When the other party answered, she said, "Brian, what time are you planning to get home? The wind is up—I want to get in an hour of sailing."

Even before "trouble" started, Kate, Meredith, and Erica were not content with comfortable lives provided by husbands, easy routines governed by children, or burgeoning bank accounts resulting from long, hard hours at the office. Both Kate and Meredith felt a need early in their marriage to prepare themselves to earn a living, to become accomplished in their fields. For Kate it was the work itself: "I love to work: when I am in the middle of a project, even at five in the morning, I feel really alive. Maybe that's selfish, but that's me. I know I don't have to work for the money, but I do have to work for my soul." For Meredith it was more a question of doing her share, but she clearly enjoys the work as well. "I couldn't ask Ted to do it all. There were times when the money was so tight that I hated not being able to pitch in more. But I also know that, if I can get my degree and teach, I'll be a much happier person. I'm beat from doing so much, but I love it." Erica, who was working overtime, needed more balance in her life. She faced the fact that even a strict career path is not always the answer. She had to set aside what once seemed to be the perfect job—with status and excellent income—in order to find a better fit between her ambitions in her career and her desires as a woman who is in love and who may want to be a mother someday.

All three women are happier now. They are in control of their lives. They may regret the loss of a lovely home or of a prestigious title and salary, but what really counts for them is that they wake up each day eagerly anticipating the future, despite the fact that the future is uncertain.

"I don't know what will happen. We may get divorced," said Kate. "It all depends on whether or not Peter can be honest about what happened to us and what has to change. But whatever happens, I'm not afraid."

Meredith echoed her words: "I hope Ted recovers, but until then the kids and I are just fine. Their daddy's drinking had them so quiet and afraid when he was around the house—nobody's afraid anymore! Gosh, I'm glad I followed my instincts."

Erica's situation is unsettled as well. She may decide she doesn't want to marry Brian, or he may decide he doesn't want to marry her. But she feels so good about pulling back on her career that the changes she's made will doubtless make her happier in the long run, even if that long run is far different from what she had originally anticipated.

Regardless of their financial, marital, and career situations, each of the three women:

• recognizes the importance of love in her life, but insists on a relationship in which the parties see each other as equals.

• is discovering the rewards of keeping an open mind toward all the options available, searching for those that will work best for them, even if no one has tried them before. In order to be sure of her choices, each is taking time to test and examine every opportunity. If something doesn't work, these women don't despair—they take a different approach, confident a solution can be found.

• is experiencing a terrific burst of energy and excitement as her self-esteem soars and her confidence grows in her newfound independence.

These are women of courage and foresight—the kind of women many of us want to be, spirited players in the game of life and love. Yet it is easy to remain complacent, hesitant to rock the boat of familiarity. That's why I've pulled together some fascinating reasons to review your own ambitions—in your career and in your personal relationships.

## Eight Reasons Why You Should Feel Comfortable Making Tough Choices—and Settling Only for the Best—in the Game of Life and Love

### 1. Believe It or Not, the Statistics Are in Your Favor

• According to the U.S. Census Bureau, the male/female population in our country is undergoing a radical change as the number of marriageable men, who have been in short supply for the last twenty-five years, now exceeds the number of marriage-able women—and that number will continue to rise.

While there were 93 men for every 100 women in 1970, by 1990, there will be 108 men for every 100 women! Many social scientists see the increasing scarcity of women as a factor encouraging men to marry earlier and make stronger commitments to their marriages. Whether or not that might naturally occur is beside the point; the media will make sure that men know about the shortage of women. It may also encourage them to accept marriage *as women want it.*

• Today nearly one-third of all doctors and lawyers and business executives are women. Within those groups and other professions another major change is happening. *American Demographics* reported that women between the ages of twenty-one and twenty-nine are earning 83 percent of what a man earns for the same work (a whopping increase over the national average of 68 percent of a man's income earned by working women of all ages). Add to that the fact that women now make up almost half the total work force of America.

This means that even though women and men are not yet paid equally, that fact is rapidly changing as more and more women enter the top professions in America. Thus, not only is the woman's income increasingly more valuable to her and her family, but she is becoming more valued in the work force. No wonder she is finding more and more companies ready to help with child-care programs and other benefits such as job sharing and part-time work options. Employers must make it easier for her to stay employed while raising her family—or they will suffer.

• The U.S. Census Bureau has other exciting news. The median age for a first marriage (the age by which half the women who will ever marry have done so) has risen to 23.6 in 1987, up from 20.3 in 1947 to 1962.

Another significant plus for the woman who marries later are recent studies showing that the over-thirty bride has a much better chance of having a lasting marriage. And a final boost to feminine morale is an upswing in the number of women and men marrying for the first time after the age of forty. This means a

woman should feel comfortable about taking her time to find a
husband or to choose to have children (the greatest increase in
the number of new mothers is seen among those aged thirty to
thirty-nine).

## 2. The Happiest Women Are Those Who Try to Do It All

A recent *USA Today* survey of a total of 100,000 people showed
that the happiest women are those who combine a job, marriage,
and motherhood.

"The more roles women play, the more satisfied they are
with life overall and with their performances as spouse, parent,
or at work," said Ohio psychologist Helen Cleminshaw in the
article. She pointed out that women with "multiple commitments" are those most likely to seek out and get help quickly
when they need it, are in a position daily to interact with more
people, and, as a result, they get constant feedback and satisfaction in what they are doing.

A recent study by NBC, reported in *American Demographics*, showed that when asked to pick their ideal lifestyle, over 80
percent of the women questioned, aged eighteen to forty-nine,
chose "to combine working with homemaking."

However, the *USA Today* study also reported that women
doing "triple duty"—job, home, and children—tend to feel the
greatest stress, so they may be happy, but they need to find some
ways to avoid carrying too heavy a load. And what better way
than negotiating to share that load with a partner who wants it
all as much as you do.

## 3. Women Who Balance Their Ambitions May Be Our New National Leaders

Women aren't the only ones who feel that they should be allowed to pursue their work and careers simultaneously with
their roles as wives or mothers. Consider these words from
*Fortune* magazine: ". . . the rise of executive women promises to

give the United States a significant edge over its global rivals in the increasingly acute international economic competition of the late 1980's and the 1990's . . . this should greatly expand the nation's pool of talent and merit, the group from which it chooses its business, political and academic leaders. With a larger group to choose from, the nation seems destined to select better leaders."

## 4. Women Are Finding Unexpected Financial Advantages

Obviously, the career couple is in better shape financially than the couple in which only one partner works. But it turns out that just being married is an advantage: a recent study by two economists, Sanders D. Korenman and David Neumark, reported in *American Demographics*, showed that "married white men who live with their wives earn about 12 percent more than never-married white men and married black men earn about 20 percent more than never-married black men." Another positive note is their finding that "the probability of a promotion for a married man is 11 percentage points higher than for a single man."

However, I hasten to point out that most of these are not men in old-fashioned, traditional wife-at-home marriages. They can't be, for the simple reason that over half of all marriages today are now "dual-career couples." And by 1995 *nine out of ten couples will be dual-career families.*

So the great news is that the man is no longer expected to bear the entire financial burden of his family, even when children arrive. Already today, for example, 61 percent of married couples with children are also dual-career families.

## 5. Everyone Gains More Flexibility in Career Choices

If you both work, it's a lot easier for one of you to explore a career change, or just take a break, if the other is there with a regular paycheck. Already the increasing number of dual-career couples means that, when a man loses his job or chooses to make a career change, the chances are 50 percent or better that his wife will continue to bring home full-time earnings. That relieves exactly the kind of stress that has been known to shorten men's lives!

In a less direct way, having more women in the workplace continues to lessen the pressure on men, as economists are predicting that future economic recessions will be milder and briefer due to the increased numbers of wage earners in the work force.

## 6. An Equal Partnership Is Becoming a Popular Goal

A report in the *Wall Street Journal* on behavior patterns among the very youngest people entering the work force showed that both men and women are more dedicated than their predecessors to having full, rich lives outside their work—they are actively searching for a better balance between their work lives and their love lives. They are doing this in stages. First, they are seeking out positions with companies that offer more flexibility in work hours, child care, and other benefits.

At the same time, many are looking for an equal partnership in love and work and family life that may provide the answers to what they feel they value most highly today. What do they value? A nationwide survey by *Family Circle* magazine found that more than half those surveyed said the most important factor in personal happiness is a loving relationship with a partner.

That option was seconded by *American Demographics*, which focused its inquiry on baby boomers currently entering their forties. Of these couples, over 90 percent say marriage is the best lifestyle and two-thirds want an egalitarian marriage in which husband and wife work both *inside and outside the home*. What they mean—or think they mean—by the phrase "an egalitarian marriage" is what this book is about: what an equal partnership can be, how it can work, and why it makes people happy.

## 7. *What Works for Mom and Dad Can Work for the Kids, Too*

The decision of many women to delay marriage and childbearing has resulted in higher earnings and more savings available to support their families when they do choose to have children. This means more money is available to provide for the children, especially in the area of good child care.

Furthermore, the life of a child with two parents who both feel as though they are in control of their lives is a much better life than in a family stressed by money worries or emotional problems.

Last, setting the old traditions aside—and finding happiness while doing so—means that today's parents are providing their children with wonderful role models. No longer do young girls see mothers tethered to the house; nor do young boys see dads constantly burdened by all the bills generated by family life. Instead it's a manageable, expanding world in which the adults share the pleasures and the stresses of life—and the kids learn how to do it, too!

## 8. *The Media Are Making It Easier*

One of the easiest ways to monitor social change is to look at what is happening in the media today. What promises are being made by advertisers? What glossy images and tantalizing headlines are being used to lure buyers to new products? What television sit-coms are designed to appeal to the dual-career couple?

We need to look no further than the pages of popular women's magazines, where hundreds of products are promoted, to see what society thinks of women's new "split ambitions." The answer is succinctly—and beautifully—packaged:

"Smart is beautiful . . . the more accomplished you appear the more gorgeous you become. . . ." (ad for new clothing)

"He thinks it's fine for me to make more than he does. . . ." (ad for liquor)

"The Professionals . . . they're tough, not toys." (ad for copiers, though photo is of a beautiful working woman)

"The New Traditionalist . . . she loves to cook . . . she loves family dinners . . . she loves Christmas so much that she spends a whole week trimming the tree . . . she also loves her job—because it lets her contribute financially to the family structure." (ad for a magazine)

These ads serve an important purpose: they are a clear sign to the people who see them—men, women, and children—that society is accepting and encouraging new roles for everyone today. The same is true on television, where women, beautiful and not-so-beautiful, from "The Cosby Show" to "Roseanne," now deal with bosses, babies, *and* the financial facts of life.

"The very first thing I felt was relief," said one woman when asked by *Adweek* magazine how she saw this "new wave" of advertising. "I had reached the point of asking myself, 'What is wrong with me, and why am I always rushing around?' Putting myself in a group gave me a feeling of proud camaraderie. Then I could laugh. There's some comfort in numbers. I can have it all, and it's okay if I stumble along the way."

Rochelle Udell, associate editorial director of the ten Condé Nast magazines, which contain some of the most influential advertising reaching American women through *Self, Mademoiselle, Vogue,* and *Glamour,* said recently that she plans to redirect the kinds of articles appearing in those magazines because she believes women should quit complaining and take control of their lives.

"I think women's magazines need to move away from negative assessments. Women are regarded as victims in magazines—screwed by their father, screwed by their boss— . . . the starting premise is that there's something wrong with you. You're damaged goods. I think that can shift in my lifetime, and I'd like to be involved in it. The question is how to reframe your life so you have the opportunity to design it instead of bandaging it." Exactly.

And Udell can begin to "redirect" articles by assigning them to writers like Gwen Collins who took this vigorous stand on the subject of the infamous "mommy track" in a recent issue of *New York Woman*:

> I once believed in a future where women could have babies and keep their dearest career goals too. Now I live in a world where you can't have it all. I'm ready to make concessions. Maybe you can't be secretary of state and breast-feed. But I'm not going to throw in the towel so that the boss can select from a growing pool of mommy-serfs and workaholic zombies.

## Figuring Out What You Want

If you're like most human beings, you want changes, not just year to year, but sometimes day to day. And you've probably found at one time or another that what you wanted wasn't always what made you happy. For these reasons it's usually easier to look at "what you want" in broad terms (I want to live in the city) rather than specific terms (I want to be president of I'm Perfect Enterprises). Doing so enables you to revise your goals easily as you go along, helps get at the real question of what makes you happy or unhappy, and simplifies the situation when the choices and the goals seem pretty far apart.

Answering questions such as "Do I like my job?" and "Is my husband the kind of man who will let me do what I need to do to be happy?" can be tough. One question often leads to another, and soon you can feel your whole life is a mess. It's easy to get bogged down in what's wrong instead of what can be right or even how close things are to being right already. If you can keep a sense of perspective on potential or actual life changes, you'll save yourself a lot of grief. It might help to remember that:

- you've been through rough times before and come through fine.
- events that looked horrible at the time frequently turn out to be the best things that happened to you.
- you don't *have* to make any changes in your life if you don't want to; it's *your* choice.

• if you *do* decide to make changes, you don't have to do everything at once—unless you want to.
• finding serious problems with your life doesn't have to be depressing—it's the first step toward getting rid of them!

## How to Use This Book

1. Complete the quiz at the end of this chapter so you can begin to have a better sense of the specific issues you might want to rethink as you read.

2. Keep a notebook on hand in which you jot down information pertinent to your particular situation or pages you wish to return to for further consideration. You may want to keep the notebook for a year or more, using it as a diary or calendar for monitoring your own changing attitudes, expectations, goals, and progress. If you don't want to use a notebook, give yourself permission to mark pages in the book. Because everyone's life is so different and our subject is so complex, it's likely that the comments you'll find particularly helpful are scattered in various chapters.

3. Contrast the stories you will read with your own life. Read and question. Don't try to fit any particular pattern; just observe how these men and women move through the changes and pressures in their lives. As you do so, you will learn about the good times they share, but you'll also see how they fight, how they decide who does the laundry, how each couple deals with frustrations. I've included the kinds of details that you can investigate, ponder, experiment with, or reject in order to enable you to achieve changes you may want.

Little has been written about those successful, remarkable relationships in which both people operate as equals. Like most people, I always imagined "equal partners" to be a two-career couple, both earning the same, both sharing household expenses and chores evenly, both sharing child care evenly—all on a day-by-day basis. But equal partners come in many variations, and learning about these couples helps each of us feel more confident about pushing for the kind of relationship we want in our own lives. Because this book focuses on people who want it all—career, love, and family—I have dedicated chapters to *couples* who are trying to make things work. I regret that the scope of this book does not enable me to fully examine the life of a single career woman who does not want a partner but who does desire balance.

    4. In the following chapters, take the quizzes that appeal to you. Each is designed to help you look at your personal ambitions and the state of your relationships in order to judge better whether or not certain options might work for you. Be honest as you answer the questions.

    5. Be aware of new trends and statistics. Apart from the individual stories, each chapter will show you ways in which society is changing—often ways that make these relationships easier for more and more couples to achieve. This kind of awareness can help immeasurably when you run into a brick wall.

    For example, let's imagine you are a woman asking the man you love to accept your need for a career—and he refuses. That's when it really helps to know there is a growing surplus of men in the country! Suddenly you are sure to feel more confident knowing there are plenty more men around who may be very willing to go "equals" with you. And if you are the man, the same fact might encourage you to rethink your position and consider a compromise. (Of course, that's an extreme position.)

    Another example of why statistics can be reassuring: your husband confides to you that he would really love to stay home for a year or two until your new baby is in preschool. Outlandish thought? Something the two of you might want but feel slightly embarrassed about? Not if I tell you that one out of every five American fathers is taking full responsibility for child care in the home. Doesn't that make you feel more comfortable about your choice?

    Or what if you are in business and want to cut back to a four-day workweek so you can enjoy your baby more? Won't it make it easier to approach your boss if you know many women are doing so, even if they are the first in their particular group?

    These kinds of trends and statistics that can be so helpful in making personal decisions are often "hidden"; it takes time for them to surface. Once a major social trend is under way, it takes at least five years for evidence of it to show up in the Bureau of the Census statistics, our only true indicator of change. It may be another couple of years before a trend in one area, such as the increasing number of working parents, is written or talked about in terms of its relationship to other changes, such as an increase in the number of company-sponsored day-care programs.

That's why I believe it is very important to be aware of the trends that are giving terrific support to men and women who are juggling new roles in radical ways. Frustrations and even failures are easier to handle when you know you are not alone, when you know your expectations may be new but not unique!

6. Remember the rewards! The first and finest is *freedom*. The freedom to be whoever you want to be, whether that is the opportunity to go as far in your chosen field as you wish to or to be a full- or part-time parent.

The next reward is *friendship*, the option of being best friends with your partner, when you have one. After all, you can't even begin to change and grow as a couple unless you are willing to resolve your problems together. And in the midst of doing that, something wonderful happens—conflict no longer means dreaded confrontations. Instead, it turns into "exercise periods," a time to "jockey for new positions," to try different tactics, to allow each other room to test and grow.

"If we're having difficulty with conflicting schedules, we'll probably have a big argument about it—but our fights are looked at by both of us as 'healthy combat,'" said one husband, a surgeon married to an obstetrician. "I know it makes a difference in our family that we're able to tackle different problems openly, to show our kids how to have a big argument with loud voices and anger but end up, also in front of the kids, as the best of friends, the best of lovers. I can't remember the last time one of us 'lost' an argument in our house."

The third reward is *financial flexibility*—enough money for you to live your life the way you wish (well, within reason!). In a partnership the rewards are excellent; two people who can reach a mutual understanding as to the kind of money they need to live on can negotiate life's toughest crises together. Just as satisfying is the confidence that comes from both partners recognizing what is needed to generate that income and agreeing on how to share that burden.

And last but not least is sheer *fun*. We've all known the exhilaration of success when we collapse happy and exhausted after a hard game well played, whether it's basketball, swimming, a yoga class, or a brisk, long walk. The same feeling is experienced again and again when you share a rich, balanced life.

Some of the questions you'll encounter in this book are easily resolved, others are more difficult, but never have we had so many ways to balance our lives better. As we move closer to that balance, we discover the kind of independence and self-sufficiency that makes it easier to deal with the setbacks that every one of us encounters. And, with luck, we'll be able to enjoy the success and happiness that two ambitious people can experience together.

## Quiz: Are Your Ambitions Split?

I developed this quiz to help you assess your own split ambitions. These questions are similar to ones I asked during my interviews. Please check the appropriate box.

### *Section A: Career Ambitions*

|  | Yes | No | Not Sure |
|---|---|---|---|
| 1. Do you take risks easily in your professional life? | ☐ | ☐ | ☐ |
| 2. Do you see yourself advancing to a high level of accomplishment in your job or career? | ☐ | ☐ | ☐ |
| 3. No matter how old you are or how long you have been working, would you welcome a chance to get more education? | ☐ | ☐ | ☐ |

4. Do you think you may want to
   change careers someday?                    ☐    ☐        ☐

5. Are you frustrated in your current
   position and considering a change?         ☐    ☐        ☐

6. Do you work more for the personal
   satisfaction gained than for the
   money earned?                              ☐    ☐        ☐

7. Are you uncertain about what it is
   exactly that you want to accomplish
   in your career?                            ☐    ☐        ☐

8. Have you ever been very torn
   between two or more possibilities
   job-wise or career-wise?                   ☐    ☐        ☐

## Section B: Personal Ambitions

                                             Yes  No  Not Sure

1. Do you take risks easily in your
   personal life?                             ☐    ☐        ☐

2. Do you see yourself as a reasonably
   happy, well-adjusted person?               ☐    ☐        ☐

3. Do you worry about the future?            ☐    ☐        ☐

4. Have you already made some painful
   decisions in your life, such as
   choosing to divorce or end a long-
   term relationship?                         ☐    ☐        ☐

5. Do you consider yourself an
   independent type of person?                ☐    ☐        ☐

6. Do you enjoy puttering around your
   house or apartment?                        ☐    ☐        ☐

7. Do you like to spend time enjoying
   leisure activities such as sports, the
   arts, hobbies, or just a good book?        ☐    ☐        ☐

8. Do you enjoy friendships with people of both sexes? If so, do you see yourself as a cooperative, enthusiastic pal? ☐ ☐ ☐

9. Would you like to have children someday? If you have them already, are you glad you do? ☐ ☐ ☐

10. Do you feel a need for an intimate, committed relationship in your life? ☐ ☐ ☐

## Section C: Amount of Role Conflict You Feel

*Yes* *No* *Not Sure*

1. Have you had to make a significant compromise in your life—e.g., in taking a job, attending a college, or buying a house—because you could not financially afford to do otherwise? ☐ ☐ ☐

2. Do you feel your personal life conflicts with your work at times, or vice versa? ☐ ☐ ☐

3. Do you often feel frustrated by not being able to give more to either your personal or professional life? ☐ ☐ ☐

4. Do you think you'd be better off if there were thirty-six hours in the day or ten days in a week? ☐ ☐ ☐

5. Do you have trouble finding time to take a vacation? ☐ ☐ ☐

## Section D: Potential for Balancing Roles

|  | Yes | No | Not Sure |
|---|---|---|---|
| 1. Do you adapt easily to change? | ☐ | ☐ | ☐ |
| 2. Do you view new challenges with eager anticipation? | ☐ | ☐ | ☐ |
| 3. Are you free from anxiety over what your parents think of you, your goals, and your lifestyle? | ☐ | ☐ | ☐ |
| 4. Can you accept failure when it happens and be willing to start over? | ☐ | ☐ | ☐ |
| 5. Do you feel you have some control over your environment? | ☐ | ☐ | ☐ |
| 6. Are you willing to speak to your boss about matters that trouble you at work? | ☐ | ☐ | ☐ |
| 7. Are you unafraid to speak to a person you may be intimate with about problems in your relationship? | ☐ | ☐ | ☐ |
| 8. Can you honestly say that having a lot of money is not all that important to you? | ☐ | ☐ | ☐ |
| 9. Do you enjoy discussions with close friends on major decisions you are considering? | ☐ | ☐ | ☐ |
| 10. Do you enjoy handling some "nontraditional" responsibilities (managing finances or household repairs if you are a woman; cooking or child care if you are a man)? | ☐ | ☐ | ☐ |
| 11. Would you be willing to consider a major change in your life, assuming that change included key | | | |

improvements over your current
situation (more time to yourself,
better earning potential, better day
care, etc.)?                          □    □    □

12. Are you reluctant to give up any of
the responsibilities, hobbies, or
friendships that complicate your life?  □    □    □

*Scoring*
Give yourself 5 points for every "yes"; 3 points for every "not
sure"; 1 point for every "no."
*Totals:* If you scored 140 to 175 points, you are an individual
with a high tolerance for risk taking and, therefore, more likely
than many people to feel the tension of split ambitions. However, your personal courage, strong sense of independence, and
high level of self-esteem make you an ideal candidate for achiev-
ing a unique and rewarding balance in your life.

If you scored 75 to 139 points, you are typical of many of us
who are slowly, carefully loosening the bonds of tradition. You
are becoming more aware of new options daily, but you need
"proof positive" that these are right for you.

If you scored 35 to 74, you are remarkably inflexible in
these changing times. Be sure you aren't setting yourself up to
be a victim of stereotypical thinking that may sabotage your
personal, career, and financial future.

Note as well the particular sections of the quiz in which you
answered "yes" most often. A high score in section A and a low
score in section B, for example, shows that your career ambitions are great, while your personal ambitions are quite modest.
Is that, in fact, how you prioritize your life? A high score (over
21) in section C combined with a low (under 30) score in
section D suggests you are experiencing considerable role conflict but seem unsure of your potential to work things out. The
couples in this book should help inspire you with confidence.

# 2
# The New Entrepreneurs of Love and Career

Want a quick trip to a halfbaked career and a half-hearted home life? Choose 'the Mommy Track' and that's what you'll get . . . ," implied a spate of recent newspaper and magazine articles. It seems that everyone is up in arms over how to handle working moms. Should they be left to fend for themselves? Should companies make special allowances for them? Should these special allowances be given only conditionally, so as not to antagonize men and childless women? Is it fair to stratify your workers—those with real career potential and those with children?

While these are all very real issues, especially from the standpoint of company policies and the law, all the hoopla has caused us to overlook the fact that, despite the inherent conflicts among career, love, and children, there are people out there who are making things work. It's certainly not everybody, and their lives are not perfect, but there are some women out there who, along with their partners, have invented new ways to balance their work worlds and their personal worlds. The key for women trying to balance their split ambitions lies in choosing a partner capable of sharing everything from romance to raising the kids. Until society—especially corporations and other employers—"figures it out," these couples are doing things their way.

## Two on a Seesaw

Their way is often remarkable, based less on formula than on thinking of life as a seesaw, a teeter-totter. Remember the old-fashioned kind? The red board, balanced on a wood block, that went up and down? Then the modern one that came into vogue in the fifties—a miracle of design using a metal plank on a cylinder inserted into a steel tube so you could whip around while you went up and down. The secret to getting the fastest ride was to go around and around while staying as evenly balanced as possible. That meant picking a partner close to your own weight, with the same skill for coordination. And if you wanted to go really fast, you practiced a lot, on sunny days and rainy days, even on humid days when the seesaw could get stuck.

Love between equal partners is a modern kind of love similar to riding on such a seesaw. You do it the same way: first you find someone young at heart who's willing to ride with you, who mirrors your values and your ambitions, and then the two of you get ready to coordinate your lives under all conditions.

Among people who are equal partners, every couple is different yet the same in one essential way—they see their lives as a fluid continuum where change is the only rule. Theirs are lives filled with ups and downs, with days when they speed along, days when they barely creep forward, days when they fall into each other's arms exhausted from the challenge of keeping a good balance between them.

Personality-wise, these couples can be characterized in a remarkably singular way; although they may come in all sizes and shapes, ages and stages, single and married, they tend to be spirited and full of energy. They are couples who have the confidence to treat each other as equals. They tend to be creative self-starters in every area of their lives.

# The Armstrongs: Choosing a Different Path

Laura Armstrong lives life from the inside out. She is a woman who questions and tests, reorganizes, then questions and tests again. Her husband, Ben, meets her more than halfway—but for neither has it always been this way. They met when they were both "committed" to other people. Both had put their whole hearts into their other relationships, yet both were short-changed.

How they came together, the extraordinary way that they suit each other, and how they maintain their marriage under significant pressure make for an excellent demonstration of the realities and rewards of being equal partners.

Few people are as well matched as forty-three-year-old Laura and thirty-eight-year-old Ben: both were married before to partners who couldn't give each what they most needed, both are physicians whose medical education was pursued in ways considered radical at the time, both love their work, both love children and an active home life, both love the sea, both love the northwest coast above Cannon Beach, Oregon, and they are mad about each other.

Their life is simultaneously disciplined and riotous. Right now they have just moved for what they hope is the last time for a long time—yet they are poised at the precipice of one final major change in their lives. Now that Ben has completed his surgical training at long last, now that son Charlie has passed his first birthday, now that they have moved into their house by the sea in a small, thriving community, *now* will Laura return to medicine, from which she has just taken an eighteen-month sabbatical as a part-timer, a twelve-year sabbatical as a full-timer?

Laura usually speaks first—her voice a rich, throaty velvet, her laughter quick and roaring. Ben listens intently, then interrupts, nudges, acquiesces, or considers. Language and laughter are the currency of their love.

And that is what both missed the first time around. But it is seeing them through their history, together and individually, that shows you what their love is all about. And their love is of a kind that every one of us can achieve—if we are willing to work for it.

## "We See the World Through the Same Eyes"

"When we first met, I was an instructor in the emergency room," said Laura. "Ben was one of my residents." Her lively face, framed with shoulder-length straight dark hair, beams with humor and happiness as she bounces one-year-old, chubby, blond Charlie on her lap and talks about Ben, who has just opened his practice as an orthopedic surgeon only ten minutes from their new home.

"It was August. He came down to the emergency room, and it was just one of those things. I remember standing at the x-ray machine as he walked behind me, stopped, and pointed to the screen I was studying. 'Hey, what do you think that is?' he said, pointing to a little fracture. I said, 'I don't know.' 'Look carefully,' he urged. I had almost missed the fracture. He walked away, and I turned to the person beside me and said, '*Who* was that?' And they said, 'That's Ben Armstrong.'

"Then I learned he was a new resident and soon it would be his turn to rotate through the emergency room where I was the instructor." Little did Laura know they would soon fall in love. Several years later they would be the proud parents of a new baby boy—as well as a large "blended family" of two girls and two boys from each one's previous marriage.

But that morning it was business as usual.

"Right after I saw him by the x-ray, I watched him sew up a little boy's face, and I was in awe of his technical skills. I clapped for him. Very good surgeons can be made, but excellent surgeons can't. And to see an excellent surgeon work—it's beautiful; tissues just fall into place." A breathiness in her voice tells the listener that what she loves about the man goes far beyond his lean, fair-haired good looks. That long after his stalwart athlete's body makes its peace with age, she will revel in his talent, his hands, his mind, and the determination that makes him who he is.

And Ben? What did he see in that authoritative, funny, smart woman who spent her weekends in the Life-Flight helicopter directing the small hospital's trauma team—and her weekdays raising her two young boys?

"She's an unbelievable doctor," he says of the woman who was his mentor in emergency room medical procedures. "She's good at everything she does, but medicine is what she most wants to do and where she receives her finest accolades.

"Laura knows what it's like to make a decision and be responsible for the decision. That's why her decision to take this year off to be home with Charlie and the boys while I completed a one-year fellowship in my specialty has been scary for her.

"When you've devoted an incredible amount of your energy to learning a body of knowledge and you know that that body of knowledge is subject to such scrutiny, especially with today's lawsuits, your profession can be very scary. I know because I'm amazed at how, when I have not done a procedure for a couple months, or I have taken a vacation for ten days, I always wonder, What have I forgotten?

"As a physician, you live on the edge. For example, the physician that I trained with is seventy-three years old and still operates. He doesn't do some of the real difficult cases that he once did, even though he's a master craftsman. I think that the reason he doesn't do some of the more difficult ones is that there is no room for error. When you don't operate frequently, you get out of practice. That's scary.

"I know that's why Laura questions herself constantly as she plans when and how she'll return to medicine. She wonders what's going to come in the door and whether she is going to be able to muster up all that she has learned. Yet that is exactly why she is a very good physician. Only the wise worry."

In addition to sharing a dedication to the science and art of medicine, Ben and Laura were both attracted by the opportunity to help mankind. The common belief in a greater good, a reason for living and doing that is beyond themselves and their family unit, is typical among equal partners.

Some couples find it in religion, others in a certain way of looking at the world. My husband and I, for instance, share a belief in what is fair and what is not fair in this world that compels us to write the way we do. All the happy couples I've studied in researching this book draw inspiration from a similar source.

Laura: "I love medicine. It's why I am the way I am with my kids. I feel toward them the way I feel toward my patients: I love staying up with them at night, I love holding their hands, I love writing orders to help patients get better. I'm in a beautiful profession.

"Medicine is so much fun, yet at the same time it's so stressful and hard. It's frightening in a lot of ways. Imagine having a mother bring in a three-year-old who is having seizures, telling you, 'She's dying—save her,' or having an ambulance holding three people mutilated in a car accident careen into the emergency area. You're in charge. I know deep down I love the control, but I'm also a very open doctor—my patients can ask me anything."

Ben: "My uncle was a plastic surgeon. When I was in high school, he got me a job at the hospital. I was fascinated. I enjoyed it immensely. I saw plastic surgery, orthopedic surgery, and general surgery. Then there was a methadone maintenance program, an offshoot of one of the original methadone programs. I spent a lot of time with the addicts and recognized that I'd really like to help people for the rest of my life.

"I also realized that being a doctor doesn't require the same kind of effort and energy that getting an A on a test does. You have to relate to the patient. It's a certain relationship that you establish with the patient. It's not something you perform and the patient gives you an A."

Nor are marriage and family life automatic. The secret is out: you do not get married and live happily ever after; you get married and work hard to stay married!

And in order to do that, you must want it very, very much. Ben and Laura do.

But even though Ben and Laura share goals and seem able to work things out well together, Laura's interest in mothering *and* working is hard to balance. And Ben knows it.

"We're happy now," says Ben. "We do most of the things we

want to do. Since we moved here three months ago, we've both felt a strong sense of community that's really making a difference for us. For the first time I have a sense of putting roots down. The lack of money isn't a big worry—I know that five years from now we'll be in great shape.

"We have been through a lot these past five years. We moved our household three times in the last two years, and we've moved emotionally from other marriages, so this has been an incredible time of change.

"But through it all," said Ben, his light brown eyes easy in his wise, open face, "we've had each other, our work, our kids, and now it's all paying off. I think that's because we've tried to honor our individual priorities as well as what's right for the family as a whole. For example, the decision to be home full-time has been more Laura's decision than anything I've pushed," said Ben. "I want her and our kids to be happy, and that's what we have right now. When the kids go to bed, it's like summer camp every night. They're different ages, yet they're in there laughing like they're at Boy Scout camp—they are the best of friends. I don't think you see that very often. Sure, they have their percentage of bickering, where it's like animals practicing for the kill, but basically I think they're very happy kids. They have good self-esteem, and I think it's because their mom is home paying attention to them.

"On the other hand, I know that Laura loves medicine. We're looking at alternatives now for how she might feel better about what she's missing. I know she's talking to the people at the emergency room. . . ." In Ben's voice is an air of pleased anticipation that underscores his eagerness to see Laura maximize her potential as a mother and as a physician.

Ben knows Laura acutely misses her involvement in her work, because they have discussed it, are discussing it, and will continue to discuss it. But contrary to some who might balk at exploring all sides of a problem, the Armstrongs know the wisdom of investigating it fully. They give themselves time to work out a solution. Why? Because in the long run, that is what a shared view of the world and its people is all about: an abiding respect for one another's life goals.

## *"I Guess You Could Call Us Renegade Realists"*

Laura and Ben live beyond the rules. Long before they met and fell in love, they discovered that as individuals they were unique not only in their expectations, but also in how they pursued their goals. They learned early on to capitalize on this, to see it as an advantage. In fact, the people I found in my research who are "successful" equal partners rarely hesitate to describe themselves—albeit with a shy pride—as "unique," "risk takers," "unafraid of the future," "willing to bend the rules in order to find new solutions."

Laura flaunted convention the day she chose not to go to college.

"I was accepted to Smith, and I didn't go," she said, "not something a San Francisco debutante is supposed to do. I went to nursing school instead. I was president of my class at a private girls' high school, and our headmaster said, 'I can't believe you're doing this!'

"But I went off to a three-year nursing school. In the second year of nurse's training I realized I wanted more, so I went over to one of the top California universities, which was close to the nursing school, and said, 'This is my history, and I really should go to college,' that I was frustrated that I couldn't do more as a nurse. But I also said I'd like to finish nursing school since I started it—so how about letting me come and take some courses?

"They said they'd never done that before, but 'okay.' So I took college courses, finished nursing school, and three years later I started medical school. I found medical school, my internship, and my residency unbelievably rigorous but unbelievably fun. It was superb. And I did very well—I was one of six women enrolled, and I graduated first in my class! I wasn't a whiz kid, but the clinicals—my love of nursing and my rapport with patients—pulled me way up."

In moves parallel to Laura's—though five years behind her as she is five years older than he is—Ben, too, followed a less than predictable route to his medical degree.

"I started at a major midwestern university, where I did

pretty well the two years I was there," said Ben. "I got all the credits that I needed to get into medical school, but I also got disillusioned with the whole process and dropped out.

"I spent a couple months in an Outward Bound program, got hired on, and went through the ranks to become an instructor. Then I also decided to go back to school. But this time I went to a private college, where they had a different system: a work/study plan where you could concentrate on studies, take a break, then go back to studies. Then I transferred to another college, where the education process was even more unusual— there you progressed by getting a committee together, forming a question, and then answering the question in the form of a paper. It was sort of modeled on doctoral programs. It took me two years to do what I needed to do."

So both Laura and Ben began their medical careers in unusual ways. However, it was just at this juncture in both their lives that they did the expected: they married while still in their twenties. At the same time, both were trying to continue their educations, and that's where you see the critical effect that being equal partners can have or—equally important—not have. What happened next to each of them resulted in a great deal of personal pain, but it also paved the way for a deepening awareness of what love truly is.

"My first marriage was very calculated," admitted Laura, her vibrant, authoritative voice registering incredulity at her naïveté thirteen years ago. "I was still in my internship and had been living a really hardworking—and celibate—life when I made up my mind that I wanted to have kids right away.

"I remember thinking, I should have them during my residency and then go right into medicine full-time. Then I met Alan. I had decided to have kids, and he was there. He was a very nice guy: 6′5″, attractive, fun to be around, a kind man, intellectually stimulating. So I married him during my third year of medical training and got pregnant right away. It was insane, it was conniving, it was so calculated."

Though she had had a fairly conventional marriage, Laura had not hesitated to continue to bend the rules in her professional life: "So here I am newly married and starting this fantastic residency. And what happens? First of all, I started working with rhesus monkeys, and I thought, My talents are clinical; I'm a doctor because I love working with people, not monkeys and microscopes!

"I remember it vividly," said Laura. "I was trying to get pregnant and had just started my residency in the prestigious gastroenterology track when I realized how difficult it would be to specialize and be a mother too. I was getting the feeling now that this wasn't all going to be so simple. It didn't help that I was the first woman ever in the department at this very famous hospital.

"I went in to the chief and said, 'I just got married, and I want to have kids, and a number of them, and I just can't see this ever working.' Knowing my personality and being compulsive and wanting to be right up there with the best, I knew I couldn't do that and fulfill my expectations of being a mother too. It's funny, it's the first thing I ever quit in my life. Even a book—if I start an awful book, I'll finish it.

"But I said, 'I'm leaving, I can't do this. It's my money, it's my grant.'

" 'You have no integrity,' said the chief. 'Do you know what you're doing to women in medicine? Everyone is going to know you've quit.'

"Yet I knew I could never be a good gastroenterologist; I'd never be able to give my heart and soul to it. I knew that family would be making enough demands on me that I couldn't go wholeheartedly into a specialty. So I went back to the chief of medicine at the hospital where I had interned and asked him to take me back as a senior resident.

"He said, 'I can't do that—we haven't a place, we haven't the money,' but the next morning he called and took me back into the program.

"I completed the residency during my first pregnancy. Stephen was due June 14th, and that April I was asked to join this very snazzy private practice. When I went in for my interview, they asked how often I would want to work the first year after the baby was born. I said, 'At least three full days.' Well, Stephen arrived June 14th, and my world changed! I had no idea I would feel so attached to this child. I wanted to take him everywhere with me! That's why I think the same qualities that make me a very compulsive doctor make me a good mother.

"So I'm supposed to start in private practice after three months. I had everything arranged—my mother had agreed to watch the baby; I was nursing, so I'd put my milk in the refrigerator and bring it over to my mother's; the office was only two miles away from Mom's—I had the perfect situation.

"It didn't work out at all," Laura recalls with a laugh how ill prepared she had been for the strains of motherhood.

"Alan couldn't help out very much, but that wasn't the problem. I may be different from many women because the two men I've been married to have been in surgical training, which is incredibly rigorous. And if you're a kind person and you love the person you're married to, you can't ask him to help when he already has his hands full! Maybe I'm more aware of that because I've been through similar experiences, even though it was internal medicine, not surgery. But I strongly feel it's just inhuman to say 'It's your turn tonight' when someone has just been in the operating room for thirty-six hours. So it was never a question of asking Alan to do more. I didn't want him to.

"It didn't work because of me—I felt so responsible for this child. I just loved being there and caring for him. Being there when he woke up from his nap and seeing his big smile. It all felt right. So I went to the head of the private practice and said, 'I cannot do this. Is there some other niche you can find for me?'

"He said, 'Why don't we try three mornings a week?'

"Then I said, 'Okay, but no hospital rounds. I'll just come here nine to twelve. So we tried that for three mornings. That worked a little bit. But then I said, 'No, two.'"

And so Laura, recognizing her driving need to be an at-home-and-there-at-nap-time mom, forced medicine to work for her: "I was a doctor two mornings a week for two years. Stephen would sleep, and I'd call Mother twice in the morning and ask how he was doing. She was wonderful, very attentive, hovered over the bassinet."

But nothing stays the same for long. Soon Alan made a job change, and another baby arrived. Again Laura did not hesitate to take her life apart and put it back together in a new formation.

"My second son was due at Christmastime. Alan had finished his surgical training and been accepted to do heart surgery, so we moved to a new city and a new hospital for his postgrad work, and I stopped working the summer before son number two was due. In the midst of all that tremendous change over the next year with the move, the new baby and Alan's intensive training, I didn't realize that I was kind of unsettled. I knew I was getting a little lonely, but I don't think of myself as a lonely person, so I ignored a danger signal.

"I got this urge to work again. So I went to the medical center, to the head of the emergency room. I said, 'I'm an internist, I have my boards, I worked for two-and-a-half years in private practice. I have no emergency room training, but I really want to get back to work.

" 'However,' I said, 'I have to have something that won't compromise the kids. I want this clearly understood because I did start in private practice, then had a baby, and it was awful. I don't want that to happen again.'

"So they said, 'Here's what we can offer: you come to work about four in the afternoon on Thursdays and Sundays and work through the night.' That suited me. I went home and worked it out with Alan. I said, 'I'm going to work only when you're off, even though I will have someone to sleep at the house in case of an emergency.' That was fine with him, although in retrospect I can see I took all the responsibility for working it out.

"I had a wonderful baby-sitter who would come half an hour before I was to be at work. Even though I really got after Alan— 'Get home at six, I want you with the children'—I couldn't realistically count on him. Too many emergencies come in for heart surgeons. And I remember getting very disappointed when something would come up. Inside I'd be thinking, Wait a minute, I'm not working that much. Can't you at least try to be there for the kids? But most of the time I would understand because I understood the pressures. The sitter would be there all through the night, and then I'd race out about seven or eight in the morning and take little Stephen to kindergarten. I did it for four years—and it was great!"

What happened next taught Laura a great deal about the kind of balance she can manage—happily—in her life. It also taught her what was missing.

"At first I'd go to the emergency room about four o'clock in the afternoon and work nights. Then I started flying around in the Life-Flight helicopters—if we weren't busy I'd have the helicopter pilot circle the house so I could wave to the kids. Eventually I was asked to help run the trauma team. That was great, because the kids would go to bed about seven, a few hours after I left the house, and there I'd be in the morning! I'd just miss out on some sleep. It was only Thursday and every other Sunday. Since it was a sixteen-hour day, I got a lot of medicine under my belt without really being away very much.

"I had the days to take them skating or swimming. We really didn't miss out on anything together except that one Thursday afternoon. Recently I asked the boys if they remember missing me. Stephen said, 'No, I really don't.' So it was a wonderful balance for me.

"At the same time, I was doing very well financially. Alan was still earning a very low salary, while I made $40,000 that year just working one or two sixteen-hour days a week. And it wasn't long before I was on the staff myself—I was assistant chief of the emergency room."

Almost all the ingredients were in place for a true equal partnership—both were doing what they most wanted to do as Alan completed his training in heart surgery and Laura worked part-time as an internist while being a mom too. But something was missing!

Laura held up her end—she helped out financially and made sure that her schedule allowed the flexibility that Alan's could not. And more than anything, she nurtured her husband and her children.

But no one nurtured Laura. No one listened to her everyday worries. No one patted her on the back for a job well done when the baby was clean and sleeping happily or when a gravely injured young woman felt that she was going to be safe with Laura leaning over her in the Life-Flight helicopter on its way to the emergency room. No one folded his arms around her and rocked her gently in a cradle of marital intimacy.

"I felt so desperately alone, I fantasized a wild affair with the butcher at my meat market," she said, her eyes moistening in memory. "Even though I knew my feelings were absurd, I didn't know what to do about it.

"What I'd learned after we were married was that Alan is a man who doesn't understand emotion," said Laura. "He never really talked to me, got angry with me, laughed with me. For instance, I never argued with Alan—ever. It was like I just did my job and he did his.

"When I would take the kids swimming, I would see other couples with their kids playing at the edge of the water, and the couples would be lying on their towel, giggling together, or they'd get up to go be with the kids, and they'd walk holding hands or they'd put their arms around each other or kiss each other. I would imagine they'd probably had a nice time the night before—they were probably still flying on that, sexually. It's such a wonderful bond. I remember how mad that used to make me. I didn't even *know* the word intimacy. So I would say, "Whatever they have, I don't care. Alan and I are good friends— *not best friends, good friends.*

"I was very conscious that I was always the affectionate one, that we never shared any real conversation together. Sometimes I'd find myself really coming on to another man, and instead of saying, 'You really seem distracted away from me; we'd better pay attention to this'—as though he might be the least bit jealous—Alan would put me down with 'God, get your act together. You're doing embarrassing things.' Of course," she said, adding a phrase that echoed through the empty chambers of her heart, "we never fought."

"It was so disheartening, too, because I always had this image of what love is supposed to be. I remember in the eleventh grade going to visit a good friend, and her father had fallen asleep on the couch. We were sitting at the table, and my friend's mother turned to us and said, 'Oh, look what I married.' She was so in love with him. It could have been the first time she saw him. And they had been married twenty-five years! 'Look at the hunk that I married,' she said with so much tenderness. And I thought, Boy, I want that. I want to be able to say that.

"When I was with Alan, it used to kill me to get anniversary cards. Most of them have sexual innuendos—those were out of the question for us! The ones I ended up with were 'Thanks for being my friend.' I'd always wonder why only about one out of a hundred cards were appropriate for me to get. I hated buying anniversary cards!"

Laura was married to Alan for slightly more than ten lonely years.

"When I finally saw a psychiatrist," said Laura, "I asked him to tell me to stay in my marriage. But he said, 'The worst thing you can do for these children is not get a divorce. These kids are seeing a cerebral relationship between a man and a woman. You talk with your heads, not your hearts. That isn't what life is about.'

So Laura discovered her limits: she could force medicine to bend to her needs, but she couldn't get her man to be an equal partner in both work and love. Silence is a weapon of power. Refusing to talk about the feelings of your partner means that you don't consider them important. If you don't consider the person's feelings important, you have conveyed the most critical message: "To me, *you* are not important." End of relationship, end of marriage.

Ben experienced a similar problem in his first marriage. He too had two children born during the years of his medical training. He too had a spouse with an outside job. And he too had a partner who refused to share on equal terms.

"My first wife was very hard-nosed about how we should split our responsibilities," he said. "She went back to work two months after each child was born, and she was a real fifty-fifty person. I *had* to pick Samantha up at day care at certain times. And I *did* it, even though I'd be tense because of some change in the hospital schedule that made my superiors angry or irritated with me. On many occasions I compromised myself and my schooling in order to make it all work the way she wanted. But my wife refused to listen to my reasons for needing things to work differently at times."

Again, one partner receives the message from the other: your needs are not important, you don't count.

"On the other hand," said Ben, "it was hard to tell what a good split should be. There was a couple in my class who had a child and went on to share a residency, which was going to last double the normal length of time because they were each going to take a half-time position and spend the other half of the time taking care of the baby.

"In some ways it looked like they were sharing, but actually they never saw each other because one was home with the baby while the other was working a half-time equivalent. And a half-time equivalent in medicine is the most ridiculous statement in the world. Even if you work two hours a week, it generates about three hours of time that you have to organize, learn, and study. So I put up with what my wife decreed partly because it was confusing and difficult to decide on a good split. The consistent pattern, though, was that she refused to be flexible."

That was the situation in both of their lives when Ben's residency led to his assignment in the emergency room where Laura was the instructor.

It was a *coup de tonnerre* — a thunderclap of two kindred spirits.

"When I got to know Ben, I experienced such a flood of emotion that I was really alarmed," said Laura. "What began as a mutual enthusiasm for each other within our profession — he thought I was a great teacher, I thought he was a terrific student — turned pretty quickly into a strong attraction. I thought he was brilliant and handsome, and he thought I was brilliant and beautiful — and we felt the same way about so much. It was damned frightening and confusing.

"What is happening? I asked myself. Am I doing the wrong thing? Am I going to hurt my children in some terrible way? That's what prompted me to see a psychiatrist.

"We took our time before deciding to leave our marriages in order to be together. We are both the kinds of personalities that like to make the best of everything, and that's what we had been doing for ten years. But when all of a sudden the best appears, then you think, God, what have I been putting up with?

"And Ben was so much younger. Here I had survived cardio-surgical training with Alan for five years, and now I was attracted to a second-year surgical resident who had all those years still ahead of him. Wow! Could I go through all that again?"

And so, suddenly attracted to each other, both of these

unfailing optimists were caught at a difficult stage in their lives. The two had the same ambitions—excellence in their profession and happiness in their family—yet neither had been able to find the deep, centering balance between themselves and their spouses that could make it all work. Both lived with a void of affection and intimacy that threw everything else off kilter. Try as hard as they might to fill life with work and family, without passion, they couldn't flourish.

A painful year passed during which they ended their marriages and grew more confident that the strength and love and passion that they shared would make everything work out the best for themselves and for their children. Finally, on an April day, they were wed.

Now, suddenly, Laura and Ben had each other and more—challenges to meet that others might find daunting:

Could Laura, in her late thirties, postpone her career goals yet again so that Ben could complete his surgical training?

Could Ben find a way to complete his training without jeopardizing Laura's future in medicine?

What about the fact that together—even though they faced the daunting challenge of "blending" a family of six, including her boys and his girls—they wanted to have another baby?

All of this at a time when neither had any money!

"It might seem like it would be impossible," says Laura today, "but we knew we could do it. We didn't know how, but we knew we would."

## *"We're Best Friends . . . We Make Love—and We Fight—Easily and Often"*

"We're so happy right now," said Laura six years after their wedding. "Some weeks we make love almost every night."

How did they do it? How did the Armstrongs get through the maze of education, kids, careers, and a cramped lifestyle to their golden cottage on the Oregon shore, where the baby tootles happily along on the freshly waxed floors and the boys come crashing through the open front door at the end of the school day, all while Laura is on the phone coaxing her banker into one more loan so she can hang out her shingle as a "part-time doctor" soon.

How is it that, when other couples in dual-career households are finding that the first casualty of their pressure-filled routines is their sex life, the Armstrongs exude a cozy sexuality that makes it clear all is easy between them? Years after they met, gentle hugs and soft strokes still accompany even their most mundane conversations.

They know exactly why that is. Nor do they hesitate to be blunt about it. Both feel that what was kindled by intense emotion in their first encounters flourishes at the same level of intensity—and not at all by accident: "We are always talking to each other," they say in unison.

Laura and Ben deliberately avoid the fatal mistake of their first marriages. They refuse to lose touch with each other's feelings and needs. The most trivial matters are handled with tenderness and sensitivity to each other's moods.

"We must talk on the phone at least four times a day," said Ben. "We're unique in the amount of communicating we do. I used to be kidded because I would always be on the phone— during my residency they'd say, 'Armstrong's on the phone again!' I don't know of anyone else who does that. The guys that I worked with during all those years of residency and the fellowship—there was no communicating with their wives. Sure, they did 'business' with their wives but with no sort of emotional contact. Our office doors were open all the time, and I didn't see it."

"He's always in touch, maybe between operations or seeing patients," said Laura, who spent the year of Ben's fellowship at home full-time with new baby Charlie, her two boys, and Ben's two daughters, who spent weekends with the family. "I tell him what's happening with me and the boys, and he tells me what's going on at the hospital. I live medicine through him."

Unintentionally, Laura and Ben have locked into one of the most essential ingredients of a strong equal partnership: simple, direct, open, and ongoing conversation. Not "meaningful," carefully scheduled half hours of "communication" but frequent, untidy chats that don't just cover the day-to-day minutiae of life but keep each one tuned in to the excitement and discovery and pleasure in the other's life. It is conversation as a currency of intimacy. It is a conduit of feelings and ambitions that carries news integral to their mutual fascination with both medicine and family. Casual though their conversation may seem, it is an ongoing source and "maintenance" of a constant tension of interest between them. Furthermore, to express interest in each other, to listen actively to each other, is to validate and approve what each one is doing. This repeated appreciation is as soothing as a physical caress. It's also an opportunity to share anger or disappointment so bad feelings aren't allowed to fester. Quick as they are to share good news, Laura and Ben stay current on bad news as well.

On any given day Ben may call from the hospital, upset about some turn of events, uncertain which decision to make, yet confident that the woman he loves will allow him to expose his uncertainty. He knows that he can be tender and sensitive and wondering—that he doesn't have to be strong all the time.

Laura, on the other hand, finds Ben a source of information that she dearly loves to hear and a great sparring partner to boot. Even as she relished her year at home with the baby, she hated being away from medicine. To make up for it, she thrived on sharing the news of the operating room, rounding out his tales with her opinions or recommendations on a specific treatment. Ben welcomes her assertive ways. On numerous occasions her recommendations have made a difference in the way he practices medicine. For her the doctor talk made baby talk a treat.

And when the home front has turned into a battlefield of crying kids and spilled Cheerios, he good-naturedly takes over to cuddle and hold her and restore her natural good spirits with exactly the same warm nurturing she's dispensed to everyone else all day.

The payoff? The reward for each? An intimacy and friendship that allow each to feel as confident and loved in moments of anger as in moments of ecstasy.

Laura smiles softly as she says, "You know, people don't realize that work talk can be stimulating. I find that intellectual conversation can be an aphrodisiac—if you're interested in what you're saying, your eyes light up, you're more animated. Talking about what excites you makes you exciting! So, sure, we're talking medicine, but it's when you're talking and making eye contact that you can be kind of attractive. Plus, you've got a reason to give each other attention—otherwise, what's your connection?"

At times Laura might be the aggressive listener. Another time she may be the teacher. "Or," said Laura, "because we understand the pressures of the job, we often talk about politics and other problems on the staff. We can share the annoyances you encounter in medicine, like other doctors' ineptitude. We commiserate, and we have a lot to say to each other."

But it isn't just medicine they discuss.

"I feel it is very important that we talk about ourselves—our work, how the day is going for both of us," confirmed Ben. "Laura thinks that I really like her because she is a doctor. She said that to me when she was home full-time—'Now that I'm not working you won't like me, and you're going to like someone else who's a doctor'—she's up front about it. And it's really just the opposite. I'm much happier with her doing the things that she loves. Fortunately she loves domesticity, although I know that it's frustrating for her at times, because she's an unbelievable doctor with the drive to achieve in her work that you have to have in order to be good."

And so they share, openly and easily, their feelings of ambivalence and uncertainty too. This willingness to confront everything that life offers—neatly packaged and not so neatly packaged—is one of the most critical elements of a successful equal partnership.

"My decision to stay home with Charlie would feel right one day and wrong the next. Ben and I talked about it a lot," said Laura. 'Don't you think it gets scary for me not practicing medicine and seeing all these women and men practicing medicine full-time having a great time, as fun as I know it can be?' I would ask him. Or I'd be home thinking, Does it really matter that I'm here? but then Charlie would wake up with a smile on his face worth a million dollars! And it felt so good to be there. I could see that it really did matter.

"But I need to hear that from Ben: 'Tell me that it matters to *you* that I'm here.'" And he does.

But when it isn't "happy talk," neither one worries that their warm little world is about to end.

"We don't hide our problems," said Ben. "If we're having a bad time and the kids are around, we don't go and hide in another room to talk. I used to be sort of embarrassed to deal right up front with anger or being cross, and I think that's because when I look at my upbringing, I can probably count on my fingers the times my parents had overt disagreements.

"That's not right. I think it is very important that the kids see that we get over those things; that if you've got problems, you take care of them. Not confronting them is like pretending they don't exist. But if you can disagree in front of your kids, they not only see that it's okay to cry and yell and scream, but the other side of it—that Mom and Dad still love each other *and* they do these things.

"But how else can you teach your children about intimacy? If you only see people loving one another, it looks easy. But you need to show them that crying or not feeling good or feeling sad is also part of loving one another, part of a well-rounded emotional life.

"Sure we get angry—easily and often. Then it's over."

"Nothing smolders in our relationship, ever," agrees Laura. "One week we all had this gastroenteritis. Awful vomiting and diarrhea. The kids had it at both ends, and I got it about noon. But I had to go pick up the boys at school. And Charlie had it, too. So Ben called from the operating room, and I told him I had to go, and I'd have to take a towel, because I knew I was going to vomit on the way.

"I asked him if he could possibly pick them up, but he couldn't.

"So I got mad on the phone: 'God, it never works when you can go get them, does it?' And he said, 'I know.' But then that was it. As long as I feel like I can be frank, I'm not bitter.

"Then the next day I was still weak from this bug, so Ben said he would pick up Stephen at a birthday party. But within an hour he called and said the camera in OR had broken and he had better get it fixed or the OR chief would be upset.

"Ben said, 'I don't know what to do. I really should take the camera, but I'll go get Stephen.' But I said, 'No, I'll go get Stephen; you go get the camera.' So I went and got Stephen, and I made Ben go for the camera. But when he came home, I was feeling sorry for myself, so I cried—then we laughed and it was fine. I really love Ben. And I'll do anything for him. But I'm not dumping on me—he'll turn around and be wonderful to me. He's fabulous. He loves me. Yet we both know realistically what we can and cannot do for each other.

"This past year has been his for work and mine for home. He cooked breakfast on Sunday mornings, but I managed house, kids, finances, insurance—I even got the mortgage for our new house. Once in a while I'd say, 'I don't want to do all this. You call the bank today,' and throw it in his lap. And he'll do it. But he was so busy in clinic he didn't have time to go to the bathroom, so he did it out of the goodness of his heart and neglected his work."

What Laura is saying about the past year is very important because it explains their stability: each understands what the other is capable of—what the other can do within reason, and what the other's human limits are. They also know that you can get furious and blow off steam but, secure in your love for each other, settle down into reasonable levels of expectation. Why is that? Because in their hearts they are confident that each one wants the best for the other.

"Does that explain why we have such a great sex life?" asks Laura with a raised eyebrow. "I mean, you'd think that we'd ease off a little after being together almost seven years, having a baby, and putting on a little weight, but not us!

"We have sex probably three times a week, sometimes more or less. It depends on how hard our schedules are. What counts is we have a tremendous amount of fun together, whether we make love or not.

"I think for a woman, mood is very important. Evenings are usually frantic for me. I've just done math with the boys, proba-

bly cleaned up the house, and just put Charlie down. I just want
to sit back—it takes a while to change gears. Ben, meantime, has
been reading the paper, waiting for me to be free, and he's
feeling good about himself and life and the job, so he feels very
amorous.

"Fortunately, he's so good at knowing me and we're so
compatible that even if I've just cleaned up the Cheerios, as soon
as I lie beside him, I'm easy to interest. He's just a wonderful
lover, so within minutes I'm turned on. And we're not very
kinky." She sighs. "Love must come in there, too. Even after the
worst day, I can look at him and just think, Ah. There's something about the back of his head and his ears. I don't know what
it is exactly . . . it's wonderful to be continually so turned on by
your mate."

Open, frequent communication is a common thread among
couples I interviewed for this book. All of the individual partners
showed me again and again that they could disagree with their
lover openly (often in front of me), easily (with a smile of
confidence as they laid out the problem), and without fear of
damaging the relationship. A series of studies on sexual intimacy
recently reported in the *New York Times* reinforces that idea in
stating that extramarital affairs are most often entered into by
"people who feel lonely, unappreciated and unrecognized."
"Men are looking for someone to talk to . . . somebody to listen
to them," said Dr. Frederick Humphrey, a professor of family
studies at the University of Connecticut who has counseled
people who are having affairs; "women are looking for attention,
thoughtfulness and caring."

In separate studies reported in the *New York Times*, Dr.
Harold Lief, a professor emeritus of psychiatry at the University
of Pennsylvania, and Dr. Gayle Beck, a psychologist at the University of Houston, said that new laboratory research shows that
anger, followed by depression, is particularly devastating to
erotic desire—more so than any other factor, including hor-
mone levels or lovemaking skills. This new research underscores the elemental fact that our "emotional life shapes [our]
sexual life for better or for worse."

## "Ours Isn't a Fifty-Fifty Split—but a Complementary Fit"

Another of Ben and Laura Armstrong's secrets to getting through the day, the week, the month, the year: they don't take a rigid approach to everyday life. They do not divide every responsibility equally in half—from laundry to car pool to cooking. Instead they strike different balances at different times—in ways that even out over a period of time, in ways that are "equal shares" when viewed from a perspective of months or years instead of hours.

Also, and this is important to note, their balance is struck in ways that correspond to what each one wants at a given time: Laura doesn't just *agree* to be at home with the new baby—she *wants* to be at home and be free to immerse herself totally in mothering for a certain time.

This is what is unique about their approach: "We don't have a fifty-fifty split," explained Ben. "We don't even think of a fifty-fifty split; instead we concentrate on how we can complement each other's current schedules and needs." Last year, with Ben working full-time and Laura home full-time, was an excellent example. But this year the division of labor—and opportunities—between them will be quite different.

Essentially, however, their solution to the complex demands of love, home, and career is to blur the edges of who does what and why—according to the needs of the moment. The crossover between them is always in flux, whether they are trying to balance the "inside work" of house and kids or the "outside work" of their medical careers.

This flexibility, this ability to complement one another, requires trust and optimism and energy—yet it is a quality demonstrated by every couple I've studied, because they are successful equal partners. And this is why each couple's life is so unusual—they establish harmony in ways that you might never expect but that balance ideals as well as idiosyncrasies, talents as well as time-outs.

So how do the Armstrongs get started on the nitty-gritty of

who does what? First on their list is always the care of the five children, a responsibility complicated by the arrivals and departures of Ben's daughters for their weekend visits. How this worked from the beginning was the harbinger of their wedded bliss.

"I stopped work in the emergency room just before I filed for divorce," said Laura. "I felt that I needed to be home with the children full-time to help them through this difficult transition.

"At first it was very hard. Not only was my soon-to-be-former husband not making much of a salary, but he was also a tightwad, and the funds dried up immediately, so my mom helped me until I could find another job at a hospital where he wasn't on the staff. I found one pretty quickly, only I had to drive thirty miles two days a week to work nights at a little community hospital. Even so, I never had so much fun!

"Why? I suppose it should have been awful, but Ben had moved in, and we were doing it all together. And Ben was wonderful. He always made it home for me to make it to every shift. Even if he was on call, he'd switch hours so that when I'd go to work at seven, he'd careen in and I'd be off on time. Ben said he'd be there, and he was.

"And he was there in every way. He'd read to the kids, bathe them, get them up in the morning, and get them on the bus. This was such a difference from before!"

Ben could see for himself what a difference his involvement with Laura's kids made right away. "It had to do with how they related to me," he remembers. "At first they weren't very affectionate, even with Laura. I noticed that when she came home, they wouldn't run up and hug her and kiss her. She'd have to chase them around the house to hug and kiss them. And I thought, This is interesting. My two little girls, when I came home, always ran up and kissed me; they were very physically affectionate. But the boys, neither of them was very demonstrative, and my impression was they were a lot like their father. It didn't take long before they were much more open physically."

Laura has watched Ben's affectionate ways pay off richly for her sons. To a woman for whom nurturing has been a driving force, in her career and her personal life, the fact that this man she fell in love with so unexpectedly could fill that void for her and her children added a priceless measure of balance to her life—in the early days and every day since.

"My boys are very much his now," she said recently, a soft smile lighting her face. "Kevin, the eight-year-old, is into everything that Ben is, and they are all very relaxed together. Ben's girls are with us on the weekends, and he helps as much as he can because he knows it is a lot for me to manage all of them at once. I think that's why the kids have always gotten along well together."

How Ben helped—or how Laura helped—was never written in stone. Both could switch back and forth, depending on what was needed and without regard to any stereotypical expectations.

"I did an unbelievable amount of camping as a kid," said Ben, "so I learned how to cook, and I'll vacuum and clean the house. I don't do a super job. But I can do anything. If somebody's coming, and Laura's cooking dinner, I'll vacuum.

"On the other hand, Laura does anything she wants to, even the sort of male things. She cut down a tree the other day. We don't separate out the yard work or heavy stuff that much—if she has the time to do something, she'll just go out and do it. Once the entire house was rearranged on the first floor—it didn't matter how heavy anything was. It was all moved from one room to another. So I don't feel like she draws any lines either." An interesting point in a time when everyone is carefully tabulating how much housework men are doing these days.

"What's important," said Ben, "is that we'll fill in for each other. For example, when she's frustrated and says, 'I don't want to cook anymore,' then I'll cook something. I always cook Sunday breakfast too."

Confident in their early experience of shared efforts, Laura and Ben got married. But almost as soon as they had established their comfortable rhythms, things changed: Laura became pregnant, Ben was offered a prestigious one-year fellowship in a distant city. Everything happened at once.

"In a way, to have it all happen simultaneously made it easier," said Laura. "I knew that I wanted another child and that I had to have a baby soon because I was almost forty. The fellowship was in precisely the specialty that Ben wanted and would give him the best possible preparation for the kind of private practice he always wanted. So this got us both off on the right foot.

"I think what sets us apart from some other people, though, was that it meant another couple of years with very little money coming in. But neither one of us cared about that, so it was never an issue. As for my career, I was willing to compromise for a few years. Again, it wasn't Ben saying he wanted me to have a child. I wanted a child, too, and I was the one who insisted on doing it as soon as possible.

"Any relationship involves compromise. And compromise shouldn't be construed as a negative thing. You're not backing off. You're not giving up. You're working things out together. Because our relationship is so traditional in some ways, I knew I'd do anything to make it work for him that year because I knew the demands of the fellowship would be unbelievable.

"At the same time, I knew that this new little baby would really need me at home. So I didn't have to make much of a choice. We talked about it a lot. We both felt that the fellowship would put Ben into the kind of surgery he most wanted to do. And to be with the baby was what I most wanted to do, wherever we were. It was an exciting opportunity for both of us."

What Laura doesn't say is that, as much as the baby might need her, *she also needed to be with the baby*. Her nurturing instinct as strong as ever, she felt the same way she had with her first child, when working part-time and leaving the baby with a good sitter still had her muttering, "Damn it, I want to be there for that little guy."

Laura treasures the opportunity to cuddle her children through their infancy. For her, the trade-off of being able to be at home full-time during that year or two while Ben completed his fellowship was a natural one. In fact, she started off thinking she might take more than one year off—maybe five or ten. She allowed herself to wonder if she might be happy at home full-time until the baby was in school.

Within days of the baby's birth, Laura and Ben moved to Chicago and settled in with other student families. "I stopped working at the hospital just before the baby was due," said Laura, "and we moved into student housing in a pretty rough area in downtown Chicago where poor little Charlie slept in a crib in the hallway. Life in the big city also meant having to drive the boys everywhere, including school every morning, so there was more pressure on me to do everything at home. Sometimes it got to be a bit much, as I did everything for the kids—all the cooking and cleaning, all the household accounts, everything— while Ben was working just as hard at the hospital.

"But even on the difficult days, it was never 'Look, I really pulled the oar before, and you're going to pull it with me now.' That's not my makeup. I remember one day Charlie had a temperature of 103, and it would have been great to have Ben take the kids to school. But he just couldn't do it. As a fellow in surgery, you absolutely cannot say, 'Sorry, I can't come to rounds this morning—I have to drive the kids to school.' I hope that someday in medicine it will ease up, but it hasn't yet."

Indeed, for Laura in particular, a significant element of their "complementary fit" that year was the time it allowed her to rethink her own goals for the future as she could examine, test, and retest what she thought she wanted out of life. Tedious as it might have been to keep the house and kids in order while Ben was in surgery, having the time to explore her choices for the future was also a luxury for Laura. That and the chance to bounce her feelings off the other doctor in the house—Ben. Aware of how critical her concerns were to his own happiness, Ben always listened.

"On the one hand, I was concerned about the effect this hiatus might have on my career, especially since I was seriously considering spending five to ten years at home," said Laura. She may have seriously considered a long time off, but she kept her eyes open as to the effect that might have on her sense of identity and self-esteem. As much as she loved mothering, she did not underestimate her own ambitions as a physician.

"I watched two women who lived in our building. Both were internists like me, both with kids, both working full-time, and both miserable!

"One just had her second baby. Her first was only fourteen months old. She'd worked full-time since the first child was about four weeks old. And they were having the worst time. Not only had her oldest never seen that much of its mother, but finally, when Mummy was home a bit, there was a new baby too. I knew that things must be bad since every time I saw the mother or the nanny that's all they talked about. People tend not to be so verbal about having a rough time unless it's really bad.

"The other woman physician wasn't as totally stressed out, but she wasn't happy either. And her youngster was always with a nanny. Both mothers seemed to be just dragging themselves from home to the hospital and back again.

"Yet I understood why they were working. A major factor is peer pressure. I haven't been around that many women in medicine, so I haven't felt a whole lot of pressure from other women—nor do I care anyway. On the other hand, comments have been made to me by men: 'Why would you take up a seat in medical school if you weren't going to practice medicine heart and soul?'

"It's funny, when men take a year off and go on a sabbatical, everyone says, 'Isn't he great? Isn't it wonderful that he's taking a year off from medicine to delve into some things?'

"With a woman, take a year off to care for a *child*—and what could be more critical and important?—and it's considered some sort of excuse not to work!"

Another thing Laura noticed that year was that staying at home can get tedious. "No one appreciates all the housework, and the first thing to suffer is your self-esteem," she said. "That's rough if you are in medicine, where you're more often praised by your patients and your colleagues than you are by your two-year-old.

"And work really is fun. It's a lot easier than being home. For one thing, you're in control. You just give the orders, and people do what you want. Babies don't! I wouldn't be honest if I didn't admit there are times when I'm with Charlie and I think, Gee, I'm bored changing and feeding and watching him spitting oatmeal all over. Wouldn't it be nice to work tomorrow morning where I'm in control again?

"Relationships are easier at work, too. I see it in men all the time. You've got a label on—you're a doctor; you've got a certain role to fill. You come home, and there are toys all over the place, and one kid needs help with math, and the other just wants to be held—the demands are unbelievable."

Again, like the other couples interviewed, Laura and Ben are very direct with one another about their concern for each other's sense of self-esteem. Laura noted during the course of her year home with Charlie how strongly her self-esteem is tied to her work, her sense of how good a doctor she is or isn't. This recognition was acknowledged by Ben, too, to be critical to the success of their relationship.

But if Laura measured the pull of medicine with realistic eyes, she could still offset its seductive charms with the rewards of mothering: "The payoff of being a mom is terrific, too. I can see, with Stephen turning twelve, some of the responsibility is letting up, so there is light at the end of the tunnel. On the other hand, I still sit and do homework with him every night, and often I have to pick him up at school. So it's the constant pull between a sense of responsibility to your work and wanting great intimacy with your kids and your husband. Anything else you do in addition to home is going to pull you away.

"In Chicago I knew it was worth being home when I started to get unbelievable comments from the teachers on the kids. If you can take two kids from the country school system and put them in a sophisticated private school setting and have them not miss a beat, I know that comes from strong self-esteem and that self-esteem comes from having Mom there, because it shows the child that 'you are so important to me.'

"And Stephen, in the fifth grade, is so self-confident. We were at a dance at the school just before our move from Chicago, and the parents were all laughing about how the kids—fifth-, sixth-, and seventh-graders—didn't want their parents near. Not Stephen! At least four or five times he came after us, saying, 'I want you to see this.' He was really proud of the things he was doing, and it was so easy for him to share them with us." Laura smiled wistfully as she talked proudly of her oldest son. "I thought to myself that night, This is the first pat on the back that I'm feeling.

"But raising these kids full-time was *hard*, much harder than I had thought. It's taken much more patience than I ever thought it would. The challenge is to make that time full of laughter and great times with the kids, to get to 9:30 at night still happy and put them in bed with smiles on their faces. That makes you feel pretty good—to me that's really being on top of life. And it's not easy—the toilet overflows, sunflower seeds spill all over the floor, and the baby crawls around squashing them into the newly vacuumed rug—all at the same time one of the kids wants you to play Nintendo with him. But if you get through that every night, put the effort into it—along with patience and a sense of humor—then you've got something really wonderful . . . I do anyway."

But balance in life for Laura is still to be tipped somewhere between kids and career. This became more and more apparent as Ben's fellowship year drew to a close. In a truly complementary way—just as Ben's career commitment stabilized at a plateau where the demands on his time would be less and he would have more control over his schedule, Laura's career concerns intensified. It was a slow but mounting crescendo.

## Confronting a Classic Conflict

It started even before they stepped over the threshold of their new home—a complex swirl of confused intentions and mixed emotions that swept Laura dangerously close to a full-scale depression. Wisely, she refused to hold back. Instead, right away and feeling like a spoilsport, she countered Ben's delight in his new medical practice with news of her increasing feelings of uncertainty and frustration.

"What happened when we first moved here was that I could see Ben's future clear and shining, but I felt stuck in a way that I couldn't fully understand. I knew I wanted to be at home, yet I could see my future as a physician slipping out of my control. With all the details of the move and all the newness of our home here, I couldn't put my finger on what was making me unhappy at first. I just knew something was very, very wrong. I was supposed to be happy, but I felt like crying."

We are talking together, Laura and I, just four months after their move west into a picturesque bungalow by the sea that reverberates with laughter and noise. A typical day—the phone rings, the baby topples stacks of Legos, the dog barks, and Laura scrambles for the phone when Ben calls, as he does numerous times during the day.

Life for Ben has changed in bountiful ways. Suddenly his clinical pressures have eased and are under his control. The new private practice—what Laura calls his "solo shingle"—is off to an excellent start as patients are plentiful and he has been warmly accepted by the medical community in their region. And with his office such a short drive from home, at least twice a week Ben takes the afternoon off to come home for lunch and spend the rest of the day with Laura and Charlie and, after school, the older boys. For Ben, suddenly there is a need to shift the balance of his life: "Now that I have my work in place, I want to focus more on home—I want more time with Laura and the boys."

And just in time. With these newfound hours together, Laura and Ben have been talking more than ever—about family and medicine, the mortgage, the loan for the new practice. They have been striving to keep it all on the table: the positive, the negative, the testing, the caressing.

And the anxiety.

The anxiety? Wait a minute—isn't everything perfect?

Not for Laura. At least not yet.

Perched at the brink of the rest of their lives, healthy, athletic, and full of good humor, the Armstrongs admit that on a personal level they have yet to complete the physical and emotional move from the student/family life of the past year to a totally new dynamic of family and professions.

"We have been intensely vocal with each other," said Laura. "Daily. I've been having a hard time, and I've been brutally honest about it. Probably our greatest strength is knowing what each of us needs and what our limits are."

Their changing situation demanded another alteration in the Armstrong's balancing act.

"I am relying on Ben to help more with the kids and the house than I did just four months ago, when he was still in training. Now that he is set in his practice, I realize I can feel comfortable saying, 'Hey, it's my turn to think about work—I'm envious of your new office, all your new patients. How can we set this family up so I can practice, too?'"

And with that statement Laura shows how she and Ben epitomize the finest expression of "split ambitions": recognition of the importance of staying honest and open about your feelings, even though you may feel confused or intensely ambivalent, coupled with a willingness to take time to work toward a new balance, a new resolution between you. They tackled their dilemma step by step.

### Step One: Deciding what's right

Most of the practical matters of their move, which she handled, whether it was finding a new house thousands of miles away, securing a mortgage, or contracting with movers, were easy for Laura.

"When Ben and I first met, we discovered that each of us had fallen in love with the Pacific Northwest, so we knew that we'd settle out here," she said. "The last few months of Ben's fellowship, we each made a trip out to find a house. We found it—and the perfect midsize town to live in—just north of Cannon Beach, right on the water. Ben loves to sail, and now we can go out on the ocean in the summers.

"Our house has a stunning view of the Pacific, the waves crashing up on the boulders. We couldn't afford it, but we're doing it. We'll make it work. It's a gutsy thing financially, but we think a view can really change your life. We spend a lot of time watching the sea. It helps to see the water so sunny and calm and lightly breezy some days, so tormented and crashing on others. Life is like that—sunny days and stormy days. The sea keeps us honest.

"But we also picked an area where there was a need for surgeons like Ben and a doctor like myself too. It meant settling for a lot less money than if you live in a bigger city, but we don't think the money is worth it compared to the small-town comforts, like the kids being able to walk to school and knowing who your neighbors are. We love the people here!"

### Step Two: Deciding what's wrong

"Right after our move here," said Laura, "I found myself in such an emotional state, real highs and lows, that I realized I needed some professional counseling. Ben couldn't help me sort out what I didn't know myself.

"Once we got moved into the new house and Ben began driving off to the office, I found I would have free-floating anxiety about his being totally in charge of our lives now. It's like he's in control. Everything is up to him. At first I was all gung ho and thinking, We'll all open this together. But that began to feel funny, too. We've been such a team, and now he's going to be a boss, and I want to be a part of it so much. At first we'd laugh about it, and I'd say, 'I want to be your secretary; I want to be part of this.' This is my first dose of his being in charge.

"I was so surprised how it hit me when we got here. It was really hard for me to watch him put on his suit and tie and look so great and go out in his little fifteen-year-old Mercedes to his own office, which I just love—I wanted to be part of the excitement!"

Finally, as her anxiety escalated, Laura decided to see a psychiatrist to sort out her confused feelings. This is a characteristic shared by all the couples I interviewed. Those who find themselves in emotional quicksand recognize when they need professional help.

Immediately upon seeing a psychiatrist, Laura was able to pinpoint the source of her anxiety and begin to organize ways to handle it.

"With a psychiatrist as a sounding board, particularly being another doctor, I was able to pinpoint where my feelings were coming from," recalled Laura. "I had a number of different reactions going on at once. The easiest to deal with was my feeling that suddenly Ben's work placed him in full control of our lives.

"To a certain extent that was true, even if temporary. So I examined why that made me anxious. One reason is that, ever since I grew up, I've never felt comfortable totally relying on another person for everything. While the fact that my dear sweet dad was an alcoholic who could really bungle things up may explain my anxiety, I do not think it is misplaced.

"You aren't being fair to yourself if you do slip into total reliance on one person. Ben and I know that nothing is for certain forever. It isn't worry, but as a physician specializing in trauma, I've seen enough life-and-death situations to know that anyone who takes anything for granted is asking for it. I don't! Not my kids' health, not my own sense of self-esteem or even counting on what we have right now as something we'll have forever. Ben and I have often said to each other that a good life is one that constantly reexamines itself, takes time to appreciate what's there, and keeps building toward something better."

So she named that fear and took it home to talk it over with her husband. He made it clear that he welcomed knowing what was troubling her, that he too understood the fragile nature of their love and desire for each other.

"That's precisely why we really are equal partners," said Ben. "It doesn't come from vacuuming half of the living room or washing one-half of the windows or doing one-half of the laundry; it comes from a feeling that you're involved in dealing with the most vital parts of the person.

"The psychiatrist that Laura talked to a couple of times said something that I think is so true—he said that to be in a committed relationship takes an unbelievable amount of time. It's easy to love someone right in the beginning, and then, whatever happens in, say, two years, it's all over. I think that the reason it's all over is because no one is spending the time to keep it up. It takes work to keep it up. It's an emotional endeavor to keep up the relationship because love comes out of being with a person and understanding that person."

### Step Three: Understanding the problems
Once both Laura and Ben recognized the source of her anxiety as a feeling of loss of control, the next step was to understand why.

"It's *my* self-image that is obviously the most important thing to me," said Laura. "Nobody makes it shaky; nothing external seems to make it shaky—it's me that does it." Self-esteem questions were suddenly surfacing as the result of many changes in their family dynamics—and Laura's perception of who she is and what she does best.

As a mother, her role was changing. The baby was nearly a year old and more on his own hour by hour, the boys were more independent in all their activities, and yet the demands on her time still precluded full-time work by Laura's standards.

"This morning is a good example of how I still need flexible time," said Laura. "I took Stephen to school at 8:00, Kevin to school at 8:30. Stephen comes home at 2:15. Kevin comes home at 3:00. Stephen has softball practice at 4:00. Even if I find a good at-home sitter for Charlie, I'm still pulled at two levels. And you can't walk into a job in medicine and say, 'I'll work when I want to, but I'm going to go to the soccer games, and I'll never work on a holiday.'"

Hoping to fill in the open hours by becoming more involved in their new community, Laura accepted invitations to join several committees, only to find that "I don't really like mingling with a lot of mothers and planning the bazaar. I get sort of bored. Already I've volunteered to run the square dance and to be Kevin's class mother. I realized when I did that I must be getting frustrated because that's not like me. I would much rather be practicing medicine and not get involved in social functions. Then, too, every time I introduced myself as 'Dr. Armstrong' I realized how much pride I take in being a doctor, being a good doctor and having people know that."

There was another reason Laura was feeling the urge to work. "I am so torn right now because Ben is just setting up his practice, and that takes loans," she said. "Then we have this new house, and that took a big mortgage. Being a doctor, I could bring in a good solid income right now, so I very much feel the pain of being pulled between family and work. And I hate it—it is *very* painful."

Even as she realized the pull of her profession and of finances, Laura was reluctant to move too quickly. She began to explore the opportunities around her. Could she find one that would allow her to practice medicine and motherhood to her heart's content?

The search took another three months and a lot of soul-searching. We talked by phone as she explored the possibilities open to her.

"My second love is medicine. The idea of being in private practice is so exciting," she acknowledged to herself and Ben. "But even the old traditional way is hard. And yet I'm getting a little panicky, thinking, I can't stay out too long. Already I can't be an internist; I've been out too long. I can't remember that stuff. I've been out of full-time internal medicine for twelve years now.

"At first I had an idea, and I talked about it with Ben, that maybe I could volunteer. I thought I could go to the head of our local medical center, and they could put me on the emergency room staff, and I could come in one morning a week from eight to eleven. They wouldn't have to pay me anything, but they couldn't count on me for more time than that either. That's asking a lot, though. . . ."

Then Laura thought over her fondest wish if she could indeed have it all: "I'd love to go into adolescent medicine. There aren't many people in it as a field. But teenagers are a really neglected little group. They're mortified to go to a pediatrician's office, and yet they're really afraid, especially the little girls, of their first pelvic exam, their first visit to their parents' doctor. Adolescents have special needs that many internists and family medical people are really not up on. It's a field that has always fascinated me."

But even as she considered it, Laura faced the negatives— examining the alternatives from all sides and always with Ben's input.

"I think because I love medicine, I forget the demands that something outside the home makes. Therefore, in my fantasy I think, Oh sure, I'll bet when Charlie's five I'll be full-time. But then I think, Remember what full time is like. Full time is not being home when they have strep throat. Full time is not being able to go to the play at night because you're on call. Full time is not being able to take them to school that one morning they want you to. Life becomes too complicated, and therefore it just doesn't feel good. It doesn't feel like everything is getting the attention, the energy, it deserves.

"I love being home, but I've also gone through a whole lot of frustration without working—yet the one factor that really helps is knowing that Ben is with me in this. He knows how I feel. Just sharing the frustration makes a difference. I'm not sure why; it just does. Maybe because then I know he puts a greater value on what I am doing here than other husbands do." And it was Ben's support that slowly but surely moved her closer and closer to the moment when she would discover a solution.

*Step Four: Testing a solution*
Neither Laura nor Ben skirted the issues: they knew they both wanted it all, and they recognized the challenge they faced.

"I keep reminding myself of a quote I heard on television that helps me balance the urges I have between wanting to be home and wanting to be helping others," said Laura. " 'Live your life simply but keep it hard.'

"I tell myself that hard doesn't mean complicated. And when I've gone to work before, life has become complicated, and I don't like it. It doesn't mean I'm lazy or ineffective or that I can't coordinate things. If I can graduate first in my class and if I can coordinate twenty-five sick, sick people in a major hospital's emergency room, then I can coordinate a family.

"But can I be a doctor and a mother and keep it simple and hard and lovely? I feel it's hard now. I'm challenged every day to get those kids off to school, to keep them happy, to keep them feeling good about themselves, to go to their plays and school conferences, to keep the baby seeing the horses, seeing the pigeons, so he's learning, so his brain is being filled with all these stimulating things.

"What I want more than anything is my children and my family to be happy and secure. I may want my patients to prosper, but first I want my kids to be happy with themselves; I want them to have a good life. What can I do to ensure that? Who knows? But I guess you just have to set up your own principles."

Laura's anxiety eased as she confronted all her "split ambitions," even though she had not yet resolved the situation. Just being able to discuss all her conflicting desires openly made a major difference in her emotional state and, not surprisingly, prepared her to recognize opportunity when it fell in her lap.

Three months after our conversation in that living room when Laura confronted her demons of indecision, we spoke again. This time in exhilaration.

The solution to Laura and Ben's dilemma had arrived — cloaked in the disguise of an old white garage. That's right — a dingy old two-story garage just three hundred yards from the boys' school.

"I was driving past this darling old clapboard garage that I had always thought was so charming when I saw a guy put up a 'For Rent' sign," said Laura. "And immediately I thought, That could be my office! Right next door to the kids' school.

"It was uncanny, but suddenly everything fell into place. I could see opening a small private practice in adolescent medicine. I'd see patients two days a week, so I could set my own hours. I'd have to be on call for emergencies, of course, but by now I had a much better sense of how Ben is around enough to be able to fill in for me at home. It's like I had to have this six months of unrest just to see how our family life could accommodate me in a practice, too.

"I called the landlord *immediately* to see if it was feasible to renovate the building for a doctor's office, and the owner was so accommodating. The downstairs level will be my offices, and upstairs is a wide-open loft, which I'm going to convert into a playroom and study space for the boys. So they can walk over from school or ball practice and study upstairs until I'm finished. If I need to, I'll have a space for Charlie there, too, and I know I can find a good sitter for just a couple days a week."

Ben too was excited over the prospect of Laura's "solo shingle." The only remaining hassle was money. They were already in debt to the hilt for the house and Ben's practice.

"I started to worry about it," said Laura, "and then I just said, What the hell! I'm a doctor too — there shouldn't be any problem getting another loan. So I picked up the phone and called our banker, and he said I could have the money anytime.

"That was a month ago. The work on the building is going to take several months, but everything is under way. I am so excited and so happy!" The thrill in Laura's voice is testament to her delight at having a direction to her career once again. And always the pioneer, it looks as though she is on her way to a new definition of what private practice can be for the physician/ mother who wants to force it to accommodate her rather than the other way around.

Meanwhile, to facilitate her developing practice, she plans to scale back the volunteer activities that she now knows are not very fulfilling for her; and Ben's schedule promises to allow him more opportunity to fill in with child and home responsibilities, which he eagerly anticipates.

As the Armstrongs stand in the drive to their brown-shingled bungalow, the sea wind whips their hair into their eyes, heightening the glow of stunning good health and happiness that embraces them as they lean together, arms entwined. They clearly believe in themselves and in each other, and in dreams that you can make come true by, as Laura says, "living life simply but keeping it hard." The Armstrongs keep their lives "simple" by limiting their priorities and "hard" by facing the exciting challenges of getting what they want out of life. They laugh and smile with the anticipation of kids charging off to summer camp.

## The Myths of Equality

The Armstrongs make it pretty clear that an "equal" relationship can be terrific. But defining how they got there isn't easy. And how can you pick an equal partner, or change the one you're with, if you don't know what an equal partner is? Few of us understand exactly what "equal" means. I think the best way to understand equal partners is to know what they *are not.*

### Myth One: *Equal Partners Share Every Duty, Every Dollar, Fifty-Fifty*

No, they don't. Rarely is anything shared fifty-fifty. Most often the balance is a complementary one: "you fill in here, I'll fill in there," balanced according to each couple's unique situation, with trade-offs made by the week or the month or the decade.

## Myth Two: Equal Partners Keep Their Responsibilities Well Defined

Hardly. Even if they have agreed to a certain trade-off, one of the strengths of the relationship is the ability of both people to change if the balance isn't working. Neither person hesitates to speak up if he or she is under too much pressure. No one hesitates to try a different solution.

## Myth Three: Equal Partners Know What to Expect from Each Other

Quite the contrary. They always keep their options open by carefully refusing to box each other in with any kind of expectations. They take nothing for granted.

## Myth Four: Equal Partners Share a Rare and Lasting Love

I wish that were true, but it isn't. And yet, in a quirky twist of fate, uncertainty is their lucky charm. As you will see, men and women who are equal partners choose to live their lives together under a multitude of stresses—personal, career, and family. And the nature of being equal partners—that is, providing the opportunities for each person to voice his or her opinions—means they are forced to come together often in "friendly combat." They can't say for sure that they will always be together, but they are confident they have the best chance of all by working things through.

## Myth Five: If Your Parents Had an Unequal Marriage, You Will Too

The biggest stumbling block for many people is their worry that revered and reviled family traditions, or our parents' failures at love and marriage, will sabotage our own chances at happiness in love. We admire equal partners from a distance but think that our inherited "love genes" may keep us out of the game. Nothing is further from the truth. People who have seen firsthand what a love relationship *shouldn't be* are the best candidates for a fine one. They also know what *did* work for their folks, so they know what they'll want to keep in their particular balance.

## Myth Six: Equal Partnerships Are Only for the Young

Yes and no. Youth is a state of mind. You certainly have to be youthful and energetic in your approach to life if you want to succeed as equal partners. On the other hand, youthful thinkers come in all age groups.

## Myth Seven: Equal Partnerships Are for Everyone

Of course not. Some women and men prefer a traditional kind of relationship. An excellent example is a close friend of mine who was recently divorced from a wealthy executive. Gwen is forty-seven years old and quite serious about the fact that, if she marries again, she wants to be a "kept woman." She is willing to give over control of their life together to the man who is willing to pay the price, who will provide all their financial support.

What's different, however, is that this is Gwen's choice. She is fully aware of what she wants and why, whereas women of old frequently found themselves as "kept women" when it was the last thing they wanted.

The bottom line is that you choose to be an equal partner. You make the choice to be equals together. You also vary the levels of sharing according to your own goals in life.

## Myth Eight: Equal Partnerships Are Very Difficult to Manage

Total baloney. Once you are into the swing of it all, an equal partnership is the easiest kind of relationship to maintain, because your efforts are always expended with the finest of intentions—to do or choose what is best for both of you. The sorting out of options takes time and serious thought, but people who feel understood and appreciated, as equal partners do, are deeply satisfied people.

## Myth Nine: All Equal Partnerships Are the Same

Most definitely not. Although they succeed best between people
with good energy levels and people who treasure one another as
best friends, that's where the similarities end. In fact, the biggest
mistake you can make is to admire a couple you know and try to
copy them.

Instead of looking at that "perfect couple" (and don't we all
know at least one apparently "perfect pair"?) as a model of
behavior, think of them only as a couple close in ways you would
like to be close. Remember that *how* each of us establishes our
intimacy with a lover is as different as our personalities, as even
the degrees of intimacy we can or want to achieve vary widely
from person to person. I know two people between whom a
glance is more erotic and powerful than the public nuzzling and
snuggling of others.

## Myth Ten: Only the Unselfish Win at This Game

Wrong again. The selfish win. You cannot love anyone well
unless you love yourself first. Think about that. How often do
you have a great day at work and find that your exuberance spills
over to lighten every part of your life? Love works the same way:
knowing how to care for your own needs first teaches you how
to care for the needs of those you love.

## Myth Eleven: Equal Partners Never Fight

Equal partners are distinguished by the *quality* of their fights.
They fight well. As you see how the couples in these chapters
resolve their conflicts, you will understand more clearly how
love can be better between two people who aren't afraid to
differ, even heatedly!

## Myth Twelve: The Experts Don't Believe in Equal Partnerships

I had an interesting experience while researching this book that
shows you exactly what experts in the field of marital therapy
and counseling think about equal partners.

Late on a weekday night, I was returning on the train out of New York City to my home in Connecticut and happened to overhear two professors from Yale University discussing their work. Specifically, they were discussing which texts they preferred to use with their students, although whether these were students of psychology or psychiatry I couldn't be sure. However, one book was mentioned several times as the best place to read about relationships that worked: *Successful Marriage: A Family Systems Approach to Couples Therapy* (New York: W. W. Norton & Company, 1985), written by Dr. W. Robert Beavers as a guide for professional therapists. Dr. Beavers is a renowned psychiatrist who is the founder and clinical director of the Southwest Family Institute in Dallas.

I rushed to order his book. When the highly touted volume arrived just as I was completing my first draft of this book, I opened the pages with some trepidation. Would my thesis prove correct? Would this learned psychiatrist agree with me that equal partners are the best partners in life and love?

Let me share his words with you: "To succeed in intimate relationships, one must be reasonably open and honest, have equal power, and resolve rather than ignore differences . . . my definition of love is caring about another's well-being almost as much as one cares about one's own."

## The Truths

As you read the stories that follow, of men and women at different stages of their lives, with different priorities and skills and dreams, you'll be sure to notice that these people share certain characteristics—traits you may want to keep in mind for yourself as you consider changes you might want to make in your life.

1. Always hold on to your own vision of the future.
2. Always hold on to your self-esteem. If it begins to fade, know that something is very wrong between you.
3. Believe that your lover can be your best friend. Look for a softhearted man who really enjoys his mother.
4. Believe that you can find a "soul mate" who wants to be your equal partner.

5. Be sure the one you love is willing to break the rules.
6. Believe in passion—but passion last, not first. Infatuation
   may fuel your first kisses, but it's the passion that flows
   from your love that brands your heart.

The poet Rainer Maria Rilke wrote eloquently of lovers as
equal partners when he described the wonder of ". . . this more
human love . . . that consists in this: that two solitudes protect
and border and greet each other." With the right person and
some hard work, you can find that love.

## Quiz: Is the Man in My Life Ready to Be My Equal Partner?

(Note: If you are currently partnerless, this quiz should help you
think about what you would expect from a man.)

### Quiz One: Your Current Balance

Does he share:

|  | Yes | No |
|---|---|---|
| 1. the cooking? | □ | □ |
| 2. cleaning our home? | □ | □ |
| 3. doing the laundry? | □ | □ |
| 4. handling the finances? | □ | □ |
| 5. caring for the children? | □ | □ |
| 6. driving the car pool? | □ | □ |
| 7. helping with a sick child? | □ | □ |
| 8. providing the family income? | □ | □ |
| 9. planning the family income? | □ | □ |
| 10. planning my next career move? | □ | □ |
| 11. the same outside interests? | □ | □ |
| 12. sports activities? | □ | □ |
| 13. the same values? | □ | □ |

## *Scoring*

If you answered "yes" to four or more of questions 1-8, you are halfway to a good balance of sharing on a daily basis. Circle the responsibilities you would like to share on a more balanced basis.

If you answered "yes" to questions 9-13, you are a fine example of a couple with potential for being very good equal partners.

If you answered "no" to the majority of questions 1-8, you are with a man who is likely to need to know more from you about what you want. He will also need to be shown how much you will appreciate his help. I think you will find some good ideas in the following chapters.

If you answered "no" to questions 9 and 10, you will want to consider why that is. Is he not interested in your work? Does he not welcome your opinions on his? If so, you have a more traditional type of relationship, which may work for you in some ways and not in others. Jot down in your notebook, as you read this book, a list of what works for you and what doesn't. The last chapter in this book is designed to help you prepare for major changes that may be necessary.

If you answered "no" to questions 11-13, you may have picked the wrong man. Is it too late to reconsider? If so, let this book help you find ways to make the choices you can make and feel better about the choices you cannot make. Being aware of what your options are and knowing how to "cut your losses" is part of balancing your ambitions.

Many of us cannot "have it all," so if you have more "no" answers on this quiz, you are not alone. You are, however, becoming aware of the many options open to you.

An equal partnership is a dynamic that takes time to grow between the two of you. But even minor improvements in your relationship and the level of communication between you can make a huge difference. Not only will you find yourself feeling more in control of your own life, but you will soon discover interesting ways to negotiate between you that will allow your balance of power to improve slowly and steadily.

## Quiz Two: Negotiating Skills

| | Yes | No |
|---|---|---|
| 1. Are you afraid to discuss what isn't balanced in your relationship with the man in your life? | ☐ | ☐ |
| 2. Does he often walk away while you are talking? | ☐ | ☐ |
| 3. Does he put down your opinions? | ☐ | ☐ |
| 4. Does he stay angry longer than you? | ☐ | ☐ |
| 5. Does his anger make you anxious? | ☐ | ☐ |
| 6. Do you fight often but remain good friends afterward? | ☐ | ☐ |
| 7. Do you think of the man in your life as your best friend? | ☐ | ☐ |
| 8. Do you talk together, just the two of you, at least once a day? | ☐ | ☐ |
| 9. Do you laugh together once a day? | ☐ | ☐ |
| 10. Can you tell the man in your life your deepest worries and fears? | ☐ | ☐ |
| 11. Can he share his worries and fears with you? | ☐ | ☐ |
| 12. Does he take care of you when you are sick? | ☐ | ☐ |
| 13. Do you enjoy sex together? | ☐ | ☐ |
| 14. Do the two of you do something together once a week? | ☐ | ☐ |
| 15. Do you tell him how much you appreciate what he does do? | ☐ | ☐ |

*Scoring*

If you answered "yes" to questions 1-5, you need to work on building your self-esteem so that you have the courage to be up front with the man in your life about your needs.

Where does self-esteem come from? Two sources. We feel good about ourselves when we know we are listened to and understood, and when we know that we do something well.

Think about things you do well, no matter how unimportant they may seem. Make a list in your notebook. In the last chapter we will talk about some specific ways that you can help yourself feel more confident about establishing an equal partnership—with suggestions as to how to get the man in your life to listen to you better.

Meanwhile, if you have a hard time thinking of anything you do well, please consider getting professional counseling. If you have limited funds, please check with your local government to see if you might be eligible for state or federal assistance for counseling.

If you answered "no" to more than half of questions 6-12, you both need to improve the communication between the two of you. Try not to assume the man in your life is wholly in error. Begin to work at talking with him more frequently. Begin by sharing one funny or pleasant experience with him at least once a day. Then share a frustration. Encourage him to share the same with you. In the last chapter we'll look at what to do next if he doesn't respond.

If you answered "yes" to question 13, that's a good sign that you have a thriving relationship—only people who treat each other as equals can be deeply, satisfyingly intimate. If you don't welcome making love with the man in your life, think about why. Are you fatigued? Resentful?

If you answered "no" to questions 14 and 15, see if you can change that. See if showing appreciation will make a difference in the relationship between you.

# 3
# The First Balancing Act: Love vs. Money

Independence is a fine word. We named a national holiday after it. We ache to turn eighteen because of it. Yet we encounter enormous confusion when we fall in love and try to merge two different versions of it! That's what equal partners are really all about. How can you come together in desire and affection, steady yourselves in ways that will fuel your need for each other, but protect your independence?

You're in love. You're together. You both work. You may be married or still exploring whether or not you have a future together—and you've run into a few snags, such as these common dilemmas:

> *Question:* "Which is more important—love or money?"
> *Answer:* "Both."

That's not much help. Let's try some more questions:

> "Who comes first—the man or the woman?"
> "What comes first—the marriage or the career?"
> "What's at stake—security or self?"

How's that for a real nineties twist on the old chicken-and-the-egg quiz? Even your questions generate questions.

After all, aren't you really asking: "Whose goals are more important and why?" "Do I have to choose between love and work?" "Must I put off falling in love until I can afford to risk my career?"

The answer to all of the above? Confusion.

And not surprisingly so. Never have the issues of love and money been more complex, more intertwined than now. No sooner does love bloom, it seems, than it wilts at the bank.

Couples marrying for the first time debate over separate or joint checking accounts (not to mention the *charge* accounts); couples marrying for the second time spar over prenuptial agreements designed to protect accumulated assets but even better designed to deflate love and devotion.

Everyone, it seems, disagrees about who should do what housework, especially in a dual-career household, where time most certainly equals money. Couples unsure of each other avoid the subjects, letting tensions and misunderstandings mount up like bad debts.

What was pursued in the heat of passion is too often lost in layers of confusion as lovers struggle to invest in their futures together from a vantage point of conflicting careers and money goals. All at a time when money has never been so synonymous with prestige and power, control and self-esteem—the aphrodisiacs of our time.

And rightly so: money has always been and always will be a driving force behind our perceptions of independence, self-confidence, and control over the future. Only now it is a unisex force. Now must come the realization that both sexes have an enormous vested interest in how their love affects their money and vice versa. Coldhearted? Perhaps, but the fact is that money is power—in work and in love.

## Fiscal Attraction

Who makes the money—and how?

Who spends the money—and how?

More relationships and marriages founder or flourish on the basis of those two questions than on any other, including sex.

Why? Because money and your attitude toward it define the quality of your life.

Consider the plight of the average adult American worker: in 1987 the average thirty-year-old man earned $20,100—that is, 13 percent less in real dollars than a man his age did ten years ago, according to a recent business article in the *New York Times*.

The article put that income drop into a more disheartening perspective by adding, "In 1950 the average 30-year-old man . . . could look forward to a 58 percent pay increase by 1960 . . . since then, however, the economic prospects of the young have grown dicier. The average 30-year-old in 1977 had to settle for an increase over the decade of just 21 percent." And now even that is lower by 13 percent!

What does it mean? Not only must the average man work harder to earn what his grandfather and father did, but the average woman must, too, if a couple is to raise a family, help children through school, and segue into a reasonably comfortable retirement. But even if money has never been tougher to come by, it is now, fortunately, flowing in greater amounts to women. And as the earnings gap continues to close, it is clear that a woman's career has important financial potential whether she is married or single.

That is related directly to the fact that more and more women are entering high-paying, male-dominated professions. To underscore the scope of that potential is this profile of corporate women, provided by Catalyst, an organization for women in business:

• In 1986, 72 percent of corporate women officers were at the vice presidential level or above, compared with 35.1 percent in 1980.
• In 1986, 57 percent of corporate women officers earned $90,000 or more per year, compared with 11 percent in 1980.
• In 1986, 26 percent of corporate women officers held board seats in organizations other than their own, in contrast to 3 percent in 1980.

- In 1984-85, women earned 51 percent of all bachelor's degrees in the United States.
- In 1984-85, 31 percent of all master's degrees in business administration were awarded to women.

Not only do these figures mirror women's entry into the other professions such as law and medicine, but they show how the professions are becoming increasingly reliant on women. This ensures that corporations, law firms, medical groups, and other industries will continue to find new ways to respond more quickly and effectively to the needs of dual-career couples— needs such as flextime and parental leave.

Note too that these figures indicate that the best is yet to come. Experts say that as women achieve seniority in the professions, we are sure to see the earnings gap virtually disappear. In short, the young professional female has never had a brighter financial future!

And none too soon. The flip side of that ray of economic sunshine is the dismal reality that, in the event of a divorce, the woman with four or more years of college has seen her average child support payment drop 33 percent in the last five years according to the U.S. Census Bureau. The message? The more you achieve, the more you can lose. Protect your career and your income. With half of all marriages ending in divorce, you must bank on needing both someday.

Nevertheless, what all this means in real life is that the young working woman of today is reshaping her own life and her family's even as she is forcing much-needed change in the workplace.

Don't think the fiscal attraction of this career charisma is going unnoticed. Another hefty piece of good news is that the higher-earning female is proving irresistible to her male counterpart—and the numbers show it. Proof? A recent report in *American Demographics* showed that 42 percent of the men in the professions—law, medicine, and business—are marrying women who are also professionals in the same fields. As Letty

Cottin Pogrebin pointed out in a recent *New York Times Magazine* essay,

> Wedding announcements also proclaim the new reality of male-female equality. He's a radiologist, she a cardiologist. (In my day, that would be a misprint, not a marriage.) Both graduated from Harvard and got their M.B.A.'s from Wharton. She's an airline pilot and he's a meteorologist. She's a Eurodollar broker and he's an international trade analyst. Often, bride and groom both are law associates. Or it's a bank merger: he's at Citicorp and she's at Bankers Trust. In other words, they are peers. They share common interests or workloads, understand each other's tensions and dreams.

Furthermore, this new equality endures beyond the courtship and early marriage phases of the relationship; many women are in the work force for good. In fact, a recent survey of America's most affluent couples, conducted by the CIGNA Insurance Company, found that over half of the spouses of "the main income producer" in households earning over $100,000 annually, with a net worth of over $500,000, also worked. (Since "the main income producer" is still more likely to be a man, we can assume that "spouse" means the woman.) Not only do more than half the women in the country's more affluent couples choose to work; the greatest numbers are under the age of thirty-five and over the age of forty-five. What is most important, however, is the effect her working appears to have on the marriage. Of these couples, CIGNA's sample survey showed that only 4 percent have separated or divorced—a startlingly low percentage in an era when 50 percent of all marriages end in divorce.

If love and marriage go together "like a horse and carriage," then love and money are "the shovel and the hoe that make the family garden grow." The most powerful indicator of this intimate connection between love and money, however, is what I call the "90 Percent Factor":

- Ninety percent of us marry at some time in our lives.
- Ninety percent of all marriages are forecast to be "dual-career" couples by 1995.
- Ninety percent of dual-career employees recently surveyed at a major corporation said they plan to start a family within three years, and more money is spent on children than on anything else in the typical family budget.

If nine out of ten of us are likely to merge love and career, then none of us can afford *not* to think of love and money simultaneously. Every one of us must plan how we can balance our lives between the two.

## Understand Your Reluctance to Talk About Money

Why does love so often wilt in the wake of arguments over money? Why is it so hard for a woman, especially, to talk about money?

Probably because most of us have been brought up to think the discussion of money is a crude social act. We aren't supposed to tell others what we earn, what we owe, what we spend. Money is a dirty little secret. We were told as children not to talk about it.

I know this well because I got that message watching my own parents when I was growing up. One episode is startlingly clear in my memory and shaped my attitude toward money for years.

My mother had forgotten to ask my father for grocery money, so she stopped by his office and borrowed some cash from his secretary. When he came home later that day, I saw him angrily demand to know why she did that. Before she could speak, he slammed his fist on the table and said, "Don't you ever bring up money with anyone again!"

His anger terrified me. Later I didn't blink an eye when a man I was once married to bragged that "I'll make the money and you'll never know how much." Nor did I think twice when he said, "Don't worry about the money for our children's college education; I've got that figured out." I did flinch when he also told me, "You can't work because your schedule inconveniences me, and my work is more important."

The second reason we hold back is we don't want to make anyone mad. I learned the hard way that I should have chanced anger and challenged those statements. I've made interest payments on loans for my children's education that I might have avoided if I'd started saving years ago instead of scrambling for money at the last minute. Why was I unprepared to make those payments? Because I let a man's remark go unchallenged rather than get into an argument.

And the man whose schedule was so inconvenienced by my work? He's history, while I work to be sure that I will have something to live on in my old age. Don't misunderstand; I love my work, but I'm fortunate to be doing well in a difficult profession. Many women find themselves unprepared for their retirement years because they yielded to a husband's wishes without question during years when they might have been wise to be employed. They wanted to keep peace in the home.

Few of us find money easy to discuss with another person. Knowing this is true for everyone makes it easier to tackle on your own. It is also easier once you realize that a woman's fear of a man's anger is tied to how those of us who are female have been socially "educated" to take care of the feelings of all those we love: "a good woman keeps everyone happy."

But that too is changing. The working woman has learned that to speak up on important issues is to prove her worth. She is promoted when she has proven that she can initiate, take charge, and test the limits in order to complete tasks that are vital to those for whom she works. A working woman today has learned that to be informed and assertive is to perform well. She is rewarded for that. The confidence that results is also part of the aura that attracts men.

How that confidence relates to money can be described in work terms. Often a woman is given responsibility for her department budget, for hiring others and negotiating salaries, or for negotiating her own salary. Whether she is experienced or just starting out, she soon learns to negotiate for her financial needs. She also learns that her salary or department budget is really just one small element of business within a larger business.

The finances of the dual-career couple are exactly that: two small businesses within a larger business. If both partners bring to the subject of money the same interest and willingness to negotiate that they display independently in their work world, they soon find that negative or destructive emotions have dissipated, replaced by enthusiasm for making their dollars—and their valuable time—work for both of them. They learn to complement and compliment one another with their money, making their money moves not in anger but in love.

Planning "money moves" should be as easy and pleasant as planning a vacation. After all, the ultimate goal of all the money talk is to plan for *the big vacation*—a happy, healthy, and carefree old age, to be spent together!

This is why couples must establish money as the subject of their very first balancing act: how to make it, how to spend it.

## Learning to Balance Love and Money with a New Kind of Currency

The three couples whose stories follow resolved the complex issues that are a part of this balancing act. They are all dual-career couples who met through their work and do not have children currently at home. One couple married quite young and is still very happily married, two are in their second marriages, and their years together range from six to fifteen. Their joint earnings range from $41,000 to $250,000 annually. Some keep their money in one joint account, and others keep it separate; all are very much involved in mutual planning and decision making. We will look, in varying detail, at each couple's strongest area of equal sharing and places they compromise.

You may be surprised to see how time spent together planning the future, working out disagreements, and talking over their work experiences has led to a new kind of intimacy. Unlike money, which brings only tangible goods, this is a rich well of good feeling, of "being in touch," that can flourish only because of their shared experiences. Though work keeps them apart for many hours in the day, it is also the catalyst that brings them together in a mutual sharing of fears and joys and hopes, the essence of a healthy and intimate relationship. Every one of these three couples has an energetic lifestyle, exudes a lively sexuality, and anticipates tomorrow with terrific enthusiasm.

## Taking Risks: Julie and Duncan

Sunlight just seems to dance around and radiate from Julie and Duncan, dark-haired, dark-eyed thirty-five-year-olds.

Both have wide, easy smiles and a friendly, genuine way about them. To hear them speak in calm, even-paced tones, you wouldn't believe that each is deeply involved in a high-paying, high-pressure career or that they've been on four continents, in twenty countries, and in almost all fifty states during the fifteen years they have lived together. Nor would you believe that just three years ago they were still hoping to stretch finances enough to allow for a modest vacation.

Today they own a pristine, creamy stucco home perched high at the peak of an uphill-winding Santa Barbara street, a choice piece of real estate worth well over $500,000. Inside, the warm California sun spills through the walls of windows and into the open, airy rooms, even into the basement offices where Julie's industrial film production company is headquartered.

Earning nearly $200,000 a year, in a business notoriously difficult for a woman to break into, Julie contributes more to the household finances than does her husband, who entered law school in his late twenties and is now a patent attorney. Speaking in a soft, measured voice, Julie showed me the national and international awards her films have garnered over the past two years. "This one beat out last year's Academy Award winner for short films to take first place in an international contest," she says, her eyes and smile bright with pride.

They are expecting their first child in a few months, an event sure to upset the balance they have achieved over the years they have been together, a time during which both have worked hard to build their individual careers and both have been willing to risk doing the unconventional in order to be what they want to be, individually and together. Julie broke the rules by becoming an entrepreneur in a hardscrabble, guys-only show-biz industry; Duncan put aside tradition by waiting until his late twenties to choose a professional career path. It is this willingness to test the limits that also defines the quality of their equal partnership.

What may surprise you is that Julie and Duncan met and decided to be together when they were just twenty years old. In doing so, they deflated two common myths prevalent among people who think equal partners are hard to find: first, that you can't really love wisely before the age of thirty; second, that choosing an equal partner means eliminating that wonderful, overwhelming physical attraction known as "love at first sight" and a definite indicator of that absolute necessity—passion!

"We have a real loving relationship," said Julie. "It's very close. A lot of people say it's almost like brother and sister. To this day, after fifteen years, he'll walk into the room, and I'll feel turned on, I'll feel so happy to see him. It's really special. It works.

"The chemistry was there for me from the beginning. We met at a coffee shop in college. He wouldn't talk to me the first time I met him"—Julie laughs—"and I was devastated. But it turned out that a friend had planned quite diligently to get us together, so Duncan had known about me for a while. He just didn't want her to think that she had anything to do with us getting together.

"At first I was crushed when he didn't respond. I was blown away by him. I loved the way he looked—I thought he was gorgeous."

Shortly after they met, Julie and Duncan moved in together. "We lived together for seven years before we decided to get married," Julie explained. "There has been an understanding between us from the very beginning that we wanted to get our stuff together before we had a child. We didn't want to do it in our twenties. We wanted to travel and explore. We've lived in so many places—right after undergraduate school we worked in Alaska for a while together, then we moved down to Wyoming. That's where we discovered what we wanted to do with our careers.

"We came to Los Angeles when I was hired at a major studio,

so my career was the motivating factor for going down there. Shortly after our move we were married, which was eight years ago, and about a year after that Duncan was accepted into law school.

"We had very little money, and his tuition was wholly our responsibility, but he got a partial scholarship. So for three years I was earning the money. It wasn't great—I had a terrible salary, and I was amazed that we were able to live on it. Those were tough years, because even though we had a beautiful apartment, it was very lonely. Duncan was gone all the time, and I didn't really know anybody. I did like my job—as a production assistant on feature films—which was very creative. And I was always surprised when I got my paycheck, because I couldn't believe I was getting paid for doing exactly what I wanted to do."

The same is true for Duncan. "He loves diversity," said Julie, "and he's got expertise in the sciences and physics, so the work in patents allows him to use all his skills. The first firm he went with, however, wanted him to travel, so he was gone five days a week for well over seven months, and it was horrible. Somehow we managed, but that's one of the main reasons he left that firm. He was very adamant that he didn't want to be away from me that much, and he realized one reason he was traveling so much was that the firm was poorly managed, so he left.

"Meanwhile, my work takes me all over the world, although it will be just once or twice a year for a fairly long stint at one time. Sometimes we can work in a vacation at an exotic location, so it's different from being stuck at home Monday through Friday."

Because Duncan and Julie value the time they have together as highly as the time they spend working, they made sure their careers allowed them to be together as much as possible.

"Duncan is a person you can really talk to," said Julie. "You can divulge your secrets. He's a great listener. We love to take walks, eat together, share stuff at the end of the day. But if we talk about work, it's just the surface stuff. Work can be so overwhelming that when it comes time to spend time together, we'd rather talk about other issues. We always have interesting stuff to say about things that happen to people or problems that we're having with people personality-wise. Sometimes we talk

about politics. We also love to have friends over for dinner at
least once a week. We have a social schedule with people. We
like to go to movies."

*A housework hassle*
Though they are in agreement today on so many elements of
their life together, it hasn't always been so. During their first
years of living together they were at odds over two issues—
housework and money. Their first serious difficulty lay in deciding who would handle the housework and how.

"Duncan had problems living with me at first, which I didn't
even know about until a couple years later," said Julie. "Our
lifestyles are very different. He's very ordered, very clean; I don't
have that sensibility. At first he did a heck of a lot more cleaning
up around us than I did because I didn't know how to be that
way or how to meet his standards. My parents were creative
types, and our home was always messy. His father was very much
a traditional 'company man' for a large corporation, and the
family moved often when he was transferred, and they were
extremely organized in their ways.

"This became such a source of contention that at one point
he almost wanted to break up with me. I remember crying about
it. I was very sensitive about the bathtub being dirty. It made me
feel like I was a bad person because I wasn't up to his standards."

The problems simmered until finally, after periodic fights,
the couple brought it out into the open. "Duncan and I tend to
handle things like this slowly; the solution evolves. In this case
each of us finally arrived at a recognition of what we wanted. I
had never done house things and wasn't interested in them,
while Duncan is much more domestic, is a far better cook than I
am, and enjoys it more. It has worked out that he oversees the
housework, and he does practically all the cooking. I'm the sous-
chef—I cut things up, but I don't really have a great interest in it.
I love to bake, but I don't like to cook. Duncan makes most of the
meals when he comes home, although I'll do the grocery
shopping.

"Once we were both working, we got a cleaning lady. She comes in once a week for the major work, and that's really all we need. Duncan usually takes the garbage out. As for the wash, the cleaning lady does some, I do some, and Duncan does some. He takes his own dry cleaning in and picks it up. See, all that was encouraged in his family, whereas in my family, all that was artsy, funny, witty, theatrical was much more encouraged than taking care of the home. I help out with dinners. We have a gardener that comes in once a week but he's not very good, so Duncan has taken over the yard work; he seems to love it."

Duncan's taking charge of the domestic side of their household reflects a strong trend away from the gender gridlock that has long identified housework as woman's work. Fifty-six percent of the women recently polled by Condé Nast Publications, Inc., said they don't like to do everyday cooking. A 1985 survey published in *American Demographics* magazine reported that the men have increased their share of the home work load to roughly one hour for every two that a woman puts in. That's an astounding increase if you compare it with a 1965 survey in which men put in one hour for every six hours of housework done by women! It's predicted that a decade from now most households will show an even fifty-fifty split in these responsibilities. And while interviewing for this book, I'm happy to report, I found that a solid 90 percent of the men said they do laundry and over half take primary responsibility for cooking and grocery shopping.

It is important to note, however, that money was the factor that enabled these couples to work out their "housework" problem; both partners felt it was important enough to spend money on housecleaning rather than continually disagree over standards of cleanliness or time allotted to household chores. In this case, priorities meshed and they could afford the additional expense. But resolving all financial issues was not that easy.

*Dueling for dollars*

Julie and Duncan's upbringing clearly influenced their approach to housework. It also influenced their attitudes toward money—

with some very negative results. Yet the way in which they resolved that difficulty gives us a clue to why and how their young love affair was able to blossom into such a sound, loving marriage.

"We keep all our money in a joint account, and we have both of our names on it," said Julie. "All our personal and house expenses are paid out of that account, but spending money has been a point of contention in the past.

"At first Duncan was much more frugal than he is now and much more judgmental of my expenditures. Then, a few years ago, after many years of fighting and feeling guilty about buying things for himself, he finally let go. It had a lot to do with one particular episode that happened when we were visiting my mother. I had gone out and bought an outfit for myself, brought it back to Mom's house, and was looking for approval. The approval I wanted was recognition of how good I looked and that it didn't bother him that I had spent the money. Well, he wasn't very approving. He was glum, disapproving, in fact. And that bothered me.

"I remember my mother talked to him about how important clothes were to me, and she felt bad that he was being judgmental about my having gone out and bought something. That caused us to finally think hard and talk about money and what it meant to each of us.

"Duncan realized that he projected the same feelings he had picked up from his father, who is a very successful man but still shops at thrift stores, where he can pay as little as 25¢ for a sports jacket. This is a man who was invited to meet President Carter and wore plastic shoes.

"Ever since he was a kid, Duncan was a sounding board for both his parents, who have had a sort of unhappy truce for years and live apart six months of the year. This whole money issue allowed Duncan to start seeing how unhappy his mother was and why. Even though his father makes enough money and she stayed home while the children were young, she now works so that she can have her own money. So Duncan put one and one together and just let go. He understood where his uptightness about money and control was coming from, and all of a sudden it was no longer the most important issue. What became more important was that we live happily. And that the money was there to be used—you can't take it with you.

"I still have to push him to buy stuff, because his initial urge is to put everything into our savings plan, but when he does, he is more comfortable with spending. Now he'll go out and buy new clothes when he needs them, with less worry and more pleasure. We even shop together and have a good time. He feels great, and he's learned how to enjoy material things in his life, which I don't think he did before. He was the third child out of four; all he got was hand-me-downs.

"At the same time, we took a good look at my attitude toward money, too. My family was very different—my mother was the breadwinner. When my folks couldn't make it as artists, which is what they were, my mom took a job as a secretary and worked her way up to a top administration post for the federal government.

"That caused much conflict in my parents' marriage. Finances and money were a big deal. So it's a very emotional topic for me too. I remember we would go out for pizza, and she would pass the money to my dad under the table. I think she controlled the money. They never worked it out, because they couldn't talk about it.

"As a result, I never wanted to be in a weak position of having to depend on someone else. Even though I've been making really good money only for the last few years, there have been times when I've supported my parents. But I have always had money to buy my own things. I started working at fourteen at Kentucky Fried Chicken. I did jobs here and there. And I traveled. I went to Israel when I was seventeen. I graduated early from high school, went out on my own right away.

"I paid my own way through college, and I was able to get scholarships because my grades were very good. Also, I lived very cheaply, and I had a room that cost me fourteen dollars a month. When Duncan and I moved in together, we lived really frugally, and it was fun. We are still two people who put saving first and check our resources before making any major purchases, however.

"So once we sorted out where the resentment over the money was coming from for both of us, we were able to take a more realistic and comfortable position on it. Plus, Duncan is very proud of what I do. And overwhelmed at how successful I've been. Financially, especially. So those arguments are over. Done."

On their own, Julie and Duncan reached a level of maturity that experts feel is crucial to the ability to establish a healthy, intimate relationship with another adult. It's a level of maturity marked by the ability to view your parents as separate individuals with needs and strengths and weaknesses totally separate from their roles as parents. For many people this happens in their late twenties or early thirties, while some, like Julie and Duncan, are fortunate to find that perspective on the men and women who raised them early in their twenties. It makes a big difference.

Before you reach that point, you are likely to rely on your parents' opinions and attitudes when making choices in life and trying to cope with difficult decisions; after that point "more mature young adults tend to have strong confidence in their abilities to make decisions on their own . . . they also see themselves as the best judges of their own worth and so can risk parental disapproval by expressing values that may clash with those of their parents," according to a report on several recent studies published in *Developmental Psychology* and reported in the *New York Times*. The critical point is that the mature person can draw a clear line between his or her own life and that of his or her parents.

Julie and Duncan were able to be honest about familial patterns that were influencing them and to establish new rules that work for them as a couple. They do not force each other to immediate solutions, but, as Julie pointed out, they "evolve" toward them.

### Evolving toward change and a child

A key example of how well this method works for them is their decision to reorder their carefully balanced lives with the addition of a child.

"I always said that if I was going to have a child, I knew it would be because we both wanted it," stated Julie. "It hit me in a curious way while I was on an assignment that took me to Kenya. I was coming back from a safari, and we were driving through this incredible field of baobab trees. I saw a giraffe cross the road, then another giraffe, then I looked out across the valley, and underneath one of the huge trees I saw an entire family of elephants in these concentric circles surrounding the tree. It was some sort of powwow. I could see that next to the big mama elephants were these little baby elephants. At that moment I said, 'I want a child.'

"A couple days later I met Duncan in Greece. He was just waking up when I arrived at the hotel—a very romantic moment. And right at the beginning of this romantic moment we looked at each other and knew we were both ready. I walked over to the window, and I threw my diaphragm out in the street! So there's a rubber diaphragm right in the area of the Acropolis.

"I guess there had been a process leading up to that time," she said, "but I didn't know why, intellectually. Yet we were both together in knowing what we wanted.

"It took two years for me to get pregnant. During that time we would talk about how we could find a balance to make this possible since neither of us wants to stop working.

"Duncan is extremely supportive about whatever I want to do. And he's very excited about having a child. Lately he has been expressing his own anxieties—he would love to stay home for a year. Just the other day he said that he's jealous of the fact that he has to go back to work at the office every day while I get to stay here.

"For me the issue right now is the kind of work I'm going to do. If I move away from what I've been doing, then our income will go way down, which we have allowed for just in case. Duncan makes enough so we can handle it, even though I don't want that to happen.

"I feel more ambitious than I've ever felt in my entire life. I don't know if it's good or bad. I'm concerned about it because on the one hand I want to allow myself to love this baby as much as I really think I will, which will be a lot. I know that I could easily get totally absorbed with the baby and feel that it was completely worthwhile.

"On the other hand, I feel that way about work too. I feel I have the capacity to both work and care for the baby, yet I'm not sure how I can accommodate both. Fortunately, I have enough of a base at all levels to be able to take a break, then return and start up production again if I want to. But I also find it very interesting how one stage I've reached in my work has coincided with the birth of the baby: I've finally reached a point where I've gained enough expertise and experience that I feel comfortable enough to take my work a step further. I want to develop my ideas, expand the documentaries, get into TV and some other areas of production. And having the baby is going to make the little time that I have in between taking care of it more precious. And that's what I need. It will encourage me to cut back on the daily production stuff and to give more thought to new directions. If I want to do something that's different from what I've done in the past, the next step requires a different approach, and I'm looking at this time when the baby comes as a chance to not be in production but to develop concepts."

Will it work for them? Without doubt. They have set up a good system, a constantly evolving balance between work and home that is always open to their changing needs. Work segues into love and home life and back again. That means Julie and Duncan are very likely to ease into a new series of balancing acts when that child arrives, give themselves opportunities to explore how much time and effort they can devote to the close-knit home life they treasure, yet be able to maintain the separate careers they both value.

The challenge is to do so in ways that keep their life together comfortable and mutually fascinating. As equal partners, I think they'll do it.

### Money Issues Don't Have to Cause Pain: Blair and Dan

At first glance Blair and her husband, Dan, are two intimidating people—two tough professionals in a very tough business.

Tall and well dressed with black hair and green eyes, thirty-eight-year-old Blair is a woman with full features and a lively face. She has been director of a team of investigators specializing in retrieving computerized financial information. Her husband is just as striking in appearance: a tall, dark, handsome man. He carries a gun, but it's well hidden in the slim lines of his expertly tailored suit. They met when the team he was running was involved in a parallel and confidential operation. In contrast to his wife's outgoing, active manner, Dan is relaxed, laid-back, laconic.

Though both are savvy, no-nonsense experts, both have been fooled by love. But that has changed. Now they have each other. Married for four years, they have been living in Fort Worth, sharing a quiet, ordered, very pretty home decorated in autumn colors with touches of mauve and pink. A recent assignment to Spain is, however, changing their lives. Dan is about to embark on a two-year project that will propel him into the top management of his international firm, which specializes in white collar criminal investigations, while Blair has temporarily resigned her position in order to move with him and undertake intensive Spanish language instruction so she can resume her career abroad.

At the time we talked, Dan and Blair still shared their Texas home. Its upper floor had been given over to a studio where he sculpted while she wrote or they strummed their guitars together. The story of how and why they met and fell in love shows how money can equal power, in good ways and in bad.

*Money: A promise or a threat?*

For Blair, in particular, money has shaped her life in unexpected ways, forcing her into difficult struggles with dependency and self-esteem at an early age. You'd never know it, watching her talk. She hunches forward, her eyes snapping, as she begins a funny, raunchy story with a punch line guaranteed to turn your ears pink. She is a raconteur par excellence. And quite wise about people. So how come such a smart woman got so psychologically beat up in her first marriage?

"My folks were really screwed up," she recalls, her voice level and direct. "I wasn't tuned in to it at the time because they sent me to boarding school, but both my parents were alcoholics and their marriage was coming apart during my first year in college. My mother was the worst at that time, and eventually she committed suicide.

"Shortly before they were divorced, my father went bankrupt and never paid my college tuition, so right after I met Paul, my first husband, I found myself pretty much on my own financially and with no role models for healthy relationships. My older brothers had married and were very traditional with their wives. I worshipped my brother, who was a CIA agent, and that got me interested in a similar line of work.

"When I met Paul, we were in college. I was a freshman, and he was a senior. He was interested in business, and I was planning on law school. The more we talked, the more he became interested in law, too. We ended up getting married when I was still in school, just nineteen. Marriage meant security to me. With no money coming from my father, I felt the need to be with another man as that made me feel more secure financially—at least I knew there'd be a roof over my head.

"He graduated and went into the service, while I was able to get a scholarship to finish school. After that I earned minimum wage as a clerk until he completed his years in the navy. Then we both applied to law school and got in. Things were pretty equal in our marriage at that point.

"We went into hock together with national student loans, so when we graduated from law school he owed $10,000 and I owed $13,000. We both worked part-time in school and split house stuff pretty much fifty-fifty. Whoever cooked didn't do the dishes. And I usually cooked, although he did breakfast. People who knew us then thought we were the perfect couple, the perfect fifty-fifty partners in the early seventies, when that was fairly radical. Little did they know . . .

"I should have paid more attention to our parents' patterns: mine were very traditional, but his parents were even more so. He was one of six children; his father was authoritarian and dictatorial. The boys all worked in the family business for no wages. Later, his father bought the boys stock, so they ended up with a lot of money when they got out of college. He did not buy his daughters any stock. They were the ones who did all the housework.

"I finally got it out of Paul after our divorce just how much he hated me for not being subservient like the women in his family. He never should have married somebody like me in the first place. Intellectually he thought it was nifty—he was impressed that I'd gone to a private high school, that I wanted a law degree, which put me on the cutting edge of the women's movement. I was real smart, and he thought he liked that.

"But once we were in graduate school together, he grew to hate me and expressed it in strange ways. We hardly ever had sex after the first year. I scare myself when I look back at how emotionally dependent on him I was. I wouldn't bring up anything that might cause him to make a remark that would hurt my feelings.

"Just once I pushed him on why we weren't making love anymore. At first I broached it teasingly, and he said sharply, 'I'm not keeping score; I don't know why you are,' in a tone of voice that implied 'Don't bring this up anymore.' Then I got brave and pushed him a little further, saying, 'It's been two months.'

"This time he said—and it devastated me—'One thing is, you've gained weight since we got married, and I really don't find you attractive.' That was enough to shut me up for the next eight years of marriage. I let it hurt me so bad, and it wasn't even true. I was in better shape then than I was when we got married.

"But at the time it didn't matter. What he believed and what he felt were what was important. Even though we were both working, were sharing the housework, he'd say, 'Jump,' and I'd say, 'How high?' My fragile ego and lack of self-esteem were all tied up in him. So we went to law school, and we kept house, but he never touched me.

"I'd always been proud of my achievements, and after the first semester I made the Dean's List regularly until I did this weird thing. A friend of mine was working as assistant to the dean, and she claims—and I don't remember any of this—that I took her aside and asked to be deleted from the Dean's List to avoid upsetting my husband. And I don't remember any of that, even though I'm sure she's not lying."

What had started as a subtle attack on her self-esteem in law school escalated into a full-scale assault on Blair's self-confidence and independence as she began to succeed as a young lawyer.

"Paul and I joined the firms where we had clerked. His was an established firm, and he got much more money than I did. I went to work for two guys who could barely afford to pay me. I graduated in 1975 and made $6,500 the first year to Paul's $11,500. In those days a top firm was paying $14,500, and on Wall Street they were paying only $17,000. Now they're paying $60,000 to start. But $6,500 gross is what I made with a law degree, with *Law Review*, graduating in the top 15 percent of my class.

"Again, I suppressed everything to try to keep our marriage on an even keel. When the guys I worked for turned out to be real jerks, I began looking for another job right away. My office was truly horrible to work in, so when I finally was offered a great job I went in and told these two guys I was leaving but that I would like to stay on for two more months.

"Meanwhile, Paul had been railing about how they had treated me, even though he was nicey-nicey to their faces when we socialized. Behind their backs he was saying, 'You should push and get paid more.' This is when he's making $30,000 and I'm probably making $14,000. But when the jerks refused to pay me, pushed me out the door instead of letting me finish the two months, and made fun of my new job, Paul screamed at me, 'Omigod, you're going to be without a job for two months. We can't afford that.' And he made me go and beg for my job back— which I did. It was so humiliating. They took me back for two weeks and made my life miserable. I still can't believe I put up with that—and I knew we really didn't need that money. But I couldn't upset Paul.

"My new job changed the whole ball game. Suddenly I was working for a very well-known prosecutor and making a lot more money. A lot more. I was making $28,500—within $4,000 or $5,000 of what Paul was making. Not only that, but getting the job was a big deal. I was the only woman assistant, the first and the only woman assistant. And what a job! I started meeting the top lawyers and investigators and having my own cases, both civil and criminal. It was a high like I can't tell you. And the money was what did it. I felt like a human being for the first time.

"That's when it really got nasty with Paul. Right after I got the new job, we went out to celebrate and we both had too much to drink. Paul started driving home and was kind of pawing me in the car and making suggestive remarks. It got to be a real power struggle. Then he pulled over in the middle of a busy street and just demanded that we make love in the car, two blocks from home. That's the first time I stood up to him. I said, 'Just get out of here,' and I refused. Then, a few weeks later, I won my first case—and he wouldn't talk to me for two days!"

It took Blair a year from that time to make the decision to leave Paul and yet another year to actually do it.

"Getting the money was like an awakening of self, as was the job and meeting people who made it clear they admired me and found me attractive—it almost immediately pushed a wedge between Paul and me," said Blair. "I started getting angry. I began to feel more power as a human being. I began to make lists of the 'pros and cons' of staying in this marriage. There were always more cons than pros.

"That summer I had had it. Paul left on a business trip, and while he was out of town I snuck around, rented an apartment, opened my own bank account, got the utilities turned on, then I called him to say I was leaving—with tears running down my face. I was so afraid to be by myself. To be in charge. We got back together the next day, and it took another year before I moved out.

"During that time I got more accustomed to my job. I was now making $38,000—more than Paul! And I was discovering I was attractive to other people. Maybe it's not a very liberated way to think, but that was a big part of strengthening myself. I realized all of a sudden, I'm not only a woman but a really attractive woman. I had started running and getting in shape, which was a threat to Paul. I was building my self-confidence as a woman and as a thinking, smart person, and I was slowly working my way into a mind-set that life does not revolve around a man, that I had a neat job and stuff, that I could make it on my own."

And so Blair stepped out on her own, no longer afraid she might die like her mother, sick, alone, without money, and despairing. No longer afraid to stand up to a man and tell him what she thought.

"The most significant change I made right after my divorce was to apply to my personal life the same thinking I was using in law," said Blair. "I refused to take the relationships that did not work out as any sign of personal failure. Instead I would think, Oh, this plan didn't work; let's try another. I made each new relationship an opportunity for a challenge, not a failure. Many of the people I went out with before I met Dan are still very good friends of mine, too."

*Work, love, . . . and money*
Within a few months of her divorce, Blair took a new job heading up an investigative team of lawyers and accountants skilled at tracking down specific kinds of industry fraud. She moved to Texas and soon ran into forty-two-year-old Dan, who was renowned as a savvy investigator and was directing a project parallel to hers within the same company. Dan had heard about her before they met.

"I knew other investigators that worked with Blair and said what a great ballbuster she was," said Dan. "She had a terrific reputation by the time we met. I say 'ballbuster' in a positive sense—we all felt she exhibited the same traits as a male in her job. You have to if you want to attain the goals that law enforcement thinks are important.

"I was never threatened by that. That could be because the occupation she was in was something I was very familiar with. I knew that Blair was working in a predominantly male field. In a way, it was necessary for her to fit the image that men have of women that take those roles. Brassy woman, pushy bitch. But I got to know her socially, and she was delightful."

"Leaving aside the fact that he's so very good-looking, I would have noticed him anyway," said Blair. "I spotted Dan at the perfect time. By then I was very happy with my job, had had a lot of successes, felt on top of the world, had a lot of good friends who were investigators and respected me. When I met Dan, I knew who he was because I wrote the brief on a big case that he had broken. He doesn't remember meeting me, but it was at a party in March of '83. I saw this great-looking guy who had two beers and left!

"We later began talking on the phone about the case his team was handling that overlapped some of ours. He said he had a lot of material on the matter and asked if I wanted to go to lunch sometime. I thought he was married.

"So we went to lunch, and I couldn't get over how thin he was. I found out he was going through a divorce and had lost twenty-five pounds. I lost a few going through mine, too. So we laughed about that and ended up having a lot of fun. And that was the beginning of something wonderful."

Meeting as they did, Dan and Blair respected each other right from the start. At the same time, each already knew the other to be intelligent, courageous, dedicated, and willing to take risks in a dangerous and fascinating job. They knew they shared the same perspective on human behavior and would understand each other's career pressures.

Equally valuable and also a reason that so many truly equal relationships begin in work-related situations is that when people are at work, no one is posing and the atmosphere is free of the sexual pressures and tensions so common to social gatherings. Furthermore, when people have important work information to share, they have a valid respect for each other.

And so Blair and Dan set up another date for drinks after work. Two years later they were married.

The contrast between Blair and Dan's life together and each one's past marriage could not be sharper, whether the issue is money or intimacy or just spending time together. Though they have an even split when it comes to housework (much as both did in the past), Dan takes more responsibility for cooking and Blair buys most of the groceries. But everything else is handled much differently.

For Dan one major change had to do with control of the money. In his first, fairly traditional marriage, he and his wife both worked. While he did more than half the housework and

cooking for his wife and their two daughters, she kept tight
control of the purse strings. It was a system they had set up while
he was away in the service, but she had refused to relinquish
financial control when he returned.

"I never had control of the checking account," recalled
Dan. "I'd bring my paychecks home from my job, give them to
Diane, she'd deposit them, and then she wrote all the checks. If I
needed money for lunches, I'd go to her purse to get the cash. So
when we separated, I liked it that I had my own checkbook and
finally had control over my money.

"When Blair and I got married we decided to maintain
separate accounts, and I enjoy that. We made an agreement as to
what bills I would pay. We've kept that system today. For a while
she was making more money than I was, but even then we split
our bills down the middle. Now the shoe is on the other foot,
because Blair is not working at the moment. I think she would
resent having to ask me for money, so I try not to put her in that
position. Instead I set aside expense money for both of us and
check her account every few days. If she is low, I put more in. I
try to make sure she doesn't have to ask me for any.

For Blair a major difference became apparent when she
went through a career crisis. "A year ago my division got a new
supervisor who is an old-time kind of guy who can't work with
women. He sure can't work with me," said Blair. "The pressure
from him got worse over the months until I was nearly frantic
and bringing it all home. There is a rule in business: if your boss
doesn't like you, it's over. I didn't want to admit that.

"Dan told me right away that I should get out. I contrast that
with when I left that first law firm and Paul had said, 'You've got
to go back in and do this.' Dan didn't even want me to take a
leave of absence. He said it would just make me feel worse, that I
should just cut off the job. He said my peace of mind and
happiness were more important to him than the money—and we
would just cut back if we had to. He was right."

But more than anything, they have an enduring sense of
intimacy born of open communication and understanding.

"I must talk to Blair twenty times more than I ever did my
first wife," explained Dan. "It's so totally different now just
because we have so many similar interests. I like hiking in the

woods; so does Blair. My ex-wife, if we went fishing, she'd sit in the car. I like going out and listening to music in nightclubs; that was never part of my first marriage. I like traveling and seeing new places—never a part of my first marriage. Work has a lot to do with it, because I enjoy hearing about Blair's cases and exploring things that are going on that I'd never know otherwise. Even a sense of humor is something we share—we probably have a good laugh together five or ten times a day."

Yet all is not perfect, nor do Dan and Blair try to pretend that it is.

"We are in the midst of a major career move and change for me," said Dan, "plus the pressure of the uncertainty of where Blair is with her work. She will have to find a job once she knows the language, and she worries about that. It's like we're out of step here for the time being."

"That's right," said Blair with a grimace. "This has been tough. The Spain offer came through, which was great, but with no timetable. So my 'recess' for learning the language and finding a job has stretched into a year, during which time I haven't been making any money. I have had to reassess where my sense of self-worth is coming from—I can't tie it all to money, yet there is no denying that a good income makes me feel better."

Within a few weeks of our interviews Dan and Blair were able to complete their plans for Spain by looking at all the issues. "When we were making the decision to take the position in Spain offered to Dan, it was hard because he will miss his girls, ages ten and sixteen, who live with their mother," said Blair. "He's more introspective than I am, and he hasn't talked a lot about it, but he's been in tears a couple of times. There are days when I just hold him until he feels a little better."

Dan is feeling better, and so is Blair, who was offered an opportunity to consult at a salary level that relieved her anxiety. Not only will Blair be working with an American firm on a part-time basis while they are abroad, but she has enrolled in a postgraduate creative writing program at the university. "Taught in Spanish!" she notes with a laugh. "I'm up for the challenge."

Meantime, all the upheaval surrounding this change gave them a chance to test the skills both feel are critical to the survival of their marriage over the long term. This is important for everyone, particularly since a recent survey of 1,001 young professionals between the ages of twenty-five and forty-nine pointed out that fully 41 percent feel they would welcome a career change sometime over the next five years. That means nearly half of us are likely to experience the kind of change currently affecting Blair and Dan. How did they handle it?

"The main thing I've learned over the last decade is how frightened I was of any conflict between myself and the man I thought I loved," said Blair. "That's why I never brought up anything. I was too scared, too fragile to be confrontational. Now that I know what kind of a person he was, I realize we would never have gotten married if I had been wise enough and confident enough to bring things up earlier, before we made it legal.

"So at the time I was getting serious about Dan, I was able to weigh how deadly it was not to bring things up against the very real risk of doing so. You have to have something in yourself to fall back on in case it doesn't work between you, and that's why my career at that point was so important to me. It really was my sense of self, which is the problem I'm facing now. My career doesn't mean as much to me, so now I'm trying to figure out who I am.

"Early on it was kind of the theme song of our relationship that I'm going to bring things out in the open. Dan knows it's good, but he's more of an introvert than I am. He doesn't bring things up as easily; he needs to have it dragged out. If he feels angry about something, he tends to think about it. I can tell when he's real quiet that something is troubling him."

Dan nods and smiles softly at his wife's words, agreeing with his wife's analysis of their dynamic. Then he tunes in to her dilemma, too: "I kind of miss her employment now, but it's not from a standpoint of anything other than I think she misses it. She's happiest when she's working hard and feeling productive. My advice to couples like us, who see a transition point in life coming, is to plan for it financially so no one feels like he or she is taking advantage of the other. Six months from now all this will be sorted out and we'll be over the hump, so I give her a hug and tell her to look ahead. She can't do any more than she has until we move, and that's a couple months away."

Blair and Dan have accurately targeted each other's fears and worries, so guessing games are not part of their balancing act. They may be in transition, but they are successfully tracking and making the most of their changes.

## Facing Up to Financial Responsibility: Linda and John

Julie and Duncan and Blair and Dan are couples whose joint earnings are well over $100,000 annually, giving them some leeway in sorting out money issues. Linda and John are at the other end of the spectrum: Linda earns $27,000 a year as a layout artist for an advertising agency; John makes over $30,000 as a computer technician. The two thirty-two-year-olds live in the rural upper peninsula of northern Michigan in a charming Victorian frame house they are restoring.

Blond and bouncy Linda, the oldest of six rambunctious Irish-Catholic kids raised in suburban Milwaukee, hit the skids of depression when she was twenty-seven. She had married young, only to discover she had little in common with the man she had chosen. When she divorced him, she had to face the fact that she was alone—physically and financially.

"I had never been alone before the divorce. I came from a house with six kids, and I hated being alone. I didn't like going to bed and waking up alone. I didn't like not knowing what I'd do on Saturday and Sunday.

"Financially, I was terrified. The first year I was divorced, I bought everything generic. At home I would keep the lights and heat off in my apartment—go to bed and watch TV in the dark, scared to death. I can't tell you what I thought would be so tragic. I guess I worried about what would happen in the future. I call that year of my life the 'bag-lady blues.'"

Linda's terror of being poor, like the fear Blair conquered when she started making good money as a lawyer, is no longer an unusual phenomenon. Recently, articles and editorials have been popping up everywhere, discussing the "bag-lady syndrome" as if the women who wake up in the middle of the night worrying about their finances are neurotic, somehow misdirected in their concern.

Not so. So long as women have been financially dependent on men, the nightmare of poverty has been a men-only syndrome. Now it has spread across the sexual barrier. Is it a neurosis? Hardly. Like the disturbing dreams that a new mother has of dangers surrounding her baby, these images of poverty are signs of psychologically healthy preparation by a woman planning to take care of herself. And well she should. The odds are she may have to!

Already one household in six contains a woman living alone, and nearly half of those women have incomes below $10,000. Two-thirds of the women living alone are over the age of fifty-five, hardly a time when these women are most employable. These chilling statistics were reported by *American Demographics*, which also predicted that these numbers, which rose 55 percent since the early seventies, will rise another 30 percent by 2001—a year in which 16.7 million women may find themselves living alone. Linda's fear was well grounded if out of proportion to her age and her earning ability.

"I finally settled down after I made myself imagine the very worst that could happen to me," said Linda. "I figured I can always wait tables—so big deal!"

It was a solution she may have found on her own but one highly recommended by experts who encourage people to think of their problems as only temporary. That's what Linda did, and it worked.

"I spent my winter eating soup and then one day I realized I had $3,000 in the bank, a good job, and was making it just fine," said Linda. "I had even begun to enjoy balancing my checkbook and watching my cash flow. It took six months, but my confidence returned once I had firm evidence I was managing really well."

Soon after she had eased up on herself and retired the bag-lady blues so she could get out and have some fun, Linda met John.

"We lived in the same apartment building, and I had a vegetable patch next to his. We started talking about broccoli and stuff, and I enjoyed his company. We were the same age and knew some of the same people. Romance wasn't even a part of it then, but I liked him because I knew he got a kick out of me. I'm real energetic, and he would tease me about it. So we developed a friendship. He was probably the best friend I had right after I got divorced. You could talk to John all night, but he was just a buddy. I had a lot of guy friends. So I was seeing him as a friend—no commitment.

"Over the next four years we just began to kind of grow toward each other. I had a couple of opportunities to date, but I didn't want to do it. I liked just him.

"Finally, after about four years of being together and two years when we were definitely dating, my father called me and said, 'We really like this guy; we'd like him to be part of this family.'

"My father had never done that. I said, 'Dad, I don't know.' This was right when I was thinking about breaking up with John because he hadn't given me any signs of commitment. That was in August. I told John I thought we should date other people. He said, 'You can date.' I responded, 'What about you? I think you should date other people.' And he said, 'No.'

"So I asked him if he wanted to get married. 'Do you think we're ready?' he asked me.

"I said, 'Of course we're ready; we've known each other four years!' We got married at Christmastime."

Nothing much changed after they were wed. Linda and John knew each other well. They kept their separate checking accounts and worked out an even division of expenses on their home. "I wanted to be independent. My folks had a traditional marriage, and that wasn't the answer for me," Linda explained. "Too many years were so unhappy for my mother, but she couldn't change anything, because she didn't have any money. My father hoarded cash on her, too. She was always poor, and we kids started working early because it was the only way to have things."

Linda and John agree that it's important to spend time and money on their hobbies and vacations. They love to take two long ski vacations every winter. Linda, who trains horses as a hobby, boards an Arabian stallion close to their home. "I keep that bag-lady image in the back of my mind, although she doesn't

terrify me like she used to," said Linda. "On the other hand, she
is why I put so much into my savings every week. That way, I
don't feel like I'm risking the future. And I see even my horse as
an investment and not just fun.

"We both like to ski, John with a vengeance. I love the look
on his face and the sound in his voice when we're on the slopes.
That's the one pleasure I could never take away, as much as I
want to get mad at him over it sometimes, when he insists we go
every single winter weekend. We also like to go to the lake and
spend the day sometimes.

"Those are things we always budget for. Other than that,
how I felt about money before I was married has a lot to do with
the way I am about it today. I feel that, if it's for a good cause, you
should spend it—don't give up something important to you just
to have the money in your pocket. I got over that panic about
money, and I never want to be like my father, who still hoards it.

"John and I are different from my parents because we trust
each other's ability to save money steadily and to spend it
conservatively on things we both appreciate. We don't assume
the money will always roll in. Right now, for example, he is
encouraging me to open a shop of my own. I can't do that yet,
but I'm taking two years to see if my client base will grow large
enough to make that possible. My concern over money is no
longer neurotic, but it is there and it is wise. As long as I pay
close attention to it, I relax, because I know I handle it well. And
we're alike that way: we spend some on expenses, some on fun,
and we save the rest.

"We have separate accounts, and I keep up to date on what
he's earning. Right now, he earns more than I do. He's been
getting lots of merit raises. I was making more than he at one
point but not recently.

"We keep our money separate not because I don't want to
put it together—it's a matter of convenience. We have different
paydays and different banks, because we work in different
towns. So this is simpler. John pays the mortgage and major
house bills: the lumber company, the water bill, his car insurance. I am on his health policy. He buys all his own clothes and
pays for his Y membership. I pay all the groceries, the gas, the

phone, and I buy the furniture. The mortgage payment is pretty high. So everything that's in our house—furniture, chandeliers, etc.—I've bought.

"We don't owe any money on anything other than my car loan and my car insurance, which I pay. I probably save more than he does. We do have a money market fund, in both names, in case anything happens. He knows I'm proud of saving. Even if it's $10 a week, I put something in the bank. And he never, ever says, 'What are you doing with the money?'"

## Quiz: Are Your Ideas about Money Up to Date?

You may be earning an excellent salary but still have some very old-fashioned ideas about managing your financial resources. Often dangerous attitudes don't show up until you've got to make your spending and investing decisions in tandem with someone else.

Consider the following and circle your answer:

1. Recently married, Gary and Amanda earn the same amount of money. You think their money should be handled this way:
   a. He pays for all necessities; her salary is used for extras.
   b. They should pool all their funds in one joint account with Gary in charge.
   c. They should maintain separate accounts but consult regularly in order to keep up to date on shared expenses and any partner's special financial needs.

2. In your fantasy marriage, the higher salary is earned by:
   a. the man.
   b. usually the man, but on occasion the woman.
   c. whichever partner has the most advanced career or is in the higher-paying field.

3. When a man finds it necessary to make a purchase costing over $500, he should:
   a. go ahead and do it.
   b. make the purchase without checking with his wife, but let her know what he did and why.
   c. check with his wife beforehand to be sure she agrees with his choice and the price to be paid.

4. Recently divorced, Alicia is thirty-eight years old. She is concerned that her current savings habits won't provide all she needs for retirement. She should:
   a. not worry about it—she'll probably get married before she needs to think about it.
   b. open an IRA and put something away every year at tax time.
   c. establish a retirement savings plan that is at the top of her list of monthly financial priorities.

5. The best way to manage family finances is to:
   a. put the husband in charge.
   b. put the husband in charge but have him review the annual expenses and budget with his wife each year as he does their taxes.
   c. trade off taking full responsibility every six months; trade off doing the taxes each year.

6. Money matters should be discussed:
   a. once a year.
   b. monthly.
   c. weekly.

7. A prenuptial agreement:
   a. really isn't necessary if you love and trust one another.
   b. is necessary only if one of you has children from a previous marriage.
   c. is mandatory. Each partner should have *his or her own lawyer* review the document before signing.

8. The family member in charge of monthly cash flow should be:
   a. the highest earner.

b. the woman if the man doesn't have time.

c. the one who has the time and gets the greatest satisfaction from the job; even so, the responsibility should be traded off or shared regularly.

9. Bob and Anne are angry with each other because her expenses are twice what he spends on discretionary items each month, even though they earn about the same amount. Anne should:

a. ask Bob before she buys anything.

b. let Bob know when she needs something so he isn't surprised by her purchases.

c. sit down with Bob and not only review their finances but also talk over what makes each of them feel better about themselves; then reach a compromise on how much they will each spend independently before needing to consult on a major purchase.

10. Shortly after their wedding (the second for each), Alice discovered Tyler had not put her name on stock certificates purchased with family funds. Alice should:

a. just forget about it. He'll get mad if she brings it up and accuse her of trying to "take him" like his former wife did.

b. sit tight and wait a year or two until the right moment, when Tyler is feeling happy and secure with her.

c. tell him she finds the omission very disturbing and suggest they each hire a lawyer to draw up a "postnuptial agreement" designed to protect both their financial interests. If he finds this upsetting, she should ask him to seek counseling—as a couple or separately.

11. You both work full-time, and although you earn different salaries, you share your living costs fifty-fifty. Your bill from the shop where you buy most of your clothes arrives—and your husband opens it by mistake. He is shocked that you spent $500 last month and tells you so. You say:

a. "I'm really sorry, but it was an outfit I needed. I'm paying for it on layaway, but I promise not to spend that kind of money again without asking you."

b. "I agree I should have mentioned it to you, but I was rushed last week, and I forgot. Will this jeopardize the money you wanted to spend on new skis and boots? I know it's about the same amount. . . ."
c. "That's just for my new shoes and purse. The entire bill will come in at $1,500." End of conversation.

*Scoring*
Give yourself 5 points for every (c) answer, 3 points for every (b) answer, 1 point for every (a) answer.

*Totals*
11-29—Too traditional. You need to learn how to take better care of your personal financial matters.
30-44—You seem willing to take responsibility for your finances, but only to a point. Keep working at it—the payoff is worth it in more ways than one.
45-55—You've most likely got everything under control, financially speaking.

## Money Matters

Too many couples seem to feel that, if they're in love, everything will fall into place. But it's unrealistic to think that any two people, no matter how much they have in common, will have identical feelings about how to spend every dollar. It's tempting to want to throw everything into one big pot, but too often one person feels resentful when she contributes more or he spends more. It's also tempting to keep all finances separate to maintain a sense of autonomy and financial independence. But one of the most wonderful things about sharing your life with someone is that you share the good (if lots of money is coming in) and the bad—no partner is going to let his lover starve because she's temporarily out of work! For these reasons, happy couples find they don't just make a decision on their bank accounts and leave it at that. They remain open about their needs and feelings, and they work together to be sure both are happy. The couples we've just seen, though very different in their levels of ambition, share the following characteristics:

● relationship priority—the couples' happiness together is

more important than the career or salary of either partner
- individual maturity—each person in each couple has individual goals and has worked or is working through past influences or money hang-ups
- a sense of personal confidence not dependent on being part of a couple—this kind of confidence is most often gained through work at a job that is enjoyed and generates an acceptable salary
- the urge to work hard—at home and in the office
- trust—these couples have a solid foundation of mutual respect that enables them to work out solutions to their problems
- a willingness to compromise—each does what he or she reasonably can to make the other happy
- a need for constant communication and monitoring of feelings—the hallmark of any good relationship
- acceptance of change—none of these couples sees life as static

As we've seen, how couples work out the details is as individual as their circumstances. If you feel that your situation is so much "worse" than those of the people you've read about, or that you and your partner lack many of the characteristics listed above, take heart. With love and a desire to work things out, you too can resolve work and money issues in your relationship. But remember, this requires constant vigilance.

I have a close friend who once made much more money than her husband. Now he earns several million dollars a year, while her salary of around $80,000 has remained relatively constant. With that kind of money coming in, you'd think there wouldn't be a conflict.

"We talk about money all the time," she said. "I just wonder if we'll ever stop. I wonder if we'll ever resolve this constant discussion over who is contributing what and how much control each of us should have over decisions about the house and vacations and other purchases."

Worrisome though that kind of conflict may be, it is typical in any relationship. What was worse was that money issues seemed to be interfering with their emotional life.

"My husband's business is up and down. One day he thinks it's all down the tubes and tells me to watch household expenses; the next day he gets a big check and wants to fly to Hawaii."

By her own admission, my friend still has a tendency to slip back into the old pattern of thinking that a woman should be taken care of. Though she makes $80,000 a year, she didn't want to be involved in her husband's finances. But as his fortunes fluctuated, so did the total family income—and the tension was beginning to affect the family. So they decided to do something about it.

One day my friend went to her husband's office to discuss their family "business." He spent a good deal of time detailing the office finances, explaining his work, discussing his hopes and his worries. Their four hours together were something of a revelation. For the first time, she understood his wildly changing moods. She received an education in *his* business that made it much easier for her to cope with *their* finances. She stopped feeling so out of control, because she was able to put their mutual financial future into some kind of perspective. Most important, both she and her husband were able to start thinking of their money as a "personal business" problem rather than a personal relationship problem. They were able to talk about money as two rational, intelligent businesspeople. And their relationship has improved immeasurably.

If you're concerned about love and money, you will want to review the quiz in this chapter every few months to see how much work you need to do in this area. If you need a lot of help, you may want to skip to the last chapter for advice on working through important issues together. You may also want to get the help of a financial planner. Sometimes it's nice to tap the wisdom of an objective outsider as you begin to solve your personal business problems. But nothing and nobody can take the place of loving, trusting, and open communication about your needs, wants, and fears.

In a recent *New York Times* story on prenuptial agreements a lawyer describes a client—a bride who was also a lawyer—

who was asked to sign an unfair financial agreement just days
before her marriage to another lawyer. She finally turned to the
bridegroom and said, "Darling, I suppose this means the wedding's off, and I'm so sorry, but I cannot sign this paper. It would
be unfair to me and to our future children."

According to the *Times*, the bridegroom tore up the contract, which had been pushed by his father. They were married
in defiance of his father's wishes and went on to have children
and a strong, long-lasting marriage. The moral: Think of yourself.
Love is caring for the other person almost as much as you care
for yourself. When preparing to share your wealth, be selfish yet
fair.

## *If You Need Somewhere to Get Started*

Ideally, it's best to work through financial matters before you
commit to each other. But it's never too late to start.

*Budget basics*
Separately, list all your assets, including income from all sources,
all savings and checking accounts, life and health insurance
policies, investments, and real estate holdings. List all debts,
including mortgages, outstanding bills, child support and ali-
mony payments, outstanding school loans, car and personal
loans, annual taxes, and insurance policy premiums.

Now list current or future commitments, such as school
tuition for yourself or children or responsibility for aging parents.

Compare your lists and draw up a model, one for the two of
you, including a savings plan and a retirement plan. Ask yourselves how much you plan to spend for a car sometime in the
next five years. How much do you spend on clothes annually?

Now list which items each of you will be financially responsible for and for how long. Will you have separate or joint
checking and savings accounts? Separate investment and retirement plans? Do you need more insurance coverage?

List those assets that you must protect for children from a
previous marriage.

Now decide which of you will be the FFO—Family Financial Officer. Will this person keep the files in order and pay all the bills? For how long? I recommend you trade off doing this every six months so that both of you stay well informed.

Decide on your financial objectives for next year, five years from now, ten years from now. How often will you sit down to review your finances together—once a month, every three months, or every six months?

Establish a policy and method for making spending decisions. What size purchase should require a prior discussion between you and your partner? Fifty dollars? One hundred dollars? Should you both agree not to make any major purchases unless you are in agreement? Perhaps one of you should prevail in household purchases and one on items bought for the children. Under what circumstances will you change these rules? If you are both working, consider keeping three checking accounts: one joint account for usual expenses and two "discretionary" accounts so each of you has flexibility, privacy, and control over agreed-upon amounts of money.

Are you still talking? Good. Now decide how you will handle disagreements over your finances. Will one of you make a unilateral decision and ignore the other? Will one of you hesitate to speak up even if you disagree over money?

### Core issues

If your budget discussions are not going as well as you might hope, it may be because the two of you have not adequately articulated your priorities to each other. Discussing your life priorities—work, kids, parents, friends, leisure—may be in order. And don't assume that your partner knows your thoughts or that you know his. People change, even married people!

If you still find yourself at loggerheads or communication just isn't what it should be, think about why. Is one of you afraid? Are you both being stubborn? Take a break from it for a while or try approaching the situation differently—with humor, for example. Consider seeing a therapist. Don't just give up because it's getting tough. Your life together is worth fighting for.

# 4
# The Hardest Balancing Act:
# Two Full-Time Careers
# Plus Kids

**B**oy, are you into it now! Never again will your life be as complicated as when you are both working full-time and have just stretched your jam-packed daily schedule to include one more challenging new project—your first child.

Even if you choose to add second and third "new projects" to your family, the most significant challenge is the first: learning to balance two careers with a baby.

This period is critical, because the highest incidence of divorce occurs soon after the birth of a first child. But it's also exciting, because so much change is taking place in the world around us today that choosing this lifestyle has never been more accepted or more rewarding.

At the same time, however, it has never been more controversial. Over the last year, news of an emerging "Mommy Track" has alternately amazed and dismayed many of us. Some of us see the growing corporate awareness of the need to accommodate working parents with more flexible work hours, parental leave, and part-time options as an exciting trend that can enhance our quality of life. Others warn that such plans might too conveniently allow the same corporate entities an excuse to sidetrack working mothers and refuse to promote them into upper echelons.

This debate over whether a "Mommy Track" exists is sure to continue until corporate good intentions have been proven. However, in the next decade the sheer need for qualified people in the highest ranks of management and the professions may render some of the concern moot. Nevertheless, it is sure to be a case-by-case situation for the near future: each woman, each parent will have to measure, plan, and judge for himself or herself, balancing family needs against career risks.

Meanwhile, the facts are these: In just over a decade, the number of mothers who work full-time has skyrocketed from one third to over half—and that number, especially among mothers with very young children, is increasing. It is increasing at the same time that more and more women are making it to the top in all the professions, succeeding in positions where they now *make* policy—not just follow it. One out of every four newborn babies has a mom who is between the ages of thirty and thirty-nine. And by 1995 one of every three babies will be born to a mother over age thirty.

Clearly, the women's movement of the sixties and seventies made a difference; women today have an opportunity to make it in a "man's world." While we still have a long way to go in terms of salary equity and (in some cases) discrimination, legislation, progressive corporations, and women proving themselves have made it possible for determined females to have careers—not just jobs—in almost every field. Women can now enjoy the satisfaction and increased self-esteem that comes from being valued employees and productive members of society. In fact, today's working mother is a lot more satisfied than her stay-at-home predecessor, even if she is stressed out from time to time. A recent Gallup survey of working women showed that "working moms are more satisfied with their careers than working women without children—39 percent compared with 29 percent." Informal surveys in magazines and newspapers back that up even more strongly.

Recently, however, women with partners have begun to see their work with new eyes. Whether they want to work for self-fulfillment is secondary; many don't have a choice. Most recognize that they must work just to keep family incomes "livable." These are grim economic times: our national economy has caused incomes to drop just as houses and the basics of life are costing more than ever. A recent report by Frank Levy, an economist at the University of Maryland, pointed out that the pressure on women to work reflects "deep problems in the economy." He says that the average person's income has dropped 15 percent now that a home mortgage takes 44 percent of your annual salary. To put that in perspective, consider that not only did our parents raise most of us during a time when Dad's income was increasing healthily, but they had to spend only 21 percent of that income on their home mortgage.

Fact: you cannot feed and clothe a family today on the same money your dad did. Furthermore, over two-thirds of today's working mothers support their families themselves or have husbands who earn less than $15,000 a year.

Fortunately, women aren't alone in their need to balance career ambitions with family ambitions. Men, too, have changed over recent years. Chances are, their mothers work, or their sisters grew up expecting they would work and be able to take care of themselves. At the very least, they take a significantly different approach to sharing family responsibilities than their fathers did. Slowly but surely, men are accepting responsibilities for everything from meals to kids, from cleaning bathrooms to stocking the refrigerator—even as women opt to manage family accounts, haul wood, or construct a new rock wall. Role reversal, role overlap, role relay, role delay—from macho to mutual, whatever you call it, it's happening.

Since I have discovered that men are sharing child care and home duties in much greater numbers than the latest "official" statistics report, I am convinced that the statistics are five years behind the current reality. In other words, the statistics are so hopelessly out of date that I encourage you to believe me, not the government.

What *is* currently acknowledged by experts, however, is a momentous change in family life: both husband and wife are sharing home and child responsibilities to a much greater extent than ever before. Coupled with this is greater mutual concern for each other's job and how the demands of each job affect the family. Most important, both husbands and wives are communicating this to their respective employers—loudly, clearly, and emphatically.

A recent survey of fathers among a major American manufacturing company's 100,000 employees yielded a startling fact: over 65 percent of the men said that they were concerned with child care. Nor was it just "concern." They made it clear that company policy on child care would influence their career plans as well as those of their wives.

Add to that the fact that the U.S. Census Bureau reports in a recent "Current Population Report" that one of every five dads takes full responsibility for child care today—that's over 20 percent of American working fathers! Again, the statistic is five years old, and my hunch is the numbers here are rising rapidly as well.

Just as exciting from an economic point of view is that the birthrate in this country has plummeted 40 percent since 1957. That fact alone will soon make it clear to employers everywhere that they have little choice, if they want to develop a productive work force, but to work *with* full-time parents. That may explain why more than 3,500 American firms now provide child-care services in some form, up 40 percent since 1984, according to *USA Today*. In fact, almost every day I see press releases announcing yet another company's benefits for families in a determined effort to attract the working mother or father.

It isn't all good news, however. Some firms are cutting back such services because expenses are higher than expected, and others are simply refusing to address the need for more flexible child care. I think we are bound to see a "two steps forward, one step back" dynamic in this area over the coming decade, so be prepared to fight for the options you want.

Almost daily, newspapers report yet another group of working mothers who are making breakthroughs that allow them time to work and be moms simultaneously. Stories in the *New York Times* recently reported on two law firms establishing emergency day-care centers, others in which working mothers are accommodated schedule-wise yet allowed to participate as lead counsels on critical cases and as equity partners in demanding areas such as mergers and acquisitions, tender offers, and sophisticated financial deals. It may take more than just asking, but the time to ask is now.

## The Agony and the Ecstasy

But if the working mother and father are here to stay, how can they balance their lives?

It can be done. Here's how.

Let me introduce you to two women who work in the same office. Each has a baby and each is a manager. However, while one is happy and relaxed, thoroughly enjoying her work, her home, and her child, the other is very frustrated.

Karen is twenty-eight years old and head of production for a midwestern advertising agency. A slim blond, attractive in jeans and an Armani jacket rolled up at the sleeves, she dashes between the drafting tables of her production crew with a tense, harried look on her face. She has just returned to the office after a three-month maternity leave following the birth of her first child, and she is really strung out.

"I'm not sure what's worse," she told me, "the sheer weight of responsibility that I wake up to every morning—with the baby, the job, and everything I'm behind on at home—or the fatigue that hits me about five o'clock every day when I've accomplished exactly half of what was on my list. I can't even think about whether or not I'm doing a decent job—I know I'm not doing anything well. Even nursing is a bummer these days.

"What really makes me mad, too, is how my husband goes blithely off to his neat little office every day. Here I am putting some stuff on hold that could help me become a creative director somewhere, while his office business isn't hampered in any way. Something isn't fair about all this—I mean, I love my baby, but I feel like I'm giving up everything for her."

Alicia is an account executive in the same company. She is forty-two and has also returned from a recent maternity leave. Her baby is the first child born of her second marriage. She also has two teenagers.

"Things aren't bad," she told me with an easy grin. She's wearing a softly pleated skirt and a tailored silk shirt. Her face below her wash-and-let-dry permanent is calm and rested. "But I'm not beating myself up either. I have a hectic schedule during the day while the baby is in day care, but I make sure to be wholly home when I'm home. No work, just kids and husband. I'm confident about the way things are working out because I've done it before and I know what to expect.

"Work-wise, it helps that I have set things up to make room for the baby. I'm not making this my year to bring in the biggest account of my career—I did that two years ago, and I'll do it the year after next. Right now I feel like I have cooked up a good emotional casserole: the baby satisfies me up to a point, I am deeply in love with my husband, who pitches in with baby et al., and my work takes me the rest of the way. I am a very happy person.

"My secret? I'm not alone. I married a great guy with a teenager of his own—and he helps me with everything. I help him, too."

There lies the difference: Alicia isn't alone. Her entire life—her daily routine, from office to home to crib to bed—is a series of trade-offs, of shared chores and responsibilities.

"I tried to do it all in my first marriage. You can't. You just can't. And if your husband won't help, then you are going to have a hell of a time making it as a couple," said Alicia.

She's right. As I talked with Karen, I heard familiar refrains. These are the concerns of all working mothers:

- impatience and fatigue that result from all it takes to manage the home and baby
- envy of a husband's ease at keeping his career on track because he doesn't have as much to do at home or as many problems on his mind while trying to work
- shock at the sudden increase in responsibilities with the baby's arrival—not just lining up child care, but the extra attention that must be paid to groceries and meals, laundry and housework

However, among some couples these are very much the concerns of someone else too: the working father. And that makes a difference in the quality of all of their lives. With both adults sharing responsibility, the family reaches a balance, a rich bonanza of mutual energy and satisfaction at helping one another that makes all the effort and stress worth it.

It's especially nice if you have, as Alicia did, experience with—or examples of—how to do it. Since experience is much harder to come by than examples, I've profiled several families who show how you can balance full-time jobs with raising children in order to get the most out of both. You will be able to see significant differences and amazing similarities among the couples. All experience successes and failures, laughter and tears. Some focus more on the children and less on the careers; others do the exact opposite. Whichever they choose, they are especially remarkable because they can debate cleaning bathrooms and cooking dinner in the same breath as they debate the need for more intimacy, separate checkbooks, or more time with the children—and stay in love. They don't believe in easy, static answers. They do believe in each partner's having the opportunity to choose what he or she can do most easily—or cannot do—in the family and work routine. These couples are proof that love flourishes best right in the midst of "trying to do it all." And it is here—in the shared doing of it—that they discover their deepest pleasures and rewards.

"But," you may ask, "do we have any real proof that this arrangement is good for the kids?" Good question. This chapter concludes with some words from Gabrielle, a twenty-year-old whose legacy is the equal partnership forged between her parents, which makes her one of the wisest young women I've ever met.

## A Tale of Two Lawyers, Two Husbands, and Two Kids

At first glance, Sarah and Phoebe could not be more different. Sarah is tall and dark, her wiry body solidly, determinedly planted over her feet as though nothing could knock her off balance. Phoebe is petite and small-boned, her coloring much lighter and her demeanor less imposing. Sarah lives in Chicago, Phoebe in Philadelphia.

Yet they are incredibly similar in other ways. Both are thirty-two years old, earned undergraduate BA degrees, and went on to graduate school immediately after college. Then, a few years later, each one picked up a law degree. Now they are both trying hard to balance full-to-brimming-over lives that include practicing law full-time, coordinating schedules with working husbands, and sharing the demands of having young children at home.

## Sarah: Support and Self-Knowledge Keep Her Sane

The day I first met with Sarah, her son, Ned, was six months old. She was back on her job as an attorney for the EPA with a heavy travel schedule, she was nursing, her mother was seriously ill, and her 40-year-old husband, also a lawyer, was expecting her to host a 6:00 P.M. cocktail party for forty of his office colleagues before she returned for a late business meeting at her own office. She also had to coordinate the next day's car pool for her husband's fourteen-year-old daughter from his first marriage, who was visiting. As we sat in Sarah and Patrick's sprawling, two-story house, I asked how she was managing.

"Minimally," she said frankly, her mouth smiling, her eyes seeking sympathy. "You're talking to one of the more shell-shocked specimens of motherhood you've ever seen."

In spite of the fact that she is the daughter of a full-time working mother, Sarah's expectations of motherhood were skewed. "I'm not sure why, but the effect this baby has had on me is a real shock. I didn't think it through, but I doubt if you ever can know what a pregnancy really means before it happens. How can you know? It's like a barrier that you pass through to the other side, and afterward you look back at the people who don't have children, and you're just amazed at how different your life is."

The arrival of a child is guaranteed to cause problems. Immediately. For Sarah, even her maternity leave became a frustration, because she desperately missed the work she loved: "I guess I thought when this baby was born that Patrick would be here doing as much as I was. Of course he wasn't, because I was the one at home, and I should have been taking care of the baby because I wasn't working. And when you're breast-feeding, there's a limited amount of stuff that a husband can do.

"But I was very angry with Patrick because I felt like he wasn't helping me out at all. I really got on his case, saying he wanted this baby and here's the baby and why didn't he take the darn baby and go do something with it? Looking back, I think my reaction was a combination of postpartum depression and unrealistic expectations.

"I don't know what I thought would happen. I guess I thought I'd have this baby and then I would be totally detached from the baby and run my own life. If you can believe it, I thought I would get a lot of work done during my leave! To a certain extent I was right, because I am in my early thirties, and I am focused on continuing my career, so I think I will be more detached child-wise than younger mothers. I have my own life, and I'm happy to have the baby—he's adorable and I'm proud of him—but he's not my whole life. He improves my life."

Sarah, like all the people who love what they do, found that taking care of the baby wasn't enough. "What I was really missing was all the bustle and action of my work. That quickly led to big fights between us, because the minute Patrick walked in the door, I landed on him with a million questions. And he didn't want to talk about his day—he wanted to play with the baby. He really is very nontraditional in terms of the amount of time he loves to spend with his daughter and the baby—much more than other men we know.

"So it was tense, because I was ready for something besides the baby and all he wanted was time with the baby. It wasn't until I returned to work that I could see some humor in that. Now that I'm back, I don't want to come home and talk about work either! So we had a hard time getting through that period, and that's one reason I know I'm much better off working full-time: it keeps me healthy.

"On the other hand—the positive side of our fights during those three months—I learned that the hallmark of a good marriage is to be able to give your partner the freedom to keep private what he or she wants private and to discuss what your partner wants to discuss. Many people think that when you come home Partner A recites everything he did and Partner B tells everything she did and they have this communion of souls.

"I disagree. I think the hallmark of a good marriage is respect for each other's need *not* to talk about some things. Give-and-take. What Patrick and I really love to discuss is everything but work. Right now we've been talking a lot about politics. But it wasn't until I got back to work myself that I was able to gain a better perspective on that.

"I'll try to have lunch once a week with three women who are lawyers and who all have had babies within the last year. We talk about how we were before we had children—how callous and indifferent we were about women with kids who were having work problems and how we thought to ourselves, That will never happen to us. And now it is happening!

"One woman had to leave the office early the other day because her child was sick. She hadn't finished a brief and had to give it to an associate. She said, 'When I was the associate on the other side, I wouldn't have tolerated that very well.'

"I thought I would be very adept at this," added Sarah, "and I never thought that I would stop working when I had a baby, because my mother and grandmother worked. My mother had five kids and was a physician and had a really hard work schedule. So I always assumed that I would do that, have her boundless energy and be able to accomplish everything that she has.

"So here I am in a job where there's a great deal of contempt for women who take time off. I thought I was well prepared. I developed a specialty in litigation and established myself well enough to be in demand. Also, judging from how neurotic I got when I was on maternity leave, I think it's good that I'm back at work. I love the work—it's just that right now it's awfully hard. Maybe because I'm pushing myself."

She is. "I had this fantasy that I'd be able to breast-feed the baby until he was seven months old," Sarah related, "and I'm getting close to it. He was three months old when I went back to work. I breast-fed him continuously up to that point. After that I pumped during the day, froze the milk at work, and carried it home in canisters, so the next day he would drink my frozen milk. I did that for two more months, and this month I started him on formula during the day and breast-feed him morning and night. I don't know if I'd do it again. It's a lot of work—the pumping and freezing. I did that instead of lunch."

Interestingly enough, though Sarah admits that this has been hard work, she is clearly comfortable with it as she talks. The fact is that she had a choice and chose to put out the extra effort.

"I would definitely like to have less on my plate." Sarah laughs. "But what has helped incredibly is advice from my colleagues who are in the same boat and terrific support in unexpected ways from my husband, who has wanted this baby since we were married seven years ago. For me, finding a balance among my many lives as lawyer, mother, daughter, wife, and artist is how I view perfection."

Sarah admits that her demand for perfection was the most serious problem she faced. She expected to keep her work performance at the same stellar level it had been at before motherhood, only to discover that that was impossible.

However, unlike many working mothers who complicate their lives even further by extending the demand for perfection into the home, she was much easier on herself as a mother—she didn't expect perfection in that arena because she never viewed her own mother as a "perfect mother." In fact, her mother's ease with her role as a "detached mother" is viewed as a plus in Sarah's eyes.

But when Sarah felt the pressures of motherhood undermining her perfection standards at work, her first reaction was typically female: she blamed herself. She immediately thought that her frustrations and depression meant something was wrong with her. Once she got another point of view from her colleagues—and her husband—she took a more realistic approach (and a traditionally male way of handling this kind of pressure): she blamed external elements such as the heavy travel schedule and the extraordinary demands of a newborn. That canceled her feelings of inadequacy and allowed her to focus on what she could change to relieve the stresses.

"For example, I've always been an evening person and would accomplish much of my work between four and seven at night," said Sarah. "Now I'm starting to get used to leaving every day at five, but it's not easy. That's something I brought up at my weekly lunch with my fellow mommy lawyers.

"It turns out that all of us felt like we were going to be fired when we first left at five. We're all workaholics, and we all worked hard to get where we are—most of us are the only women in our departments. So at first we would creep out to the baby-sitter feeling really ashamed. Now we realize that no one in the office really cares as long as we get the work done. If we have to take it home and do it at night, that's fine. But I sure was paranoid until I found out everyone felt the same way.

"The real difference now is that I fully realize I am not going to do work as perfectly as I did before. I can't. What keeps me sane is that, even at this level, I'm still doing superior work. That's a real big difference from doing everything perfectly. But I have learned—from my colleagues, from my mother, from my husband, who is in the exact same field—that doing perfect work isn't really required.

"Men have known this a long time. I don't think women realize it as quickly. Now I know that my bosses want an overall pretty good performance, and it's my attitude and enthusiasm that are more important than being completely perfect."

Yet even as she credits others with helping her gain perspective, she firmly states that she could not do it without a husband willing to share the physical burdens of career-home overload.

"In one sense our work patterns are quite complementary," said Sarah. "I have many more trial settings than Patrick has. Fortunately, most of Patrick's cases are settled, and he rarely goes to court, which means as much as I'm gone, he's home.

"In our personal lives too we are very complementary. We don't take each chore and split it up—there are just certain things I do, such as paying our bills and handling finances, while Patrick does laundry. We have certain specified household tasks that we split up.

"I would say that our marriage has evolved. I found that I

was just better at certain things, or more interested in them, and he was better at other things. By the time we had the baby, he was doing most of the cooking, while I do most of the shopping once a week. We are both concentrating on eating low-cholesterol diets, so I just figure out main food groups and buy them, and he prepares what he wants. We don't have menus—Patrick decides what he's going to cook when he comes home around 6:30, even though I'm already home because I picked the baby up at day care at 6:00.

"I'm a good cook, and I can do all the things he can do, but I really don't enjoy it," said Sarah, "and he hates doing bills, which I like to have control over. When we've got decisions to make, like a major purchase, we always make it together. Sometimes we disagree, so we compromise a lot."

One area where they disagree is child care: each is convinced the other does more!

"She does 60 percent when it comes to the baby," said Patrick.

"He spends more time with the baby one-on-one than I do," said Sarah.

While each couple I interviewed for this book certainly had times when one partner carried more of the load than the other, they always recognized that and tried to make up for it in other ways. Meanwhile, Sarah and Patrick are feeling happier with their family time as the baby gets older.

"I am enjoying this baby more than I did my first child because I'm so much more aware of what's going on than I was fourteen years ago. So much more attuned. I wish that I'd been more relaxed with my daughter at an earlier age," said Patrick.

"Even though work-wise I have less time now, I realize this has less to do with time than the lifestyle I want for my family. What I don't want is a rigid time schedule. I try very hard to have four hours a night with the kids, but it's the environment that's most important—I want an easy, spontaneous atmosphere. I want our time together to be warm and full of paying attention to each other. Quality time, to me, is relaxed time—not tiny intense chunks scattered here and there."

While we were talking, Patrick's words reminded me of a recent story in *Rolling Stone* magazine in which Keith Richard had spoken eloquently about his kids.

"Family is a special thing . . . you can't really talk about it, except to say that it's one of the most special things that you'll ever get on the face of this earth. It gives you that final missing link of what life's about. While they're looking upon you as the most wonderful person in the world because you're 'Daddy,' they do more for you than you do for them."

"That about sums it up," said Patrick. "It isn't what I give to my children—it's what I get from them. And the more I'm with them, the more I get.

"And when Sarah and I have spent time trying to find someone to be with our child during the day, we interview people less in terms of child-care skills than how they feel about kids—what it would be like for our child to be with this person, how this person will make our child feel about himself—so you might have a person who doesn't speak English so well but you know she loves little kids. We are very concerned about this and always conduct these interviews together."

Sarah takes an approach to their baby that reflects her upbringing as well as a considered opinion of our societal attitudes. "I think that much of mother love and much of the concept of the closeness that you're supposed to have are a typical American faddish concept of reality," said Sarah, her dark eyes serious. "There's much in America that's pop culture, and 'mother love' is an example of a myth that has been built up.

"I believe that you can love your child a lot—and I'm not talking about careful doses of limited 'quality time,' which is B.S. too—but you can love your child a lot and not spend full time with him and he'll still grow up perfectly fine. It's better for the child because it gives him more of a chance to be himself. That's how I was raised, and I think I turned out fine. The fact is my mother spent much of the time away from me. If she had been around me, she would have driven me up the wall. I'd like to give my own kid the same space. I think that in order to really do so, we'll probably have to have another child.

"Most of my friends feel the same way, especially the other mothers who are lawyers. Sharing our experiences is letting me see how children are at various stages, too, so I'm seeing that things will get easier.

"At home now, as the baby is eating more cereal and formula, Patrick is able to help with the feedings more. When it comes to child care between the two of us, we don't have any regular job assignments, just a basic give-and-take. What might be one person's job one year may not be appropriate the next year, but only in a good marriage could you have the give-and-take."

In spite of the conflicts they may experience because of the drain parenthood now makes on their time, what works for Sarah and Patrick is their willingness to confront the problems.

"We know we haven't been getting enough time together one-on-one," said Sarah. "But we're talking a lot about getting more sitters in and having a regular time that we're together almost every night. One idea that came up during my lunch with my lawyer friends was to get a sitter every night for an hour. Just pay a high school student to come over for an hour so that you can go for a walk and talk. It would probably be at some time that the kids are sleeping, like 9:30 or 10:00 at night.

"I'm also planning for someone to come in and cook for us. Even though Patrick likes to cook, it's a chore. I've found these women who will come to your home, cook two weeks of meals and freeze them, and you just defrost dinner every night. So that will free up more time for us to be together."

Sarah and Patrick are also working on a more serious conflict that arose immediately upon Sarah's return to her full-time schedule.

"I returned to a work load that was incredible—I had cases in six different cities requiring that I be out of town every other week for several days at a time," said Sarah. "What Patrick didn't understand about my traveling was that I appeared slightly gleeful about it. He thought that I was happy to get away from him.

"We had a long talk, and he realized that I was just happy to get a little bit of space. I pointed out that my glee was in finally getting seven hours of sleep a night. I had to be honest—it was delightful! So it was a misunderstanding that caused him to be so angry, and he's a lot calmer now that we've straightened it out.

"But the travel is very, very difficult for both of us to work out, given all the pressures we're under from every direction. This season's work schedule has been the worst we've ever had in our marriage. Patrick has a very complicated trial starting in a week, and he has been traveling, too. When one or the other of us travels, the one at home has to do everything, so it's an awful lot to contend with."

Sarah recognized that she was the one who had to instigate some kind of change, since her schedule was the most unpredictable. Because she knew she wanted to work out a balance that allowed for her family's well-being as well as her career success, she didn't sidestep any issues. "Philosophically and rationally, Patrick is oriented toward my having my own career, but he wonders how we are all going to bear up emotionally if I have to focus so much of my energy on my work because of this heavy travel schedule.

"I'm torn, too, because I work to make a living, but I also work because I enjoy it. I love my work. I even love the travel when it's reasonable. And I agree with Patrick that, if I'm out of the home for more than a week a month, it's not good for the baby, who seems to have a lot of separation anxiety. So I'm trying to work out a less intense travel schedule, where I go out for only a few days a month for the next year or so. And we both agree that if I'm out of town most of the time, that does not bode well for the future of our relationship.

"Since I have the largest individual work load of anyone in the country who is doing this kind of work, it's very rough right now. And my bosses recognize that. We've been talking over several options. Part-time work is not an option—I don't want it, and they said it wouldn't be fair—undoubtedly they would end up paying me for part-time work while leaning on me for full-time effort. All of us know that we have unpredictable hours with much too much overtime work. That causes tension for everyone in the firm, including the men."

Then Sarah made a very interesting point. She said about her firm that "if they're inflexible, I may leave. I have suggested to them the cases I can handle and be able to keep my travel time to a minimum, and they are due to get back to me on this in a week."

As it turned out, during that week two things happened. First, Sarah's regional office agreed to let her handle cases in one city. Sarah is articulate, very bright, and outstanding in her field; the office could not afford to lose her.

But also during that week, a private law firm offered her a four-days-a-week position. Sarah found the offer of more money and better hours tempting. The difference was she would no longer be the lead litigator on cases.

"My specialty is unique," said Sarah, "because I lead the fight for the people who cannot pay the big bucks. I love being one of the good guys, so I'm going for my ideals and less travel, not my checkbook or eight more free hours a week. I'll combat the bad guys and risk the overtime."

So her schedule remains rigorous. "I keep thinking that when I become hardened to it, when I become inured to all the things I have to do, it will be easier. Already it's easier than it was last month," Sarah admitted. "I know it's not because I'm a woman that I feel under the gun so often; recently Patrick has had feelings of being overwhelmed too. So we share a lot, especially the pressure."

Sarah, especially, is open about her thoughts, whether it's emotions, conflicts, or potential problem areas. She is nothing if not very direct.

"For me that's great," said Patrick. "It's a better way, even though we may end up discussing things more than I would like. But the fact that Sarah tells me when she is angry or upset doesn't make me angry. It makes me feel a lot more secure, because I know what she's thinking and feeling. I tend to hold back, but she calls me on it immediately."

Sarah agrees: "Some of our best moments have been our worst moments, explaining to each other our fears or our worst upsets. I find that it's in those times that seem to be the most negative that we realize something really important about each other or understand how things have to work."

"You know," continued Patrick, "you cannot expect to be

the closest of friends if you don't keep everything on the table. It isn't having everything always settled between us that really counts—it's the energy it takes to get there that means more. If one of us is upset over something, then the upset is worthwhile in itself."

"I get my greatest satisfaction out of good, hard work," elaborated Sarah. "I think a good marriage is built on the same idea: confrontation sometimes, compromise sometimes, but the marriage that endures and comes through all that is a stronger, more interesting marriage."

"We have a lot to deal with," said Patrick, glancing fondly at Sarah as she bounced Ned while we talked, "and I really like the situation. I like being challenged, and I like being brought to task about everything."

His eyes twinkle as he says with a happy grin, "This is the most exciting time I've ever had."

## Phoebe: Reprioritizing and Risk Taking

Phoebe, like Sarah, is thirty-two years old. She, too, is a full-time practicing lawyer and the mother of a young child. Her husband, Taylor, who is thirty-five, runs his own package design firm from an office in their spacious Philadelphia home.

When Phoebe ran up against the horrendous pressures of the legal field, the same pressures confronting Sarah and Patrick, she and Taylor decided to "downscale" their lifestyles in order to "upscale" their personal time so they could maintain a balance between their home lives and their careers. Phoebe opted for a four-day workweek. However, it is still a full-time, forty- to fifty-hour-a-week work schedule. Taylor also works a four-day week. Their decision to scale back came out of a conscious decision not to let work run their lives.

"The biggest conflict that we've had in our marriage oc-curred my first year out of law school, when I was making a lot of money but working at a breakneck pace," said Phoebe. "Tay-lor was working out of the office in our home on projects he loved, while I was in this miserable sweat job. It was so terrible. I was so unhappy. I would come home, and in the little time that I was there I would complain about my job. The end result was that I became a whining, unhappy person—no one you'd want to be around.

"Taylor knew what the problem was, but we weren't sure what to do. He encouraged me to list my alternatives—to think about what I could do, put it down on paper, and then see what kinds of changes I could make."

Phoebe today recalls her anxieties of two years ago: "On the one hand, I knew I could be a waitress, but once you write it down, 'waitress' doesn't look so good, especially after you just passed the bar exam.

"Plus, we had bought a house, and I couldn't take a job that paid no money. I also had student loans to repay even though I'd gone through a work/study program where I studied three months, worked three, and so on, to pay for law school. So I had to be realistic about what other job I could take. We talked it out a lot, and in the end what helped most was all that talking.

"First we examined just exactly why I went into law in the first place. That's because we had moved to Philadelphia when the novelty of the New York advertising scene had worn off. Even though we met when we were working for the same agency— Taylor as a designer and I as a copywriter, I didn't see that many opportunities for me. I wanted a field where I could make more money.

"So during the time that Taylor was developing his company, which he has now had for eight years, I was in school and working part-time. It was a wonderful period—he was working at home, and I'd get back from class and we'd have lunch together. That's until I graduated and took this high-powered job."

"That was bad," said Taylor. "The first year Phoebe worked an average twelve- to fourteen-hour day, almost seven days a week. I never saw her. It was terrible. There was a lot of short-notice travel."

"I'd go in one day and they'd say, 'We want you in Nashville this afternoon,' " said Phoebe. " 'We think you'll be there about a week'—but I'd end up staying a month and not be able to come home on weekends. It was a real sweatshop.

"After six months, I knew I enjoyed being with Taylor too

much to keep living like that—and it was impossible even to think about having a family under those conditions!

"Together we made a choice to live on less money, and I found a new position at a medium-sized and much more relaxed law firm where I had done some work while I was in school. I was there for about a year and a half before I became pregnant.

"During that time the firm had the opportunity to see my work, to get to know me and consider my value to them on a long-term basis. I did very good work during that time. So, after my maternity leave, I designed a four-day week, which is forty to fifty hours of work, just like before, but gives me a three-day weekend. It is a full-time schedule by normal standards, but it is 80 percent of my former workweek and I'm paid 80 percent of my former salary. After I planned every detail, I presented the plan to my bosses, who listened, talked it over, and decided to let me try it out. And it has been working out extremely well for everyone.

"Now I do general corporate litigation Tuesday through Friday. I'm home on Mondays. I picked Monday to be my day at home so I don't get Sunday-night anxiety. Taylor works Monday through Thursday and has Friday off. That means that Amy, who is thirteen months old, is in day care Tuesday, Wednesday, and Thursday from nine to five, then each of us has one day alone with her."

Taylor's attitude toward sharing the work of their household—whether that's caring for baby Amy or keeping up with the daily tasks that crop up in a family household—is crucial to their happy balance; it takes two to make it. Like most men sincerely dedicated to establishing an equal partnership with their working wives, Taylor finds it easy to cross over from traditional male tasks to female tasks or to let Phoebe do a "man's job" if it pleases her. This flexibility may be a result of his upbringing. Not only is he one of six children, all of whom were expected to pitch in around their house, but he is the son of a very busy working mother who now averages twelve hours a day in her career.

"What you do and how you do your work is so important to your self-image," said Taylor. "Not working makes you a nobody.

In the long run you are making yourself dependent on somebody forever. Somebody who could become disabled, who could leave you, who could become mentally ill. I don't understand why more women aren't realistic about that fact. That more women don't see how easily that could happen comes as a big surprise to me.

"I also wonder why they don't see the link between feeling good about themselves career-wise and being a good parent. Phoebe and I know that because we love our work and love the way it works for us we are much better parents. We relax when we are with Amy, we relax when we're at work. Each part of our lives that goes well makes the other part succeed, too.

"Right after Amy was born," said Taylor, who is as dark as his wife is fair, "I made the choice to cut my business back so that I could also work a four-day week. Let me put it this way: I can take on four major design proposals a year, work six and sometimes seven days a week, and make a lot of money—or I can take on three proposals, make half to three-fourths the money, but have the time I want to with Phoebe and Amy and keep things humming. I chose the latter—and I love it."

"Taylor does the grocery shopping, most of the cooking, and the laundry," said Phoebe. "To a certain extent, it depends on who's got the time that day, and on weekends I make sure to buy groceries and go to the drugstore. But if you make a list of tasks that are associated with having a baby—like diapers and fixing bottles—Taylor ends up doing more of those tasks simply because he's at home more than I am. He also takes Amy to and from day care because I leave at 7:30, an hour before she goes, and I work a long day, until 7:30. When I get home, Taylor usually has something very simple on the stove or fish sticks in the oven or a pot of chili ready. It's just great, because we eat at the table while I feed Amy in the high chair.

"When I met Taylor, I knew he was different right away." Phoebe chuckled. "On our first date he invited me to dinner—at his house—and he cooked! He enjoys it. Recently he even sewed new curtains for our house."

Both hate housework, however, so they contribute jointly from their separate checking accounts to the cost of a weekly cleaning person. Other bills are also split up, with Taylor making sure that everything has been paid.

"We rarely have sitters, because we never go out," said Phoebe. Because I'm out so much, I find that I enjoy being at home more. I try not to bring work home so I can just enjoy our time with Amy. I have really changed my feelings about work and how much time I'm going to spend on it since Amy. That has made me much more efficient at work now that I'm on four days, too. I organize my time better and I do as much as or more than I did before.

"I'm much happier with my work life now than I've ever been," Phoebe went on. "I used to feel—especially that terrible first year—that there was no room for me. Now, though most of my time when I'm not at work is spent with Amy, I feel that is time for me. I'm more relaxed. I don't feel like I have to cram everything into two days on the weekend. I think everybody should do a four-day workweek. It would help considerably."

Even though Phoebe knows the conservative world of law is slow to change, she said, "I wish that more employers would think that allowing for flextime and providing day-care options are the right things to do. It's funny, but at work when I started to go on a four-day workweek I had comments from one of the managers who is a working father. Snide remarks like 'I wish they'd let me do that.' The only difference between the two of us is that he has never been brave enough to ask for it. No one offered it to me—I went in with a detailed plan and made a case for flextime. Maybe if others did, they could have a four-day workweek, too. You have to do it yourself; it's chicken to wait around and expect to have it handed to you."

Nevertheless, Phoebe and Taylor recognize they haven't solved all their problems. For the time being, they are "doing without" financially—a balance they agreed on mutually. Once Amy is older, they'll probably go back to five-day workweeks. I asked them both if having less money coming in was a hardship for them. Do they have a sense that the men who have reached partner earlier than Phoebe is likely to and who are making a lot of money are happier individuals?

"No, I don't," Phoebe answered firmly. "The difference between their life and mine is maybe that they have a house on the shore for the weekend. They may be able to send their children to very expensive private secondary schools and colleges, but they don't have much time to go to the house on the shore and be with those well-educated kids. All the extra money has no bearing on what they can do when they're not sitting behind a desk, because they don't have any time to enjoy it."

"Fortunately, our idea of a lovely evening is reading together by the fire," said Phoebe. Taylor pointed out that while they make a deliberate effort to save money by not going out to dinner or hiring sitters for evenings at the movies, they still maintain an active social life by having friends over for dinner or going to their homes, children included. "We don't feel like we're missing anything," said Taylor.

"We also love to run together," said Phoebe. "In the summer we put Amy in the baby jogger and try to run every day of our three-day weekend. Although lately we changed our schedule so I could work on a special project of my own every Sunday morning for five hours—a novel." She grinned. "I have always wanted to write fiction, but I found that I don't do well when I feel economic pressure on my creative work. So right now Taylor takes Amy somewhere all morning on Sunday so I can complete this. Then it will be his turn."

Phoebe's news about her novel explains why she feels less pressure regarding her law practice than Sarah does. "I have another outlet with financial potential," explained Phoebe, who already has an editor anxious to see more of her book. "I am ambitious in terms of my legal career in the sense that I want to do good work and be paid well so that I can afford to spend time on other things I dearly love, like my family and my writing."

"That's the trade-off that we make," said Taylor. "Look at me. I've been an independent entrepreneur for eight years. At first the tendency is just to work all the time. Somehow it lessens the anxiety about making ends meet, as though the harder you work, the more likely you are to succeed. But what I've found over the years is there is a certain amount of work that you should do and must do—and beyond that you can keep yourself occupied with busywork that doesn't further your goals. That's why I've decided to cut down a little bit even if it does cut down on my income. Basically, between the two of us, we've cut our income considerably."

"My biggest fear now is that my firm will decide that they don't want me working this way," said Phoebe. "If that should happen, I'll find some other way to do this even if it means changing jobs, because it is our best solution to the constant hassle of day care, which is true for everyone.

"Amy is only thirteen months old, and we're already on her second day-care provider, which I didn't expect to happen. I thought we'd found someone who was perfect and that would last for four years. But the first person we had got pregnant. She already had a child, and it was obvious she couldn't take care of a newborn, a fifteen-month old, and Amy. But it was a wonderful arrangement while it lasted.

"Right now we're very lucky that we had Taylor's cousin to help out until I found a new person through a friend of mine. But when we found out that Amy's first sitter was pregnant, I was just beside myself. It's a terrible problem. Good day care is the biggest problem that there is for working couples.

"You have to work really hard at finding a good person and just have faith that it will work out even if it does take enormous energy. Just figure it's a problem you must be determined to solve.

"Something else that's important," added Phoebe, "is that we've been careful and delicate about trying to be equal partners with a baby for a year now. I'm very happy it's working out, but I think we have to keep thinking of life as an experiment and an adventure, because there's uncharted territory and you aren't going to get any support from anybody because nobody else has done it.

"You'll get people who'll say, 'Isn't that nice?' or 'Isn't that odd?' or 'Good luck,' but nobody's going to say, 'This is a good thing—we did it and it worked out great,' because nobody's been doing it.

"Taylor and I have been taking risks forever. It was a big risk for us to get married when we'd known each other for only a year. Yet I take pleasure in that. Right now I enjoy the fact that I'm doing something that is a challenge. Taylor left a nice job to go out on his own. I took a big risk leaving one profession for another one. We take a lot of risks, and we like it this way." Phoebe paused, and a soft smile crept over her face. "It's scary." But she doesn't look frightened.

## Balancing with a Bigger Brood

The Sorkins and the Greens have a lot in common even if their family incomes differ by $300,000. Both sets of full-time working parents lavish attention on three children, succeed at full-time management careers, travel together or with their children, and spend their extra hours lovingly decorating and maintaining their homes—in that order.

Life in a rural area makes it easier for the Greens, while the Sorkins flourish in the big city. Both mothers feel a constant pull between children and career but admit to being "bored" when not working full-time. Both fathers cross over the traditional line of "men's work" at home in unexpected ways. Both couples have been together for over fifteen years, and both echo the same singular need: "We want more time alone—to read, to think, to be creative."

### *Meg and Will: The Truth Behind the Superwoman Mask*

Meg Sorkin speaks straight from the heart. A slender woman with black eyes who wears her dark hair in a simple shoulder-length bob, she looks much younger than her forty years, perhaps because as she speaks her voice is soft, her manner wistful and girlish, almost sad. But that's because we are chatting in the living room of her elegant Boston home just a few days after the death of one of her closest friends, a time when she has dropped her usual bravado to carefully reexamine the choices she has made.

Don't mistake her softness for lack of ambition. Meg is not a mild-mannered manager with limited vision. She is a top administrator for one of America's largest companies—a position she is

surprised to find herself in since she resigned what was to be a
better-paying, more prestigious post ten years ago in order to
have more time with her children—only to emerge in this high-
paying, significantly *more* prestigious position.

"It's amazing," she told me. "I thought I was making this
sacrifice, and here I am successful—with exactly the kind of
strict nine-to-five hours I wanted. And the prestige and the
money to boot."

Yet she is the first to say that with the big bucks come
greater personal costs. The more responsibility and prestige she
accepts, the less time she has to give to her children, her husband, and herself. However, she has discovered the solution that
makes it work most of the time: less pressure on herself to do it
all, more help from her husband to share in everything. It's a
delicate and tentative balance.

Because of her apparent success, Meg is often invited across
the country to speak on the subject of combining career and
family. But she does not gloss over the reality of what it takes to
do what she does. If anything, she is harshly honest about her
own successes and failures and how well prepared she thinks
the world is to help the average working parent, female or male.

"Am I, Meg Sorkin, the perfect working mother?" she asks,
raising her eyebrows to emphasize her point. "You ask the
people who work around me, and they'll say I've got it all
together, but the fact is it's really, really hard every single day,
and I can't imagine how people with fewer resources do it. I've
got all this ability and help, yet there are days when I'm coming
apart at the seams. But I'm going to keep living this way for
another fifteen years because this is how it has to be while the
kids are at home. I can do it because I've chosen to do it—I just
don't like to think that everyone has to live this way.

"When I look at our society and the divorce rate, I'm so
sorry that we've set up a system where women are in a position
where they *must* work, whether they want to or not. It's one
thing if you have a high-powered career that you really want
because it gives you a lot of satisfaction, but I don't think that's
the case with all women. To know that women all across America, of all ages and incomes, are trying to do what I'm doing is

real serious. Our expectations have been skewed—what you think before you have children and what in fact you feel like afterward depends so much on you as a couple, not just you the person, not just what the popular magazines say. And I'm not sure how many of us know that ahead of time.

"A working mother doesn't know how she's going to feel after her baby comes, because it'll depend not only on what her husband literally *does* but on how he *feels* about what he does—and vice versa—not to mention what is actually done versus what should be. I am fortunate because my husband thinks just like me. We agree together on what we do, and we're convinced it's what we want, so we put out all the incredible effort it takes to make it work. I don't do it alone. He doesn't do it alone.

"I have one friend who works part-time whose husband really would like her to be home, and another who works part-time whose husband would like her to work full-time. They ask me for advice, but I can't say anything because their lives are very different from mine. In sharp contrast to their situations, Will and I are in total agreement on what we are doing and why.

"But it is frustrating not to be able to help. I used to think if I asked enough people, people who seemed really together, I would get answers everyone could use. I have asked, and I've read everything that's come out, and my conclusion is that there aren't any easy answers. But I'm glad that at least the myth of supermom is being exploded, because I've come to the conclusion that it's impossible for a woman to be the only one responsible for kids and home and keeping on top of her job."

That realization has radically altered Meg's attitudes toward her staff people who find themselves caught in the crunch between work demands and child-care problems, the classic dilemma of dual-career parents. "Today, for example," she said, "I just learned that the day-care person for a guy in my office quit without notice. So he's out today helping his wife find someone new. What do I think about that? It's his turn today, my turn tomorrow. It's all of our problem. It's not just that he was unlucky and I'm fine.

"My understanding as a supervisor is much different from what it would have been ten years ago—though I'm certainly not going to take half his work back. I simply understand what he's going through. Before Will and I had children, I didn't have a full appreciation of how fluid your problem solving has to be, how you have to learn to flow with constant changes. One time his job will expand in a big way, and that means I have to fill in some spaces. Sometimes mine will. Sometimes the kids will have concerns, or we'll have a new baby. Another time the sitter will have a crisis. And now we've added our parents. His father just died. My parents got divorced a few years ago. We have three more people that we have to take care of, interact with, be emotionally supportive of, and I'm finding that kind of over-whelming. Sure, it happens to everyone, but when you add that to all the other responsibilities, you can really feel pulled apart."

## Minimizing Conflict: The Joy of Being Organized

Meg and Will approach their life together in a spectacularly well-organized fashion. The precision planning that character-izes their life at home with three children—two boys and a girl, ages nine, six, and three—was forecast when they met—on a blind date arranged by a computer!

It must have been a pretty good program: "I'm forty, and Will is forty-one, and we've been married fifteen years," said Meg. "We have always thought of ourselves as 'equal partners'—right from the beginning we've divided everything. We both went to business school while working full-time—it took about five years. It was real good practice for what we do now. We learned to skinny every task down to the least amount of effort and the most efficient way of doing it. I studied time manage-ment before they wrote all those books.

"We do it all the same way today. Like we photocopy our shopping lists by aisle in the supermarket and just use a yellow highlighter to check things off, because you pretty much need the same stuff every week. We try to go to the drugstore once a year and buy all the toothpaste and other supplies we need. I just bought a dozen sympathy cards. I buy baby gifts by the dozen. All those kinds of things.

"Will does everything that I do, if not better. My schedule has been frantic lately, so he took the kids to buy all their school clothes. We are remodeling our house, so one lunch hour a couple weeks ago we met and picked out twenty light fixtures for the house, then I stopped at a store where they were having a sale and bought four cocktail-type dresses. I don't shop for myself very often, but when I do, I try to buy as much as I can see needing for a long time.

"We have a housekeeper who comes in every morning, and we've been fortunate to have the same person for six years. We overlook a few things because we know this lady is very stable.

"She comes in at 7:30 A.M. and leaves at 6:00 P.M. Exactly. The good part is she's stable; the bad part is she's very inflexible. If we're ever going to be later than 6:00, which happens, we have to call either my mother or the kid across the street; once in a while we call a sitter service or one of us will go home while the other stays at work.

"The housekeeper's responsibilities have changed, depending on whom we have at home and how old they are. She gets the older kids their breakfast, dresses the three-year-old, and takes her to nursery school; she also takes the six-year-old, who goes to the same school. She does all of our grocery shopping once a week; she keeps the house straightened up, although we have someone else to do a full cleaning every week, and she's there for repairmen. We have a big old house with a major renovation under way, so she's there for that. Sometimes she will take the kids to an extra activity, although carpooling is not her forte. Occasionally she will prepare part of the dinner."

Because they have a housekeeper, Meg and Will are able to have an early "fun" time with the children each morning. "Normally we both get up and one of us gets the kids up, so they're interacting with us while we're getting ready for the day," said Meg.

"It's nice, although some days we're harried because one is crying and another one needs something. But somehow we get our eldest fed and on the bus. Then Will and I drive in to work together, partly because only one of our companies pays for parking and partly because it's a great time to talk. But that can change. This morning I had a 7:30 United Way breakfast I had to be at, so I got up and left and Will took care of everything.

"When we walk in the house at night," said Meg with a

laugh, "it's total chaos. Not only are the kids excited, but I love for the sitter to tell us everything they did during the day. Unfortunately, all she usually tells me is what the kids ate, which seems to be the extent of what she thinks is important about the day." Meg grimaces.

"Then everybody wants our attention all at once, the fights escalate, but pretty soon it calms down, and Will and I cook together. My mother used to laugh over how the two of us would even do our laundry together—but we just do things together as easily as your right hand and left hand: he'll take the orange juice out of the refrigerator; I'll open it and put it in the container. With the kids it's not quite so even, but it's very natural."

"It's hard to put percentages on things," Will explained good-naturedly. He is a fair-haired, tall man with a direct, easy, energetic way about him. He too looks much younger than forty. He is the son of a working mother, the brother of an older sister who is also a career woman. He grew up helping out. "So much just blends over time, but I do at least half and frequently more than half the cooking and cleaning up after meals. We cook and eat very informally, although right now I'm trying to make some more organized meals.

"We operate as a team: Meg goes upstairs with the kids while I start supper. An hour later she takes it off the stove and serves it to the kids. Whoever has a free hand pitches in. I do almost all the dishes. Neither of us shops now, because the housekeeper does that for us, but I used to do most of the grocery shopping.

"Symbolic of our life right now is our decision to put two microwaves into our new kitchen instead of the double ovens most people would choose," said Will. "It isn't that we do that much cooking, but we think that the children can do more of their own. One microwave will be on a low counter so even our six-year-old can use it to make cheese sandwiches or heat up pizza. That's one way I think as working parents we are changing the American family—making it much more 'collaborative' than when I grew up."

In addition to being chief cook and bottle washer, Will takes care of the traditional "men's work" around the house. "I'm responsible for getting the cars repaired, for the basic house maintenance, and for our finances. We keep one checking account, and everything we earn goes into that. I handle the checking accounts and the investments.

"Meg likes to spend more time with the children, especially when they are very little, with the diapering, bathing, personal care. I'm perfectly capable of it, although we joke that while raising three children I've probably changed fewer than a hundred diapers myself. But I can do it, and I don't hesitate when Meg wants me to. I take the kids to buy their shoes. So it's a 'where a free hand is needed' routine around here."

### Assessing and reassessing

"As soon as we got our MBAs, which was when we were just over thirty, I wanted to start having children," said Meg. "Will would have been happy not to have children, but I wanted a lot, so we compromised with three.

"Getting pregnant was no problem, and I continued to work full-time and felt fine. I was scheduled for a cesarean, so I was able to work up until the Friday before my due date. The baby was born on the following Monday, which worked out very nicely. I took a three-month leave, and then things got a little crazy."

Meg had joined a high-pressure consulting firm and Will too was on the fast track, in a real estate investment company where the hours were unpredictable. Not only was Meg the first woman in her firm at her level, but she was also the first to try working full-time with a young child. She found little flexibility in the attitudes of the people around her. The crunch on them both prompted Meg and Will to think long and hard about what they wanted from their life. They decided they would both get out of the fast lane in order to have a stronger, happier family life.

"Within a year we both moved to corporations where we could have a slightly saner life," said Meg. "The middle of the day remains the same, but we don't have to put up with uncontrolled schedules. Working nights and weekends stopped."

After the births of each of her first two children, Meg took a short maternity leave and then went back part-time for a year and a half before returning to a full-time schedule. She did not do that after the birth of her third child, for two reasons. Not only does their child-care setup work well for them, but she loves her work.

"Part-time just didn't work for me, because I had managerial responsibilities, which meant I couldn't get home until three or four each day anyway. That's the worst time for little kids, so I would walk in on everyone's 'downside' of the day.

"I know, too, I've got this image of how ideally I would love to be home with them rather than leave them with a sitter at home who doesn't do anything educational and enriching with them. In the afternoon the boys watch TV and play. But I know when I'm home they watch TV and play, too. So I am honest with myself about myth versus reality."

Meg tackles her ambitions for her children with an approach unlike that of the traditional "perfect mother." Knowing that she isn't a mom well suited to providing the one-on-one creative and educational activities herself, she works with Will to see that the children are enrolled in good schools and outside activities. Then she spends her "mother time" finding out about what they are doing, encouraging them, letting them know how interested she is in everything they do.

"Plus, I'm just too ambitious," she said. "I didn't like getting passed over for promotions. I love my work. Will encourages me to do whatever I want, so it is truly my choice to make. When I really wanted to work part-time, I did—and he was very support-ive of that.

"Right now I like the combination of family and work. It isn't the perfect combination, but I'm comfortable with it be-cause I realize how much certain extras mean to me, such as being appointed to an executive committee, getting elected to a board of directors, getting recognition, being in a decision-making position, being part of a management team. I'd give up a big chunk of that if I went part-time. And I've worked long and hard to get the responsibility. Yet it isn't just how important work is to me.

"The other side is I don't have one quiet baby at home. I have three boisterous kids, and it's not easy being the referee. It's hectic, energetic—I'm pulled in different directions. I can't get everybody happy all the time, and frankly, it's a relief to be able to leave.

"Practically speaking, I find one role refreshes the other. Work makes me happy to get home and vice versa. I think every work opportunity has its trade-offs. Mine are crafted to my particular family. The compromises are mine—and my family's."

Still, Meg is pulled between spending time with her children and gaining more control over her personal time, while Will wants to spend more time with the children and convince Meg to take less time debating the family decisions, especially finances.

The Sorkins deal with these issues head-on and with a remarkable lack of rancor even though what they do seems to contradict what they each say they *want* to do.

The fact is Meg *chooses* to spend more time with the children than Will does. "When we come home, they jump all over her, and she can't walk out of the room without a little parade of kids following her wherever she goes," said Will, who may be less involved moment to moment, in spite of his stated wish to be a more active dad, but is nevertheless firmly ensconced as the champion "bedtime reader" every night.

"That is an irritant when I feel like spending more time with them," he admits. "I'll try to pitch in and help more, but the kids won't cooperate. We chalk it up to children reacting to mothers differently than to fathers."

Meg fusses over how much of her time the children take, yet whenever she goes out of town things run very smoothly and efficiently. "I do fine," said Will, "but I'll grant that there's probably less of Meg's type of loving attention. I won't let them fool around as much. I won't be as softhearted about letting them stay up for a half hour more. They tend to stall her more, partly because she's a guilty mother and partly because she loves it."

And though Meg loves her time with the kids, she would like to trade off some for time alone. "It isn't time with the kids I really need right now," she said, "but space for myself. Like I want to garden, but I have this baby wrapped around my knees all the time, so I end up hiring somebody to put plants in, or Will ends up gardening. Lately I have had more travel for work reasons. I can choose not to go, I don't have to do it, yet I find there are times when it's nice to get away. My time alone is almost nonexistent, which is the major problem that I've faced in the last year that wasn't an issue for me just two years ago.

"I know why—I've been doing this for ten years, and I'm tired. I'm finding that my brain can go that fast, but my system gets worn out emotionally, and I need to have some quieter time when the accelerator pedal isn't stuck down. Frankly, I'm jealous of Will's ability to find time for himself—unlike me, he's not a workaholic by nature at all.

"My problem is I've divided up my life between work and kids—and too often there isn't any room for just plain me," said Meg. "So I'm working hard to change three things." "I'm working on my perfectionism and unrealistic expectations and negativity—the fact that at the end of the day I'll always see what I didn't do, but I won't really give myself credit for having done seventy-two other things. I'm trying to meditate a little and find time to be with some people who are more spiritually oriented. This means finding some new friends. Over the past fifteen years I've sought out 'high achiever' types, but I'm realizing I'd like to find different kinds of people, ones who are more serene.

"Over the last month four people I know have died," said Meg wistfully. "It started with my father-in-law, then three friends. One was a forty-one-year-old woman, a mother and wife. Another was a colleague who reported to me. Three of the deaths were totally unexpected. They made me stop and take stock. If I died tomorrow, is this how I would have wanted to spend my time?

"One friend who has serious breast cancer has three kids under age five. So I ask myself all the time if I should *just* work or *just* have kids or *just* be independent and travel. Believe me, we talk about this a lot. Both Will and I would love not to work at all, just pick the kids up and travel; or work part-time, be with the children more, and do other things we enjoy. But I think we're pretty happy this way. Nevertheless, on bad days I think seriously about working part-time."

Will describes his view of such analysis: "I want to be

tremendously efficient even at the risk of making mistakes. When Meg reexamines choices we have already made, it drives me crazy. I think she takes too much time over her decisions, but sometimes she does come up with a better one. Even so, that's why I end up having time for myself, time to do creative things, and she doesn't. I create space for myself, and I'm even efficient in using those spaces."

When they knock heads, neither Sorkin holds back. "We talk to each other very well," said Meg. "That's the best thing we do. We really talk a lot. And sometimes we get angry with each other. It's been sort of a shock in the last couple of years to discover that we don't always see things the same way, that there are some significant differences between us. But that's okay. Until we were tackling everything at once, it seemed we both thought very much alike. I know a lot of people who have divorced during times like this, and I hope we never do."

Their expectations for each other have been and continue to be quite realistic: "I certainly always assumed that I would marry a woman who worked, not for financial reasons, but in terms of wanting a partner intellectually," said Will. "Neither one of us ever expected this to be easy. We really work at being married."

And that includes taking time together, without the kids, as Meg explains: "Unlike many of our friends, we try to go out one night a week. Something else we do that's fun, particularly in the spring when the weather is beautiful, is we take days off together during the week. It's especially nice, because we aren't sticking the kids with a sitter on a weekend. We take a vacation day on our birthdays and our anniversary and go to the mountains or the shore or to a nice restaurant. Then we're home by 6:00 as usual. We also try to have nonbusiness lunches and to stay in touch on the phone during the day."

What keeps them going in the toughest hours is the feeling that they are hardly alone. "Two-career couples are commonplace among most of our friends," said Will. "If we made a list of a hundred friends, probably no more than half a dozen are couples who are not both professionals—in business or doctors, dentists, or lawyers."

"When I'm asked how I do it all," said Meg, "I try to be

honest and say there isn't one answer. I have the answer that is right for me. I think my life is richer for all the variety. But my answer won't necessarily fit another working mother. My best advice is to look hard at what you want, talk it over with your husband, and do what you want most. Be less concerned with what work will let you do.

"And also, don't worry about it forever. Worry about it for a year. Think about what you want the next year. You keep changing anyway—it's a decision you have to remake every few months. You can't figure it out forever!"

## *Anne and Dennis: The Kids Are Part of the Solution*

Like the Sorkins, Anne and Dennis Green have three children (ages ten, nine, and three), a beautiful home (with a soon-to-be-finished spa), two full-time careers (as supervisors), and a precisely orchestrated family routine.

The differences are these: the Greens earn less than a fifth of what the Sorkins make; the Greens live in the country, on the shores of a secluded Minnesota lake, where the cost of living is lower; they cannot afford a housekeeper, so their children go to the home of a sitter when not in school; the house and yard are kept neat and trim not by hired help but by all family members. Unlike Meg and Will, for whom the decision to have a third child was not a matter of money, Anne and Dennis had to do some careful financial planning before deciding to do so. And although the Greens share very similar goals with the Sorkins, they lean toward being more child-focused than work-focused. "All our money and most of our time outside the office go for our kids," said Anne Green, "and we both work because we love having a nice home that our children will always want to come back to. We do a lot with our kids—they are our chief priority."

The Greens are kind, sweet people. She is round-faced, petite, and forthright. He is over six feet tall, stalwart, and gentle. She is thirty-six, he is forty-three, and they have been equal partners for thirteen years. Happily, their kids are their partners, too.

The children are the center of the Green household, a bellwether for all the family emotions. "When our schedules are strung too tight, we recognize it when we get a little testy with the kids," said Anne. "We can tell we're doing too much, and we'll try to get the kids to help a little more."

"We laugh a lot over our kids," said Dennis. "The things they do make us laugh more than anything. But we try to keep the line of communication open for all of us. If we have a problem, I like to bring the kids in on it. For example, Anne wanted a place in our drive to put a basketball net, and I didn't like the idea. So we went to the kids.

" 'Do you want a blacktop driveway with a basketball goal?' we asked. They said yes. 'Then you've got to sweep it off and take care of it, and each of you has to pay $25 toward it, but we'll pay the balance.' I said I didn't want it but their mother did. So everyone's vote is given equal weight. It's not like Dad said no and that's it."

"Another good example," said Anne, "was deciding whether or not to get a dog. Dennis has always had a pet that was like a brother or sister to him, whereas I didn't. We had one for a year, a big dog, and it was just too hard to take care of. He wanted a dog that would have the run of the house. I said, 'Sorry, a dog will not have the run of the house if it's a big Lab.'

"Then we got a chance to get a little Shih Tzu that does not shed and is small. I knew even if it had the run of the house it wouldn't cause a big problem, so it wouldn't involve a lot of cleanup. The kids were involved in this decision, too, because they had to take on the responsibility of picking up the dog mess. They have to brush the dog every day, and they have to take care of it and feed it. So we all help make big decisions around here."

Anne pointed out that even the anger is shared in the household. "When I grew up," she said, "my parents never argued in front of us. Nothing angry was ever said, money was never discussed in front of us—and I think that's wrong. It's not reality. We may get into a disagreement, and the kids will say, 'Stop arguing.' Maybe it's arguing to them—to me it's discussing. You need to see that people *do* need to have arguments; they *do* need to talk; they *do* need to raise their voices periodically. And you need to know that money does not grow on trees. We all work hard for what we get and we manage it carefully.

"Dennis does the analysis of things like our insurance, major things like buying our new house, then we make the decision together, but I consult him on any unexpected purchase over $100. Also, we're a relatively practical family—we do shop for sale prices.

"We're putting a lot more financial responsibility on the kids, too. They've got to cooperate if they want a new bike or something. This summer we set up a list of duties, and they get paid to help watch our three-year-old with the baby-sitter, to do the dishes, sweep out the garage, feed the ducks. And if they don't do the work, they don't get their money."

The Greens are quite relaxed in their attitudes toward the demands of family and work. They have easy rhythms, which they have fine-tuned over the years. Their full-time schedules are something they enjoy and find difficult to imagine changing for any reason. Yet, as much as the Sorkins, they maintain a busy pace that includes work, chores, vacations, children's activities, and time alone for each.

"We are both supervisors," said Anne. "I work for the state and Dennis for the feds. Our hours are exactly the same, 8:00 to 4:30, so we can take the baby to the sitter and drive to our offices in town together.

"When our first child was born, I took three months off, which was really my 'accrued sick leave' because the government didn't allow a maternity leave."

"She is very good at what she does, and she has a good boss, who let her do it," adds Dennis.

"I did the same when my second child came along, only I took just two months off, which was actually 'advance sick leave' because the babies were so close together," said Anne. "With the third baby I had two months, too. The only drawback was I didn't dare get sick, because I didn't have any more sick leave until a long time after I was back.

"I enjoyed the time at home with the babies, but by two months I was really ready to go back. I missed the social contacts. I've always expected to work, too," said Anne. "We combine our salaries and pay for everything jointly—but we couldn't have our lovely home and be able to do things for the kids like have a boat and help them buy their bikes if we didn't both work."

"We come from two different backgrounds," said Dennis. "Anne's father is an attorney, and she was used to a little different style. I'm an only child who didn't grow up with a whole lot. My father and mother were divorced, so I was rich one day and poor the next. So I came from a background where I probably had to work harder younger.

"My mother didn't have many skills, because my father had been wealthy and she was raised as if she would never have to work. But after the divorce she did anything she could and became a cook for different restaurants and resorts. She always liked her work, so I grew up thinking a working mother is pretty natural and that the rest of the family is expected to help out, too. I had to keep house for my mom and me, even after I started to work when I was thirteen."

His wife's upbringing was more privileged, but she was one of six children who were expected to fulfill their share of household duties, too. Anne started college but didn't finish. "I've worked since I was nineteen," she said. "I've always worked full-time, and when I was off with the kids, I really missed work. Even to work part-time now I think I'd be really bored and thinking I could be earning money, so that's not an option I consider seriously. I don't think I'd be satisfied with part-time work."

Both Anne and Dennis work extremely hard to be sure they get everything in—at their jobs, on their house, getting their youngest to kiddie soccer on time, their oldest to Boy Scouts, and their daughter to Brownies. "We love it," said Anne. "But you know what we take the greatest pride in? Working it all out. Not just the daily stuff. We love the work of our relationship—it's the working out of all these things that keeps us in love with each other." And they give each other a lot of credit.

"Anne is extremely well organized," said Dennis. They both are. "Every Saturday Dennis tackles the three bathrooms and the cottage," said Anne, "which is property we rent out, while the two older kids and I clean the rest of the house. We both cut the grass with a self-propelled lawn mower, although usually Dennis cuts it and I do the raking. We also heat the house with wood, so we haul our own.

"I love to haul wood," exclaimed Anne.

"Not just wood," her husband said proudly. "We have beautiful rock walls surrounding our yard and along the road and the lake," said Dennis, "because Anne and I kept a little trailer behind our car to haul rocks for two summers."

"I made those walls," said Anne with a wide smile, "and we built a deck last fall in front of the house. I really enjoy carpentry too. We've done a lot of carpentry work in the house together — the whole basement in knotty pine. It took two-and-a-half winters to do that, staining and varnishing, putting up the tongue-and-groove wall. We're making a spa this fall. This is our dream home — we go all out on it, and we love working together."

Energetic and lighthearted, the Greens go all out on everything. Together they work hard on every part of their lives, and they always have. More than any other couple I interviewed, they are an extraordinary example of the "crossover" that is true of couples who are equal partners.

Anne loves the "man's work," of hammers and nails and woodworking plans. And so through the cold midwestern winters, he saws and she pounds. "She's the artist, so she plans everything out. I just follow what she tells me to do," said Dennis who counters his wife's woodworking skills by being one of the finest pancake artisans this side of the Mississippi.

"The kids always have a nice warm breakfast in the winter thanks to Dennis — pancakes and eggs. Dinner is on me," said Anne, "but we both do the cleanup, although we're trying to get the kids more involved in cleaning up now. Grocery shopping we do together, too, on the way home from work."

Child care slots neatly into their daily routine as they have been fortunate enough to find sitters who take whichever Green child needs looking after into their home. "We're very lucky that we both have the same hours at work so we all get to go to town together," said Anne. "We stop off at the sitter's, Mom and Dad say good-bye to the kids, we work, and then we pick them up."

As with most busy, two-career families, time alone is a problem. Anne and Dennis happily addressed that issue two years ago when they decided to take separate vacations in addition to family car trips. "Last fall I went to the Renaissance Festival in San Francisco with a couple of my friends," said Anne, "and Dennis went out West hunting. In February I went to Arizona to visit my parents. It's a nice break to be able to do that.

"We avoid time-share vacations and very expensive trips so we can go where we want to go, take or not take the kids, and not feel guilty about the time and money. This year we decided we want to stay home because we'd like to get a better boat for the lake and we want to put the spa in—that's something we can use all the time. To have that and to have the kids enjoy it is a lot better than a high-priced week somewhere."

"Money is serious business around here," said Dennis. "We often talk about 'How are we going to make it?' It's difficult right now, financially and otherwise. To have another child was a big decision for us—then suddenly he came along, and he is the neatest."

Dennis breaks into a big smile as he talks about their youngest tax deduction: "We have more fun with him. I'm not sure why. They say you've had the experience with the other ones so you're a little more relaxed. Maybe that's the difference between the first and the third child—you worry less."

## Is It Good for Our Children?

"Will our pursuit of two full-time careers hurt our children?"

"Are we missing the best moments of our children's lives because we are at work when they happen?"

"Are we leaving the kids in unstimulating environments with too much TV time because we have to work overtime or lose credibility with our bosses?"

The questions were always the same, no matter which family I interviewed. Mothers and fathers alike mulled identical issues.

I know these worries because I too have had them. I have held my breath as I've watched my youngest child, Ryan, grow from a baby who went to his first all-day sitter when he was six weeks old into a teenager who often comes home to an empty house after school. Will he turn to drugs because he was a latchkey kid at age nine? I've wondered. Did he lose out on critical reading skills because he was in full-time day care at age four?

Experts have lots to say on the topic, but they often disagree. Some say at-home mothers raise more confident, achievement-oriented kids. Others say day-care babies are more independent and more cooperative. It's difficult to know whom to believe.

More than the worry, however, being away from Ryan for long work days has caused a different kind of pain. A palpable, visceral feeling of loss, for me, because as much as I give to my child, I get back so much more. He fills up my life! Just having him around to smile and laugh, to need me, means so much down deep inside that I cannot bear the thought that being a full-time working mother may have harmed him irreparably in some way. Missing moments with a young child makes you feel like you're missing an arm or a leg.

Yet I've had little choice. Like most of the parents I've interviewed, I have had to work for purely financial reasons. During my son's sixteen years I have been married, unmarried, and married again. During those years my financial resources have fluctuated wildly. I remember one year when I could afford a bed for my child but no dresser, not even an unpainted one, to hold his clothes. So I know why we do what we do . . . but I worry. Then there's the issue of maternal happiness. If I'm unhappy at home, how can I be a good mom? But am I being selfish?

And yet today I see a happy and healthy teenager who gets excellent grades in a highly competitive high school, made the basketball team, and gets himself to practices and games on time even though his mom has to miss most of his games. He is a resourceful kid who is a whiz at the computer and has paid for his own desktop publishing setup.

I also see a parent—me—who recognizes the emptiness I feel when I am away; it has made me a more careful parent. I treasure the time I have with Ryan, so I don't fritter it away on unnecessary socializing or go shopping more than I need to. We certainly watch plenty of TV in our house, but we appreciate having each other around. Whenever I can—without embarrassing him—I try to lay a hand lightly on his shoulder, my way of saying "I love you."

But there was an awful, never-to-be-forgotten moment when Maria Shriver asked my son, who was her subject during an interview on the "CBS Morning News" because he was a "latch-key kid," "Wouldn't you rather have your mother at home than working?"

I remember feeling my life twist in the wind until Ryan said, "No . . . all my friends' moms work. If my mom was home, I couldn't have my snacks and see my favorite shows." Thanks, kid. And thanks, too, for your smile—that keeps me going. And just for being you. When my work is hard and I'm dead tired, I see your energy and enthusiasm for life and know I'm doing something right.

Let me share with you what makes a good parent: *making your child feel loved and accepted.* That's all. And you can do that while working full-time. When you are home, be a good listener. Ask your child about the day. Ask about the sitter or the day care. Even if you can't do anything to change something that makes your child unhappy, his or her knowing that you care means a great deal.

The single greatest error full-time working parents make is thinking that their frantic pace and frustration and exhaustion are the result of something they are doing wrong. They aren't! You are doing what you must. The system has been wrong but it is slowly changing to make it easier for you. Be equal partners with each other and you will be doing your best.

And just in case you don't believe me, here's further proof that it can all work out okay—for you and for your children.

## The View from the Other Side

You need a string of adjectives to describe Gabrielle: spirited, self-assured, independent, and buoyantly happy. Soon to graduate from one of the country's best colleges, she is direct and honest and radiates a simple, natural beauty. She's everything you could want your child to be. She is also surprisingly wise for her age, thanks to her parents—both of them.

Gabrielle's parents have followed less-than-orthodox career paths. Her father, a physician specializing in obstetrics, gynecology, and internal medicine, made a career change in his early forties to become a psychiatrist, a change necessitating more medical education and another residency. Her mother, who was a nurse, also returned to school to earn a master's degree in psychology that would allow her to become a psychiatric social worker. They are nontraditional in other ways too. Mother is the athlete, while Dad is the bookworm; Mother does crisis intervention while Dad cleans the bathrooms.

"I always remember my mom working," said Gabrielle. "I'm the oldest. My brother was born when I was a year and a half. I guess she was home until he was two. Then she started working part-time, and she began working full-time when Mark was six.

"My clearest memory is from school where there was an emergency phone number for a friend of my mom's because we could never get in touch with my mom or dad. I remember getting sick in school and going to my friend's house because my mom was at work. I didn't feel bad about that. The person who would take care of me was my best friend's mother. I spent a lot of time there and felt really comfortable. The understanding was that my mom would have done the same thing for her, too. Otherwise, I never thought much about it—I figured everybody else's mom was working, too."

Nor did she find it remarkable that her parents split the work of home and children: "My dad cooks, although my brother and I made our own breakfasts, and once we got to be about twelve or so we made our own lunches to take to school. Dad just did the dinner, which he still does.

"He loves to shop," said Gabrielle matter-of-factly. "Dad goes to the grocery store almost every day after work. Usually he'll come home and say, 'What would you like for dinner, kids?' He likes to cook fish and vegetables and have everything ready to eat around 6:00. Our favorite is spaghetti.

"Only once did I ever notice that other dads didn't cook. I remember going to a friend's home for a slumber party, and her dad was cooking waffles for breakfast. She was making such a big deal of it, saying, 'I can't believe my dad is cooking in the kitchen.' And I thought, My dad always cooks—that's not weird at all.

"When it comes to the housework, Dad does the bathrooms and Mom pretty much does the rest. For a while they had a lady that cleaned house for them, but not right now. I wouldn't say the cleaning is well organized; it's more a kind of progressive thing.

"My mom gets on my dad's case sometimes. They have this agreement that he does the bathrooms, and sometimes he'll get kind of lazy. Meanwhile, my mom does a little after work every day, so by the end of the week everything's been done. If my dad puts it off, Mom will say, 'You haven't done the bathrooms this week.' He'll say, 'No, I haven't,' and get out the toilet bowl cleaner."

Gabrielle sees nothing unusual in this kind of balance. "I want to work," she said without hesitating. "I think it's practical for women to work. I think the whole thing about splitting the cooking and cleaning is good.

"I know a lot of the kids my age are thinking about things like that," she said. "My friends are college women who have strong ideas about wanting to work and support themselves and have an equal partnership in marriage. We talk about it a lot.

"Sometimes it comes up when someone's talking about their boyfriend and how serious they are and whether or not they might get married. Sometimes it comes up in talking about children. That leads to marriage and 'What do I want from marriage?' This year, especially, the whole idea of maternity leave and bringing up children with someone else has come up among my friends.

"We want paid maternity leave—paid paternity leave too. So that you can give birth to a child, stay with it a certain amount of time, then your husband can take off work and you can go back to work. I think you should be able to switch off.

"My male friends are really open about that kind of thing.

Most say they'd love to take a leave to be with their children, but they wouldn't want to be home all the time and have a wife be the one working. Generally the guys agree that equality is important. As many women as men at my school are going into the same kinds of fields anyway—medicine, banking, high-prestige jobs.

Gabrielle is savvy about money too.

"I know my parents' salaries," she said. "My dad makes exactly twice as much as my mom, but I have never felt like Mom's job wasn't worthwhile or just as important. She talks about her work more—I think Dad has a more boring job. He writes prescriptions, while she's out doing crisis intervention.

"But even though he makes more, they split the bill paying. My dad deals with taxes—at least he takes stuff to the accountant. But they definitely split the bills, and they each have their separate bank account." How many of us knew that much about our parents?

Naturally, I was curious to know if Gabrielle was conscious of friction between her parents.

"I became more aware of their arguments as I got older," Gabrielle said. "I don't know if that's because they were hiding them when I was little, or if I just didn't notice.

"They tend to be pretty calm and relaxed when they argue. Usually the problem is that one of them is missing some kind of information. They had an argument about taxes this year. My dad had some bit of information my mom didn't know about, and when my mom understood that, she was okay. They don't really scream and yell; they sit down and talk things out.

"I see them as good friends," said Gabrielle. "They talk a lot, they have a good time. They used to commute an hour together to work, and they would listen to taped books together. And they are careful to fill each other in. If I call home and one isn't there, the one who is makes a list of what I say to share with the other one."

As with most dual-career couples with children, home life was Gabrielle's parents' focus once they left work. "My mother plays tennis, my father loves to read," Gabrielle said, describing their activities. "And when my brother and I were in high school,

I remember the big family scene at night. We'd sit around, and they'd both be helping with the homework. Dad was better at helping with the homework than Mom.

"My family's pretty open. They're definitely both really good about talking to my brother and me about pretty much anything. I can remember sex was something my dad talked to me about as much as my mom. When I got my period, I ran and told my father. I was thrilled. And he said, 'You're a young lady now.' Both of them have been open about pretty much every-thing—partying, drinking, etc.

"I've been thinking a lot about marriage," said Gabrielle. "I like the way my mother did it. She was twenty-six when she got married and twenty-eight when I was born. I know I definitely want to get married, and I'd like to have two kids before I'm thirty—but I don't want to start until I'm twenty-seven, so I have a fairly rigid time schedule for when I want to have these kids. So I guess I'm looking at getting married at around twenty-five. And that's pretty young these days." Gabrielle smiles with confi-dence. "I like my mom's plan.

"Another reason I've been thinking about it a lot is because I just broke up with a serious boyfriend. It was a relationship that I ended gradually.

"He was too uptight. He tried to do everything and do it perfectly. He could never relax and enjoy himself. It got to be an overwhelming problem. I just got more and more fed up with his being so uptight. I couldn't really ask him to *change*. That's just the way he is, but I brought it up saying I saw it as a problem. It carried over to everything: If there was a problem in our rela-tionship, he wanted to 'fix' it.

"Sometimes problems just can't be 'fixed instantly,'" Gab-rielle went on. "You have to work on them over time. I could never get him to see that. It probably irritated him that I'd do just as well as him in school and I'd spend about half the time that he did grinding away. And he doesn't have to work that hard to do well."

It was uncanny talking with Gabrielle. What she had discov-ered already in her young life was the essence of what makes a marriage an equal partnership. I'm convinced this could only have come from the patterns she observed between her parents. Few adults that I interviewed were as perceptive as Gabrielle when it came to describing what matters between two people. And she continues to learn what works for her the only way you can—by testing and trying and giving up only when you can't change something.

"A major problem was our difference in values," she said of the boyfriend with whom she had just broken up. "He worked just to work. That was all he would do. And I feel like there's so much else to do besides work. He was not very people-oriented, either, while I have at least five close friends here at school and a lot of other people I'm pretty close to. I wouldn't forfeit that. He couldn't understand why I'd want to spend all that time with my friends.

"On the other hand," Gabrielle added with a laugh, "the guy I dated before that was *too* relaxed, so I need a happy medium.

"Definitely, I will talk things over with the person I want to marry—like an agreement between us that what I want to do is as much a priority as what he wants to do. I know my parents did. My dad said they talked about these things seriously before they got married. He agreed to help out when my mother went back to school, for example.

"Dad said the reason he talked to us so much about these things was because he really hated his home life when he was a kid. He saw his mom at home and his dad working, and he never talked to his parents about anything—so he really wanted to be involved with his own kids.

"I have two other women who are good role models for me, too," said Gabrielle. "Both are professors here at school. One I have really mixed feelings about. She has a three-year-old kid, and her husband is working in another city. She just got tenure, and she's the best professor I ever had, but she has the child all the time and her husband comes home only on weekends.

"I think it's great that she's able to be a college professor and get all the things done that she gets done as well as take care of a kid. But at the same time, I feel like she's getting shafted, because she has the kid all week while the husband gets to come home and play with the kid on weekends. I admire her for doing all this, but I think, Do you really want to be supermom?

"The other professor I think of as a role model is still single. She's got her life well in hand. I admire how successful she's been with her career, how she's respected, and how she's very involved with students.

"But nothing worries me really about being married and having a job. I know that I really want to spend time with my kids and my husband. And I know with my little time schedule that I've worked out I might have to get married and then have the kids pretty fast.

"I know it will be tricky to balance everything. But I don't think I'm going to try to be perfect in every way. I don't have to be the world's best mom or the world's best businessperson. I just have to be good. You can't be perfect."

## Being a Good Parent

Gabrielle's parents did several very important things right:

- They stayed in touch with their children even though they had demanding schedules. They were always inquiring, always interested, giving Gabrielle and her brother the warm memory of "the big family scene at night."
- They shared with them the everyday realities of life — salaries, financial pressures, schedule conflicts — and how to handle them.
- They confronted the serious side of life with open discussion of sex and drugs and other hazards. They emphasized the importance of finding an equal partner — using exactly those words — and showing how they did it.

Like all our children, Gabrielle has easier access to sex, birth control, and a fine education, as well as an opportunity to land a great job and the freedom to choose career or family or a combination of both — something many of us did not have. And while she is under pressure to plan her life with split-second timing, she has a wonderful enthusiasm and a great perspective on what true balance in life is all about. She is prepared to

handle all the choices—especially love, marriage, career, and
children, along with expectations that the roles between husband and wife should expand and merge just like her parents'
have—wisely.

## Quiz: Do You Have What It Takes to Be Half of a Full-Time Dual-Career Couple?

Consider the following and circle your answers:

1. You feel the average happily married dual-career couples
   should have a serious talk:
   a. once a month.
   b. once a week.
   c. once a day.

2. Sue and Mike have been living together for three years
   and are considering marriage, but Sue hates to spend
   every winter weekend on the ski slopes with Mike, an
   avid, expert skier. She should:
   a. put her foot down and insist he cut back his skiing in
      order to spend more time with her.
   b. try for a trade-off, where they spend half their
      weekends together doing what he wants and half doing
      what she wants.
   c. consider learning how to ski herself and going along
      on a few trips each ski season as well as finding ways
      to enjoy herself doing something on her own while he
      is away skiing.

3. Claire is concerned that she and her husband rarely go
   out with other couples or see friends, which she loves to
   do. Both work long hours, so their only free time is on
   the weekends. She should:
   a. realize a man's home is his castle and give her poor
      hubby time to unwind. He sees plenty of people during
      the week.
   b. arrange to see friends on her own if it's so important to
      her.

   c. talk to her husband about her desire to share the pleasures of outside friendships with him and see if they can compromise on time to be alone together and time to spend with others.

4. After living with Fred for a year, Janet finds herself feeling left out when his good buddy Roger is around, as Fred shares more of his thoughts, his humor, and his most charming moments with Roger than with her. Her expectations are:
   a. unreasonable. Men and women make love, make babies, make homes together—but they don't always make the best of friends.
   b. understandable, but it will be years before most men are able to be close friends with women.
   c. perfectly reasonable. Fred's inability to include her as a close friend is a signal that they may not be well suited to be each other's permanent partner.

5. Karen and Michael have been married for twenty years. He takes her out for breakfast every Saturday, never forgets flowers on special occasions, and often surprises her with a hug and a kiss when she least expects it. When she is chubby, he tells her he likes his women "healthy"; when she is exhausted, he takes over the house and the kids. Michael is:
   a. probably having an affair.
   b. too good to be true.
   c. a savvy fellow who knows a little appreciation goes a long way—like about twenty years down the road.

6. The average happily married dual-career couple should have sex:
   a. every day.
   b. whenever either partner wants to, even if the other isn't in the mood.
   c. whenever both partners are not too tired or stressed out from work and both agree they would enjoy being together. Depending on what's happening in their lives, this could be three times a day, three times a week, or three times a month.

7. Janice's maternity leave is almost over, and she wants to go back to work full-time. She loves her job. Her husband, Jack, has decided he wants to stay home with the baby. Janice should:
   a. try a part-time position instead.
   b. point out the financial benefits of both continuing to work.
   c. suggest they budget so that Janice can work full-time while Jack tries out being the full-time homemaker to see if this option works well for both of them.

8. It's 10:15 A.M. Judith is in the middle of an important conference when she is notified that the baby-sitter has suffered a mild heart attack and an ambulance is on the way to her home. The next-door neighbor is with the kids. Judith should:
   a. excuse herself from the meeting and rush home.
   b. call the neighbor and see if she can take the kids for the rest of the day—she'll be compensated, of course.
   c. call her husband and discuss which of them can more easily leave the office for the day.

9. You are a twenty-six-year-old woman, and the president of your company wants to know if you are interested in a "Mommy Track" option, which would give you time off to have a child, protect your job for two years, but require you to give up any expectations of becoming a senior executive. You say:
   a. "It sounds like the answer to my prayers, because I really need the money. Does this mean I could keep my benefits during my years off?"
   b. "I'm not sure about this. On the one hand it sounds ideal, because I would dearly love to spend more time with my children, when and if I have them. On the other hand I love my work. Right now I really want to move up the ranks and become a supervisor. Could I make this decision later?"
   c. "I can't believe this company is serious. I may consider a lawsuit if it goes any further with this sexist policy. Don't you know I intend to become president someday?

The fact that I might have five children, too, won't stop me!"

10. You are thirty-two years old, a lawyer, and likely to be invited to become a partner in your firm. You have just received a whopping bonus of $20,000 for your hard work this year. Now your boss wants to know if she can count on you for another year. Your reaction?
   a. The partnership sounds great if you can continue working on the same team, but you were thinking about starting a family next year.
   b. You aren't sure if you can accept the partnership, because the long hours this year were hard on your marriage. Your husband, a doctor, really counts on you to keep the home fires burning, and this year he had to pitch in more than he likes.
   c. You want to know what the bonus plan for next year is, especially if you make partner. You tell your boss you agree you did a great job this year and you'll work just as hard the next. Since your boss is also a wife and mother, you let her know that a chunk of your bonus will go to your terrific housekeeper, whom you and your husband pay handsomely just to be sure she's there when you both have to work long hours.

*Scoring*
Give yourself 5 points for every (c) answer, 3 points for every (b) answer, 1 point for every (a) answer.
*Totals*
10-20—Even though you probably *want* a dual-career marriage to some degree, tradition is sabotaging your chance for long-term happiness. Stop listening to your mother and start listening to yourself. Or consider part-time work.
21-39—You're making a real effort, but something is holding you back. Is it you? Your spouse? Do you need to talk things over? You're probably pretty happy now, but things could be a lot better.
40-55—No "relationship" manuals for you! You should be able to work out an equitable and satisfying dual-career partnership if you haven't already.

# Making It Work

For two-career couples with children, the nature of their goals will determine the way they run their lives. Those striving to score big on the career scene—in terms of money, achievement, and prestige—are going to put in more hours and labor more intensively at the office than those who are satisfied to stay on a particular plateau. The latter group can more easily keep work hours predictable so that time and energy are easily allotted between job and home, but that doesn't mean this approach is better; everyone must make his or her own choice. Success lies in doing it together. Ease up on yourself and share with your spouse. Be equal partners no matter what pace you choose.

As the Greens and Phoebe and Taylor show, choosing to "downscale" lifestyles by living in a rural area or choosing more flexible and less demanding routines can relieve some of your stress. On the other hand, for Sarah and Patrick and Meg and Will, professional success and self-esteem are joined at the hip, making their extra efforts well worth it to each member of each couple. Sure, their lives are tough at times, but they are also tantalizingly full of action and excitement.

The good news is that many options are open, many more than ever before. And even though the workplace is hardly perfect yet, the future promises much good news for the man and woman who want to pursue their goals as equal partners. What is making this so promising is that more and more couples are changing. He does it only if it works for her; she does it only if it works for him too. *Together* these families decide what is right for them; together they ask their employers for what they need—or together they find new employment—whether that means downscaling their lifestyles, changing careers, or striking a new, if temporary, balance between home and career. Again, this is happening not only because men and women share the same values—insistent on quality in their home life as well as at work—but because they are willing to cross over and assume duties once traditionally limited to the other sex. Mothers do carpentry, fathers cook, mothers handle finances, fathers care for little babies, mothers choose the job with the heavy travel schedule, fathers keep up with the housework.

At the same time, almost everyone has to give up the same things—outside socializing and time for themselves alone. Few regret the first, but many continue to struggle to find more personal time. Fortunately, as the children get older, that struggle does become easier.

If you are a full-time working parent, it is perhaps most important for you to get over the guilt factor. Accept the fact that you're not going to have as much time with your children as you or they would like. After all, you've accepted other facts of life—from having to work to death and taxes—without being any worse for wear. Like it or not, the world has changed since we were kids. The choices have changed, some even for the better. No matter what you decide, you're doing your best. That's all anyone can ask of you and all you can ask of yourself.

Remember that to be a good parent you must feel good about yourself. If that means making enough money to send your son to a good school, or gaining important self-esteem through work, then you should work. Good child care *can* be found. It's not easy, but I've never met a couple who truly wanted it who couldn't manage to find it.

Remind yourself what this is all for: you and the people you love. Listen to your children and to your partner. Tell them you appreciate what they are doing; tell them that you love them. And when you feel guilty about not baking those homemade cookies every Saturday, tell yourself that you can give a child an opportunity easily—by signing her up for a lesson and seeing that she has a ride to get there—but that you spur her to learn and achieve when you set an example and show her you care.

Last, don't forget that you can make changes in your life. If you're feeling stressed out, or if you're beginning to feel that all that time away from your kids just isn't worth it, consider having one of you go part-time or stay at home for a while. Maybe you'd rather wait to go full-time until your kids are in school. Nothing is written in stone. It's *your* life, and you've got only one chance to do it your way!

# 5
# The Easier Balancing Act:
# One Full-Time Career Plus
# One Part-Time Career Plus
# Kids

Short of winning the lottery, nothing makes many working mothers happier than being able to work part-time while nurturing their little ones through the rigors of childhood. These women think they have the best of both worlds: the stimulation of their careers, steady income, the delightful, rewarding company of their children, and the awareness that they are moms who can be close by for bruises and playtime, fevers and school plays.

After sorting through painful confusion and worry, many women who are deeply torn between motherhood and career find that a part-time career can be a terrific balance . . . if they can work it out as equal partners. A part-time "balance" allows the working mother to enjoy her kids without slipping into the role of traditional full-time homemaker—a role that might make her feel taken advantage of. Furthermore, she protects her own career by staying current, and visible, in her field. In some couples it is the father who chooses a part-time career (turn to Chapter Six for a full report on that option), but here we will look at the mother's choice to work part-time.

179

When a couple opts for the wife to work part-time, the results *can* be terrific: she feels great because he continues to help out, preventing her from feeling overwhelmed by housework and child care or thinking that her part-time work is not important; he feels great because she's happy, yet the financial burden of their lives is not resting wholly on his shoulders. He also feels good because he recognizes the value of her time with the children and the house and is a more appreciative husband than he might have been if he did not share the same duties himself. He doesn't take her efforts for granted. And because they are satisfied, interested parents, their children thrive.

But be forewarned—this is a balance that works for *some* women. Some of us are too strongly career-driven to be able to balance our split ambitions this way. I recently observed a close friend try to make the change to part-time. For over a year I listened to her tell me how she couldn't wait to quit her high-pressure, high-paying, high-status administrative position in a major metropolitan hospital. Marianne, age thirty-three, was convinced she wanted to be more involved with the house and the cooking and the care of her young child—all duties that her husband, who also worked full-time, was happy to be fully responsible for. It was as if his happiness in domesticity was something she envied and wanted to share—and probably felt guilty about since her involvement was so minimal.

Yet, when that chance came and she was able to be at home part-time with her three-year-old son, she panicked. Within a few short weeks she remembered that she genuinely disliked housework and that she didn't know how to cook because she really didn't want to. Soon the extra time with her child became more of a pressure than a pleasure. Fighting depression, Marianne also found herself distinctly unimpressed with the quality of the part-time positions available to her—positions that made her feel underutilized, underpaid, and just plain unexciting.

When she was offered a full-time position managing more people for, of course, more money—but in the incredible pressure-cooker environment of another hospital—she jumped at it. The part-time option was absolutely not right for Marianne. But she had no way of knowing that until she tried it out.

Be aware that, like Marianne, you may find after trying it out that it isn't for you. Like Marianne, you may find the trial has relieved a great deal of anxiety and also given you an opportunity to find a better job. In the long run, that's what Marianne's real dilemma was. She had peaked in her former position. Now, although she is more career-driven than ever, she understands her anxieties over her home and child and knows what she can and cannot do about them, and she is in a new job that provides the challenge and excitement that she craves. Though her experience showed her that part-time work was not right for her, by trying it out, Marianne won on all counts.

For lots of women, however, part time *is* the answer, especially when the children are young. Many of us want to lead lives that place work in the forefront some days, family first on others. If you are like me, you want to do your best and be recognized for it, and you want to love the best way you can and be loved for it. My twin desires led me down the road to fourteen years as a part-timer—in school or working—some of those years with an equal partner and some without, some with money and some without, all those years with children. Today I am a full-time vice president in the communications industry with a heavy travel schedule, one child still at home, a husband who is very much an equal partner, a six-figure income that ranks me at the top of my field—and I haven't turned forty-five yet.

If I can do it, so can you—I don't even have a college degree! But I do have energy and I work in a field that I love. How I got there is less a tale of carefully orchestrated goal setting than one of a willingness to allow my life to evolve, which is not always easy to do.

The first time around, I married at twenty, had two babies within two years, and expected to be happy at home. I wasn't. I went from misery to depression. Money was a problem, so I talked to my young husband about scaling back our expectations ("I don't need a dishwasher and an elevator in the building"); we found a less expensive but comfortable apartment. I quit smoking and started running, which I still do eighteen years later. That wasn't enough. Somehow, I had to break out of the full-time homemaker routine that I found stifling, even though my husband hated the idea of my working. What could I do that wouldn't take money, time, and devotion away from my family?

I pieced together an answer: a part-time job on Saturday mornings that would pay for one class at a local college per semester. To pay for the necessary baby-sitting, I volunteered for extra hours in the sitter pool of which I was a member. Suddenly I was flying! I was back in the world again. Soon I was able to add a second class. My self-esteem soared with the grades I got on my papers. I began to sound like the well-informed woman I wanted to be.

When my husband asked me to consider having a third child, I agreed, confident that I would be able to continue work on my undergraduate degree and turn a seemingly disconnected pastiche of art history, music theory, economics, studio art, and sociology courses into a master's in arts administration.

I vividly remember a moment of quiet exuberance from those days. I was six months pregnant, rocking on my knees in freshly turned dirt as I set in a pink petunia plant. As I tucked the spring soil carefully around the young plant, I thought with satisfaction, I can do this for about five more years—then I must be able to work full-time. And I was right. Five years later I took my first entry-level management job. However, the route there was more circuitous than I had dreamed it would be that sunny day.

Right after my third child was born, we moved so my husband could take a new job. Until we moved, I kept my Saturday job and my classes going on the side, asking only that my husband watch the children on Saturday mornings. But when we had completed our move to a new state, he told me he didn't want me to work part-time anymore. He thought my working made it look like he couldn't take care of his family. Since we had married at a time when men and women led traditional lives, when few women worked unless they absolutely had to, and men made the important decisions in the family, I had always done what I was supposed to do—all the child care and housework. I said little about this new request. I wondered how I could pay for school. But when I checked into the local universities and discovered they wouldn't take my hard-earned credits anyway—or allow me to attend just one course at a time—the question was moot.

What a change in my life! So confident just a few short months before, now I felt desperate again. I kept the pain to myself, because I was afraid to rock the boat. I had no money of my own, none that I could make, and none that I could get from my family. I had no power to take care of myself and my children if I made my husband angry and somehow ended up on the street. Not a logical thought, perhaps, but a very real and potent one.

What to do now? I reconnoitered. What did I already possess that could be turned into something without additional study? The answer popped into my head—my writing. I thought of all those A's on my papers. The kind words of the professor who said, "It's always a pleasure to read your work." I remember the day I made up my mind: "I'll write to save my life" was exactly how I said it to myself.

I set a goal of selling a story to a national magazine within one year. Ten months passed without a sale. Eleven months, no sale. I went to the smallest, least prestigious of the local magazines and placed a story with an editor who had bad breath and made a pass at me. Finally I was in print. Whew! And the year wasn't yet over. Would you believe that within days of the end of my "year" a major magazine called? I'd done it! That fired me up for the next year.

Now I called myself a writer. Pretty soon I had another nice project in hand: a volunteer effort turned into a small book for schoolchildren. I secured a grant to pay for production, design, and printing, assembled a team of collaborators, and within two years had a finished product that was well received in our community. Meanwhile, I was still taking care of the children and the house full-time.

But I was ready to branch out. I wanted to write more, cover more news stories, try my hand at fiction. I began to work more evenings because the kids took up my daytime hours. My young, traditional husband sat me down. "You can't do this," he said. "You can't write, because I don't want you to. It makes you too

busy, and that isn't the way I want our lives to run." This time I
spoke up. But he was firm. "I make the rules around here," he
decreed.

I took the little book that had been a volunteer project and
walked into a small communications firm where there was an
opening for a news editor. I had no background in the industry,
no college degree—just a healthy dose of desperation. "I need
someone who will try to solve our problems in new ways," said
the managing editor, who happened to be a woman several years
younger than I. "No one knows how to do this anyway, and you
seem to have the energy it will take." I was hired! Soon I had a
regular paycheck, and I asked for a divorce. Slowly I was gaining
control over my life.

In order to launch myself into full-time work, I found a baby-
sitter. My husband asked if I would seek marriage counseling
with him. I agreed, especially since this type of counseling was a
paid benefit—from *my* job.

Suddenly something fascinating happened: we began to talk.
This man with whom I had lived for nearly twelve years listened
to me and I to him. We talked about ourselves, yes, but we really
talked about our work. We shared our office war stories. Our
marriage caught fire again. We saw and heard each other for the
first time, it seemed. He pitched in to help with the kids and the
house. We shared our expenses when we were together. And
then, when we felt confident of our mutual need for each other,
we decided to stay together.

A few months after that decision he asked me to consider
working part-time, and I had been offered a very good part-time
position as a newspaper columnist. I agreed. "On one condi-
tion," I said. "We don't stop talking." I knew that the strength
between us now was that thread of everyday reality that we
could share, that understanding of work pressures, of in-house
company politics, of small victories in the office, and of the
frustrating tedium that makes up the bulk of our lives when we
are fully employed. But the day I began my part-time job, not
only did he stop talking, he stopped helping around the house.
Six months later I filed for divorce.

# Turning Terror to Tenacity

We have a tendency to think that only those couples in which one partner holds down a well-paying job can afford to have the other go to school, even on a part-time basis. But I've found even the most strapped can make it, if they explore all the opportunities and are willing to work hard. I started married life thinking I was on my road to happiness. But I was wrong. None of us is safe from this kind of mistake or from tragedy. It could be divorce, a lost job, a move, or even death that alters our best-laid plans and ravages our savings. You never know what the future will bring—but that doesn't mean you must lose control over your life.

To say I wasn't terrified as I left my marriage wouldn't be telling the truth. But I had a secret. I had waited tables when I was a teenager and knew I could do it again if I had to. Whenever anxiety clutched too tightly at my chest, which it did every morning as I woke up, I imagined myself as a waitress and knew I would never be destitute.

Within a few months I was offered another part-time job, one that turned into a three-year project with fluctuating hours. It was a well-paying position that utilized my varied background, my writing, and added other media experience to my career pattern.

Meanwhile, I had found somewhere new to live. I drove by a little bungalow that I had always thought was darling and saw a "For Rent" sign stuck in the yard. Soon I was living in a cute little house that I could easily afford. So what if the refrigerator was missing all its racks? The house was across the street from the elementary school that my youngest child attended, making it possible for him to come home to a sitter for a few hours a day. Later, when he turned nine, he became a latchkey kid. My office was five minutes away.

In the midst of all this change, I met a new man. He was a journalist, too, so we got to know each other through the common language of our work. We became good friends, then better friends. Along the way I learned that he expected to do his own wash, he could cook a great veal parmigiana, he was an expert with the vacuum cleaner, and he loved to talk. One day we talked about marriage, and I wanted to be sure that this time the man in my world understood that my work was a vital part of my life, that I was my own security. He was surprised I felt I had to mention it! He had wanted to be sure I realized I would have to work if we were going to be able to afford a life together! I was surprised he felt he had to mention it.

On the first of May, two years later, we got married. In the next year I held another series of part-time "consulting" positions, making it the third year of workweeks that could vary from twenty to fifty hours. There were also long stretches when I was anchored at my home-office desk or aloft in small chartered planes flying all over the region. I couldn't have managed without my new partner, who filled in for me as parent and cook, who never once expected me to "do it all." And, when it was necessary, I filled in for him, too.

In the midst of our juggling, I noticed something very different about our life together: it was never quiet. And I'm not talking about listening to music or having the television on. We talked. We fought. Our biggest hassles occurred when one of us thought he or she had been doing more than his or her fair share around the house to the detriment of career efforts. Or when one of us felt he or she was not getting enough attention because the other one was working too hard. And we always worked it out right away. To this day, we are a couple that argues. But no one would ever say we don't know how to have fun, either. We run together, windsurf, ski, read, listen to music, and, yes, watch TV. But what we do most is talk about our work, our thoughts, our family, our friends. We talk all the time.

Nearly ten years have passed since I changed my life. Today I can see that my curious pastiche of studies and experience has paid off. As an executive in the communications field, I work with authors and artists whose work covers a vast range of subjects. I know how to work with computers, can easily plan a party or a press conference. Who would have known I would find my way here even a decade ago? If I hadn't part-timed my life, I might have missed it.

And eight years after we met, I'm still with that equal partner of mine. We continue to split our chores with little regard for tradition. I get cars fixed and clean up a yard full of debris from our giant willows. He cleans the bathrooms and sorts the wash. I pay the bills; he manages the mortgage. For the last two months, while I have completed this manuscript, he has been doing all the cooking, grocery shopping, some carpooling for the teenager in the house, and all extra household duties, including the laundry. Next month he has a major project due, and I'll take over.

When I went back for my twentieth high school reunion this year, I realized that I had lived through the same pressures and worries about career and money that the men in my high school class had. I too had survived divorce and disappointments. But I had also achieved the same rewards as they: I've raised happy, bright kids and enjoy a lovely home. I earn as much as most of the men in my class, which is important to me because it means I met the same challenges, maybe greater. When I stood in the midst of our reunion party last summer, I recognized who I have become: a self-made woman.

And when my old friends began to talk of retirement, I had to pull back. That's where we differ—I will never retire. I have twenty more years of full-time work ahead—then another twenty or more as a part-timer. I'm having too much fun.

## The Good News

It may indeed be true that women have it tougher than men do. A man can, in fact, have kids with very little disruption of his career or his life, provided he can find a woman willing to play the role of traditional wife (which is a lot harder than it used to be). Maybe life *isn't* always fair. But since there's nothing you can do about that, and since you *do* have the wonderful option of actually carrying and giving life to a child (an option men have yet to be given), you may as well look on the bright side. If you enjoy working or feel you have to work for financial reasons, or you feel it's right to work but can't find good, full-time day care, you couldn't be living at a better time. And working part-time is a wonderful way to be able to do a little bit of everything without giving up anything completely. Not only do part-timers rave about their lives, but there's a better chance now than ever that they can find a man who shares their priorities. Furthermore, companies are more willing than they used to be to discuss part-time options with women, and it seems there may even be some hidden career benefits for the woman who chooses to get on the "Mommy Track" not because her company makes her do so, but because she wants it.

Working mothers love what they are doing! As mentioned earlier, a *USA Today* survey of 100,000 people over the last ten years showed that the happiest women are those who combine job, marriage, and motherhood. They are, however, the same women who feel the greatest stress—so they may be happy but they need to find some way to lighten their load. And they are doing that, but not in the way you would expect. Very few drop out of the work force on a permanent basis. Few want to. An astounding 90 percent of all women between the ages of eighteen and forty-nine work, 60 percent full-time and 30 percent part-time.

Also, Felice Schwartz, president and founder of Catalyst, a not-for-profit research and advisory organization that works with corporations to foster the career and leadership development of women, recently reported in the *Harvard Business Review* that a new study by a multinational corporation shows that "the rate of turnover in management positions is 2½ times higher among top-performing women than it is among men" and that "a large producer of consumer goods reports that one half of the women who take maternity leave return to their full-time jobs late or not at all." That means that millions of American women are leaving the work force to have children and then reentering via flextime, job sharing, working at home, and generally redefining their lives to combine career and family in new, unusual, and exciting ways. As one expert put it, "Many of today's working women will be tomorrow's working women and vice versa."

A recent poll commissioned by the Ortho Pharmaceutical Corporation found that 52 percent of mothers who were working part-time said they were "very satisfied" with their lives compared with 41 percent of the mothers working full-time.

Clearly, many women love their work. It's just that they love their families, too. And they are making a point of reinforcing both of those concerns by choosing a man to live with or marry who shares their pleasure in family and work to the same degree. It isn't just that these equal partners place a similar *emphasis* on the importance of career and family in their lives—they also share a personal commitment to both. As mentioned in the previous chapter, it is no longer uncommon for women to work and for men to help out around the house. Did you know that:

- A stunning 74 percent of fathers surveyed in *Parenting* magazine recently said that they should share child-care chores equally with the mother.
- Today's dad now averages one hour of housework for every two hours put in by the working mother, a considerable increase from the old routine that saw Dad willing to work only one hour to Mom's six!

The change runs deep. It has metamorphosed from an attitude that once demeaned housework and child rearing ("Oh ... you're just a housewife?") to a hearty respect, a recognition that the time spent with the children is of great value to the family, that the time spent on housework is always needed, sometimes even fun or rewarding—and definitely to be shared.

Tightly linked to this is the couple's changing perception of what "success" really is. The concept of success is linked less and less to money and the accumulation of attractive, acquired "goods" than to feelings. Specifically, feelings of balance. The good marriage is less likely to be the one outfitted with the new Volvo station wagon, expensive vacations, and carefully orches-trated Armani wardrobes and more likely to be the one in which both man and wife bounce happily along on hectic schedules balanced among the needs of their healthy, active children, their two careers, their house (in which, needless to say, the soup cans are not in alphabetical order), and a car that will be replaced next year because Andy needs braces this year.

Luckily, changes have occurred in the workplace, too. Women have come a long way from the 1970s, when the working female was so grateful to be accepted into the workplace, so afraid that her toehold in the work world was tenuous, so convinced that her professional status was shaky that it was risky to ask business for more—maternity leave, flexible work hours, or just plain time off. Fortunately, the number of women entering the work force, leaving it, being courted to return to it, and being given new benefits to make that return easier continues to escalate.

In the last several decades the American economy has become dependent on women, not just as spenders but as earners. Forty-eight percent of the country's wage earners are women, and 38 percent of corporate executive, administrative, and management positions are held by women. America's companies need women. They are going to continue to need women. And this figure doesn't include women in the professions! As the baby boom generation ages, having had proportionately fewer children than any other generation in American history, we're beginning to see a decrease in population. Demographers are forecasting a future lack of talented workers, as evidenced by the fact that in 1989 top American colleges reported applications down by nearly 20 percent. Already, management consultants are beginning to advise companies to plan for better and longer relationships with their older workers, from senior executives to on-line producers.

The more companies need workers, and the harder good workers are to come by, the better position those workers will be in. Women—and men—are and will continue to be increasingly able to get more of their needs met in the workplace. For many people one of those needs is part-time work. Furthermore, changing attitudes toward retirement, the emerging power base of older working women, and a growing awareness of how an active career makes for a healthier old age are also contributing to a real interest in the privileges and possibilities of part-time work.

The increasing popularity in part-time career options was given a healthy boost in early 1989 when Felice Schwartz made this amazing statement in the *Harvard Business Review* article mentioned earlier:

> Part-time employment is the single greatest induce-
> ment to getting women back on the job expeditiously
> and the provision women themselves most desire. A
> part-time return to work enables them to maintain
> responsibility for critical aspects of their jobs, keeps
> them in touch with the changes constantly occurring at
> the workplace and in the job itself, reduces stress and
> fatigue, often eliminates the need for paid maternity
> leave by permitting a return to the office as soon as
> disability leave is over, and, not least, can greatly en-
> hance company loyalty. The part-time solution works
> particularly well when a work load can be reduced for
> one individual in a department or when a full-time job
> can be broken down by skill levels and apportioned to
> two individuals at different levels of skill and pay.
>     I believe, however, that shared employment is the
> most promising and will be the most widespread form
> of flexible scheduling in the future. It is feasible at
> every level of the corporation except at the pinnacle,
> for both the short and the long term. It involves two
> people taking responsibility for one job.

Schwartz pushed for job sharing, but that is only one of several options. Some women find that other types of part-time work suit their individual situations better—e.g., four hours a day, one day a week, evenings only, "project-based" hours they can fit in whenever they want, even work just at Christmas or over the summer. Whichever you choose, you'll need approval from above. Even if it's hard-won, it's worth fighting for if you feel part-time work will provide you with a partial "time-out" without any loss of expertise.

"I am encouraging two young women on my staff, who are in their mid-twenties, to think seriously about having their children soon," said Miriam, a senior vice president with a manufacturing firm. At forty-five, Miriam has one child, age twenty-three, who has completed college, and one, age seventeen, nearly ready for college.

"I cut my teeth professionally by working and going to school part-time while my children were little," said Miriam. "I had to work in order to pay for school, but managing those hours plus completing my education plus doing a good job as a mother and homemaker—all at the same time—impressed the people who hired me so much that the full-time job I was offered when my youngest turned nine was above entry-level. I am sure my age and maturity were a significant factor because I was nearly thirty-five years old, which made me a natural leader in my group.

"The very young women who work for me are often stalled in lower middle-management positions because of their age. They just don't have the maturity—or the perceived maturity—for promotion into senior management, nor do we have the space for them yet, even if they were ready to handle the responsibility. They can leave the company or turn what could be a frustration into a plus by using this as a 'part-time' period to have little ones. In a sense, that makes *us* work for them!

"I have two staff members I could easily fit into a shared job or flexible part-time position if they were to choose to have babies right now—and I can practically guarantee being able to move them more rapidly into management in five to eight years.

"I felt like a traitor thinking this way years ago," Miriam said, "as if I was taking a step backward, but I want these women to get the maximum out of each stage of their lives. I am at a point where I can look back and see what worked and what didn't. You really speed up in your late thirties and early forties if management is where you want to go. If your children are already past the toddler and kindergarten stages, then you are much freer to manipulate schedules, handle sick children, and feel that you can communicate better with children about their needs."

Women concerned about losing precious career time when they temporarily put these careers on hold needn't necessarily worry. Miriam feels that her situation actually improved.

"My years out as a part-timer somehow invested me with so much energy that I'm already planning how I can sabotage that bugaboo 'mandatory retirement age,'" she declared. "I don't want to retire at sixty-five; I'm having too much fun. Twenty more years in my career seems like too short a time. I plan to work well into my seventies and eighties if I can. I love work. I'm flabbergasted every day to see how much energy the women around me who are charging ahead have. We are all redefining 'middle age.'

"Think about it," she said, "I'm forty-five, my children are on their own, I run fifteen miles a week and play tennis, I am a senior vice president—and I have twenty or thirty years ahead of me in which to push as hard as I want to in every direction. I don't know many men my age who have as much to look forward to. So time out in your twenties or thirties or early forties may guarantee 'time in' as a major player when you can most easily manage it."

Fortunately, the benefits of working part-time can be shared by men. And part-time work doesn't have to be simply a way station until you go back to full-time work. It's important to realize that working part-time can offer opportunity. For some couples, the part-time option is an excellent way for one partner to take more time with home projects, pursue a risky, creative effort such as writing or the fine arts, or have the time to develop and market a new product or invention. This is how part-time can also mean "creative time."

Couples in which one or both partners work part-time may have less money, but they seem to enjoy life more than they did when both were under a full-time crunch. One couple I interviewed, ages thirty-three and thirty-four and the proud parents of a new baby, have already decided on a part-time path for both of them. She works part-time now, and he will, as well, within a few years. "My wife is still making more money than I am," said the husband, "even though she is working part-time on her business, which is designing interactive computer software for her own small company. I hope to equal her income within the next two years."

He is a management consultant with eight years under his belt. "Right now we have a big house and live in the city," he said. "We're looking to change that in two years when we will both have enough of a customer base to cut back our hours so

we can spend more time as a family. . . . We don't need all this.
We're looking for a less expensive lifestyle that will allow us to
choose to work on only those projects that challenge us, the
ones we really want to do. We've worked hard, both of us, to gain
the skills, the reputations, and the savvy needed in our careers.
Now we have that, and it's time to invest in our personal lives
too."

## Part Time Doesn't Mean Forever

The working woman who chooses to go part-time is not necessarily leaving her career momentum behind. She may simply put
her career on hold, if that, for a short time. Then again, she may
decide, each time she reevaluates her situation, that part time is
right for her, and she may end up working part-time for the rest
of her life.

The key to making part time work for you (and, some might
argue, the key to a happy life) is to remain flexible. There's no
law that says you must make one career decision and stick to it.
For example, let's say you decide, when your first child is born,
to work part-time until that child is in nursery school. If by that
time you've had a second child, you may decide to forgo going
back full-time until the *second* child is in school. Or imagine you
try part-time work and hate it. There's sure to be a way you can
work out going back to full-time employment! For most career
women, part time is a temporary state—usually while their kids
are young—that will end in their return to full-time work later
on. Whether part-time work is a permanent way of life for you or
a way to work things out in the short run, it's not set in concrete.

The couples you are about to meet have worked out part-
time career options that include job sharing, returning to
school, and an extended time-out from the worlds of business,
law, the performing arts, and education. One term used to define
this career option today is *flextime*. Think of that as a general
description applied to a variety of flexible hourly options,
whether it's the full-time flextime that Phoebe designed in the
previous chapter or a more manageable twenty-hour week.

The women you read about in this chapter range in age from
their mid-twenties to their mid-forties and provide the perspec-

tives of both college-educated, well-paid middle-class working mothers and those of women who are less financially secure. Part-time work is a viable option for dual-career families at all income levels.

Certain characteristics are shared by most of these women and their husbands: they met and fell in love in work-related situations (even though the age at which they met varies greatly), they tend to resolve their problems with an up-front approach and by testing unique solutions, and they emphasize a close-knit family life with a minimum of outside socializing or entertainment. Most of all, they are very flexible in their roles and in their outlook on the future.

## Working Part-Time: Paying the Bills and Keeping Self-Esteem

For many couples the decision for the mother to work part-time relieves everyone of pressure and guilt. Whether planned from the beginning or, as is more typical, arrived at through evolution, the successful part-time lifestyle is usually dependent on the woman's having established herself firmly enough in her career to feel work is satisfactory, not just painful time away from the kids. It's also dependent on the couple's ability to share—housework, child care, feelings—and the partners' willingness to try new things.

### *Devon: Job Sharing and Sharing at Home*

Devon is an investigative reporter for an upstate New York newspaper. Unfortunately, the newspaper business does not easily accommodate people with families. To be an investigative reporter is to endure wildly unpredictable hours, travel at all times, and personal risk (should a story involve criminals or disaster). Furthermore, Devon's newspaper is considered "hard" on women and is almost exclusively male in its executive echelon. The few women at that level who have taken maternity leaves did so briefly and compensated by working overtime hours. These women are the ones who set policy for the rest of the employees.

Thus Devon did not anticipate a hospitable welcome when she decided to ask for part-time work or the option to share a full-time position with another reporter, a woman who was about to have a baby. She was expecting a firm "no" even though the shared job option is the most popular form of flextime and the one most frequently recommended by experts such as Felice Schwartz of Catalyst.

To Devon's great surprise, however, a number of factors dovetailed to make the shared job a reality. Certainly it mattered that her husband was also a member of the staff, so that what worked for her would also ease pressures in another area of the paper. It also helped that a majority of women employees—management, reporters, and clerical staff—meet regularly in an informal group to discuss new options in maternity leaves, work schedules, and the like. Though no demands have been made, knowing the women are exploring the issues has heightened the awareness of senior management. It also mattered that Devon was a highly respected and valued reporter—with a specialty and a unique style—the paper did not want to lose. The woman with whom Devon suggested job sharing was also a prized employee. Because the two of them were unified in their approach to the shared position, they made a strong case for themselves. And because Devon and her husband, Harry, were both convinced this was the only way they could continue at the paper together, Devon was able to negotiate with conviction.

A close look at the relationship between Devon and Harry helps to illuminate how they decided on the right balance for them. A look at their daily patterns also shows what this particular option demands from everyone involved.

Like so many couples who succeed as equal partners, Devon and Harry were friends first, lovers later.

"We met five years ago in one of our newspaper's local bureaus," said Devon, her delicate Irish beauty framed by a halo of dark auburn hair. Hers is a sweet, freckled face that belies her tough-as-nails profession; few would expect such a fine-boned, petite person to go for the jugular.

"Harry was my boss at the time. Because of that and because we knew we were both going out with other people, we were able to get to know each other without any possibility of a relationship. I remember thinking early on, Gee, he's the kind of person I'd want to marry, because we could really talk.

"During the time we were going out, I felt that he was very fair to me at the office. I didn't feel like he favored me or did the opposite. He was pretty even-keeled about everything. And I think other people in the office felt that way for the most part. In fact, a few people told Harry to ask me out! Then afterward, when we came out of the closet, they all said they knew all along, but they were very nice about it. It helped that Harry was assigned to a different position about then, so we didn't have to worry about our work positions any longer."

Their relationship grew more serious, and within a few months they had moved in together. For Devon that meant other issues should be discussed right away, too.

"I felt I had to make it clear that I wasn't going to give up my work if we had children," said Devon, "because I didn't know what he thought about that. I wanted him to know that I'm not going to do everything for house and family—I'm not going to be the one that's mainly responsible for the kids."

"But when I brought it up, Harry said, 'We're not at that point yet. Why do we have to talk about that now?' He wasn't angry, but he felt like I was jumping the gun. I don't know if we were even engaged at that point, but I thought it was important, before we got serious, to know what he thought about things." Meanwhile, Harry had taken over half or more of the housework and repairs, activities he genuinely enjoyed.

Eighteen months later, Devon and Harry got married. She was thirty years old, and he was thirty-three. Shortly before the ceremony, they bought an old home to restore and decided they wanted to have children pretty quickly. Devon had no trouble with those decisions because she now had hard evidence that Harry was planning to share the load. Already, the division of housework was more than equitable by her standards. Today, two years later, that is still true.

"One thing that was nice was we were both older. We were both totally independent. Harry didn't expect me to do any-thing, except he hated to cook. So I would cook, he would do all the dishes, he did his laundry and I did mine, and he would do a lot more. I was terrible, as I continue to be, at any sort of housekeeping, so he keeps the common areas neat and things like that. As we were living together, I found that we split most things. I never felt that I was getting stuck with any housework. In fact his level of 'accepting messes threshold' is lower than mine, so he's more likely to clean than I am when things are rushed."

The division of responsibilities settled to their mutual satisfaction, Devon and Harry charged headlong into family life: first the house, then a baby, Molly, now age one-and-a-half. Pressures mounted.

"Even as it got more difficult, we always had a clear understanding of what we wanted," said Devon. "As it turns out, Harry definitely wants to be very involved with Molly. I've always felt I couldn't raise kids alone. The sheer work of it, the responsibility. I'm one of six kids and I know that I would go crazy if I had all that hanging on me.

"Harry is willing to do whatever I want him to do in terms of figuring out a work/home schedule. If I want to work full-time, that's fine. If I want to quit, that would be okay, although we both know that it wouldn't be great financially. But he's said, 'If you want to quit, we'll scale everything down, whatever.' So being in this totally together has worked out really well."

Nevertheless, life was soon out of control. Devon grew frantic soon after her maternity leave was over.

"Originally I came back full-time," she said. "Molly was ten weeks old. At the time my leave seemed pretty good because it was better than anyone else was getting, which was just six weeks off. It took the last three months of my pregnancy for me to work out this terrific deal, but I finally persuaded management to give me an additional four weeks—unpaid.

"Now I look back and see how tiny Molly was even at ten weeks. But I was back full-time and suddenly aware that I was never going to see her. And at that age they change so much! I would nurse her in the morning, and Harry would take her to the baby-sitter. Then I'd go over at noon and nurse her and then go back to work. By evening she was ready to go to sleep as soon as we got home. I had maybe an hour and a half with my baby every day.

"Meanwhile, she was still getting up in the middle of the night—it was crazy. When I look back, I don't know how we did it. She'd have nights where she got up at two and at five to nurse, so I was going to work on less than four hours of sleep. Friday would zoom up, and I was so out of touch from stress and fatigue, I'd be saying to the baby-sitter, 'When does she eat now and what is she like?' I'd hit the weekend worried because I hadn't been around her. It was kind of like 'Oh, God, how am I going to take care of Molly?' I just wasn't spending enough time with her.

"This probably would have continued indefinitely," Devon went on, "except that my editor said to me one day, 'How is it going?' He expressed a genuine interest in knowing and invited me to lunch. I considered making up nice things to say, because no one at the paper worked part-time. It was an unheard-of thing. You either quit or came back full-time—there was no in-between."

Devon's eyes moistened as she remembered their conversation at lunch. "I was still trying to figure out what to say when I just let down and said, 'To tell you the truth, it's not the greatest.' He didn't seem surprised; he just said, 'Let's talk about it.' I held my breath: 'I really would like to work part-time.' He said, 'Forever and ever or for a little while?' I said, 'I think I'd like to do it for two years, but I'd settle for a couple of months.'

"Right away he came up with twelve different ways I could do it—everything from a different kind of job to doing my own job in various sorts of ways, job sharing, shorter hours—he was really supportive. We honed in on the best alternatives for both of us, and I wrote up a rough draft for sharing my beat with another reporter who was due to have a baby soon.

"Then my boss presented the plan to senior management. After that I went in and talked to an executive editor who was a working mother with a baby herself. She was quite nice and asked, 'Is this something you think you're going to have a nervous breakdown over tomorrow? How long can you go before I give you a decision?' That was June 15th. I said 'I'd like to start part-time by July 1', and she said, 'Okay.'

"They really didn't make a decision but said I could 'try' part time for three months. We survived a trial period, and that has been extended indefinitely because every time we review it, it's working well for everyone," said Devon with a relaxed smile. Besides the support of her boss, which goaded Devon into an action that she was hesitant to launch into on her own, she had another booster in her corner: her mom. Years before, when Devon was still in college, she had done her mother a favor, a favor whose power she didn't fully grasp until her mother had the opportunity to return it.

"I don't think I would have had the guts to do this if my mother hadn't insisted I ask for it," said Devon. "I really didn't believe there was a chance. I just assumed they would say I could only be a correspondent, with no benefits and no real job. That would have been such a huge step down for me career-wise that I just couldn't do it. But, it happened that I talked to my mother right when I was in the midst of my internal debate over asking for a part-time position."

Devon was born third in a family of six children. Her mother started working when Devon was eighteen. "She went to work as a guidance counselor more for the money than a career," said Devon. "I was in my freshman year when I heard that she had gone to work. I thought it was fantastic that somebody had hired her for such a good job. I was an English major, and I really didn't know what I wanted to do, nor did I think anyone would ever hire me for anything good. It was very reassuring to know that she could get a professional position. It sort of meant I could.

"I thought it was so neat that I wrote her a letter. I didn't know at the time that even though my father was quite supportive, she was feeling pretty bad about working because she wouldn't be home for the three younger kids when they got out of school. My twelve-year-old sister was saying things like 'I never see you anymore' even though Mom got home an hour after she did. In my letter I said how proud I was of her and how great her new job made *me* feel, how it gave me confidence to hear that she was able to be a real professional. I remember writing, 'This is the greatest thing you've ever done.'

"My mother was shocked and thrilled when she got my letter—she carried it around for years. In retrospect, I wonder, if she hadn't gotten that job, would I have pursued my career as diligently? I don't know.

"When I told her I didn't think the paper would let me work part-time, she was adamant that I ask anyway," said Devon. "'Just go in and tell them what you want to do,' she said. She was like a union organizer on the telephone. She told me not to fall into a 'plastic women's role' where you don't want to ask for anything, where you think it's just so great they even give you a job, where you don't want to ruffle anybody's feathers because 'Look, how nice they are being, letting you nurse at noon!'

"Without my editor and my mother, I don't think I would have done it," said Devon, her eyes widening as she recalled her misgivings, "which is sad because it has turned out so well." Women are often quite tentative as they move toward solutions that are right for them. As Carol Gilligan so eloquently argues in her landmark book *In a Different Voice*, women tend to think that men's expectations of how they should behave are the norm. Yet often all we need is the tiniest boost to get us where we need to be. One gentle nudge of reassurance can put us in a confident negotiating position.

Look at Devon's situation as an investigative reporter. The newspaper business has a macho image of hard-drinking, hard-driving newsroom types who are second only to undercover agents in their relentless pursuit of truth. Devon's hesitation was tied closely to her subliminal worry that to deviate from the male norm, to follow her softer, nurturing instincts while trying to compete in that fierce industry, was to do something wrong.

It helped when her boss, who was a man and a seasoned reporter himself, supported her. It really helped when her mother, who had already broken one rule by leaving her younger children to fend for themselves as latchkey kids, came to her aid as well. Devon, like more and more women, is slowly realizing that there are no "norms" for working mothers: this is brand-new territory. Every working mother has her own "norm"!

Now beginning the second year of her shared job, Devon is planning to continue part-time indefinitely. And since she pioneered the position, more shared jobs have been established.

The basics of Devon's job sharing are simple. She splits a "beat" with another reporter who is also a working mother. They both do all aspects of the job—keeping in touch with all their news sources, getting the facts, and writing their stories. Devon and her colleague are expected to cover some "breaking news" and to develop front-page stories. Other reporters do exactly the same, but they are more likely to be called in to help out on a major breaking news story than Devon might be.

"I work three full days—twenty-four hours a week. Since Harry's desk is only fifteen yards from mine, if I can't get to the sitter, whom we use from ten to six every Tuesday, Wednesday, and Thursday, he can go. It's a terrific situation. When one or the other of us has to work late, we've been known to bring Molly back to the office and then go home together. We trade off taking her to and picking her up from the sitter—it depends on who needs to do more in the office.

"Job sharing has a good side and a bad side," said Devon. "The good side is that my beat really lends itself to working three days a week. I cover an enormous number of subject areas that used to be divided among three reporters. Because it does not involve too much breaking news, I am able to take an issue and develop a major story.

"Unlike a reporter who is full-time and required to help the other desks follow all breaking news leads, I get to stick with my longer stories—so I don't get sidetracked the way I used to. For the newspaper, my working three days isn't a problem because they are always trying to free up time for people to work on the longer stories anyway.

"The other reporter and I have divided up the subject areas. Also, we'll do backup for each other on the days that we're off.

"But when I'm off—I'm off! At first I had envisioned that during Molly's naptime I would sit down and catch up on any work that I'm behind on, but I learned rapidly that it's really hard to do that, especially at her age. She takes a solid two-and-a-half-hour nap in the afternoon, and I need that time to recover.

Occasionally I'll make phone calls, but mostly I need that time for my sanity—to bring a little order to the shambles of our house, then read a book or something.

"The downside of job sharing is I do feel like now is an incredibly pivotal time in my career and I may be missing something. Now is the time I should be jumping to a bigger newspaper, and I'm not doing it.

"Harry, of course, is working full-time, and I've asked him if he would like to trade and let me do full-time. He's not up for that right now, and I haven't pushed because I'm not sure what I want yet either. At one point he said that, if I got a job I really wanted somewhere else, he would move for me, and he would figure out what he could do. I think to an extent he still feels that way—so we are flexible for each other.

"But—the upside again—what I have right now is a very good job that is interesting and challenging and I like it. Plus the salary is very fair. I'm paid per hour, the same as everybody else. That's one of the reasons that I want to keep my hand in at this level—it keeps my salary up where it should be. I want to maintain my professional standing. I went to graduate school, I invested a lot in this career, and if anything should ever happen, if Harry were in an accident or we were divorced, I don't want to be in the position of trying to scrape things together and figure out how to support myself and a kid or two."

Devon is a realist: "Many of the women my age are raised with the idea that we can do both home and career, that we have to do both and that we have to do both incredibly well. That's too much—you just can't do both well all the time," she said firmly. "Also, I have a high energy level, and I love running around, but some people might find it an enormous burden. The day begins when Molly gets up around 7:00. I give her breakfast while Harry takes a forty-five minute jog. When he gets back, she's fed, dressed, and ready to go. Then he takes her to the baby-sitter, and I go to the Y for a swim. After work I pick her up at 6:00 or 6:15. And we're very flexible. Some mornings I take her because he wants to do something.

"I hate to admit it," she added, "but maybe my career is suffering. And yet—Molly isn't! She's doing great. We both are. It's good for her to be with other kids a few days a week, and I wouldn't be much fun to be around if I weren't doing this. It's a constant trade-off. So maybe my career has to suffer in order for me to be around my kid, but maybe it will take turns that it never would have otherwise. Maybe it will wind up being better. That's something that's already happened. Because I have fewer days, I do better stuff than I used to. Because I have less time, I'm much more focused. I work on only good stories, Page One stories. My clips this past year are the best I've ever had."

Working things out at home means trade-offs too. "I like to hike and bike," said Devon. "I'd like to do even more of it, but Harry loves doing rehab on the house—repairing the plaster, taping the walls. I'm not into that kind of stuff. I'll help out painting. But I'm not into full-scale restoration. I just don't want to spend my time that way. My relaxation time I like to spend outdoors.

"When Harry fell in love with the house, I told him before we bought it that I might not be around to help too much. He said that was okay because for him it's fun. He loves to restore things, and he's a perfectionist. I'm really not into any of that stuff. For me, it's torture. It's good, because I suppose if I had married somebody that hated doing all that stuff, nothing would ever get done. But sometimes I'll have to say, 'The weekends are also time to spend time together.' There was a time when he would give me two hours off to go to the Y and swim and do whatever I wanted to do, but then when I came back I would be on 'kid care' from noon until 6:00 and he would be scraping or plastering or whatever. I would really get upset over that.

"Now he knows when I'm getting tense about it. I say, 'Look, it's Saturday—let's go down to the park and take a hike or something.' To me that's a priority. So we have a good push-pull system." Their push-pull is replaced by a more complementary dynamic when it comes to household finances.

"We keep our money separate," said Devon, "a holdover from having done that before we got married. Harry sees that our bill paying is on schedule, but we each pay our own. He keeps the books for the house and gives me a full accounting, which he meticulously divides according to how much we earn. I earn three-fifths of what he does, so that's my share of house costs, electricity, etc. We split the cost of vacations and child care.

"I guess the only thing that bugs me is I do feel Molly is more my responsibility than Harry's. I'm the one who finds the doctor and the baby-sitter. Part of that is his standards are not as high as mine—for sitters, for example. I'm the one who does all the organization of what's going to happen with Molly. But"— Devon paused suddenly—"he really does more with the house, so we are working it out.

"Right now, knock on wood, it feels pretty well balanced," she concluded. "I still have days when I haven't seen enough of Molly, or days when I wish I could spend a ton more hours on a story. Now there's where the difference in our metabolism works for us, which is good. Harry slows me down and keeps me from burning myself out. If we were too much alike, we might drive each other crazy.

"It's funny, you know, how my life is so inextricably bound up with this other person. I was such an independent character before, and I tended to be a lot more impatient about things. I've learned over the past two-and-a-half years that this is a long game and you might not get what you want today—but if you can wait a little and not pound on the other person, he'll come around to what's best for both of you."

## Natalie: Home-Based Flextime

Natalie and Fred Marshall are fiercely independent. You can tell the moment you turn into their driveway. There, instead of a manicured suburban lawn, is a vegetable garden. Right in the front yard.

Natalie is a tall, spare woman whose eyes crinkle with a wry humor behind her granny glasses. Her husband, Fred, is a dark-eyed, mustached motorcycle aficionado who will usually eschew his big bike for a plain one as the family, with five-year-old Jennifer and three-year-old Bradford in tow, circles the block on assorted bikes and trikes every evening before bedtime.

Natalie and Fred met and fell in love nineteen years ago,

when Natalie had just turned sixteen and Fred was twenty-two. She was a young and talented pianist, hired to play private parties; he was an accomplished clarinetist and a performer in the prestigious Army Band. One night they were hired for the same gig.

"When I met Fred," said Natalie, "I already knew the direction I was going. I wanted to make a go of it as a musician. The hardest way to succeed financially as a pianist is to be a performance major, and that's what I wanted. My ideal was not to be the touring concert pianist; I just wasn't genius enough to do that. But I knew I was good, and I knew I was appreciated in a lot of different ways. I knew that I could keep my options open by going into performance. I knew I could teach, and that's usually the musician's ace in the hole. And I love teaching.

"But it was also very important to me to prove to myself that I didn't need somebody with me. I made it a point to go away to school rather than stay where Fred was. So I did the year away and then I went to Boston, where I could study with the teacher that I really wanted and where Fred was working on his master's. Because of my work—and not because of Fred—I felt I could say that I wanted to stay and study in Boston. I was still concentrating on the fact that I had to study where it was going to be best for my career.

"Of course, it was a nice perk that Fred was there, but he was going to leave," said Natalie. "He had just finished his master's when I decided to come here. So I moved in with him for a month or two, figuring he would leave and I could take over his apartment. But he didn't leave—he was offered a job close by, so we ended up staying together. I finished school, and we've been together ever since. We were married when I was twenty-three and he was almost thirty. Even though we eased into marriage without any overt planning, the one thing we talked about before we got married was the fact that we both wanted to have kids, but we mutually agreed it was something we wanted to do in the future. Fred was quite adamant—I think we both were—that right then was not a good time. I agreed. I didn't want to be a twenty-three-year-old mother. I knew if I had a child I wasn't going to get on with my music. I wasn't going to make the connections I needed. And I really wasn't ready for motherhood. I had a lot I wanted to do.

"Maybe I was selfish, but I didn't want to give that time to kids; I wanted to give it to me. Periodically over the next few years we'd both say, 'Kids are great,' and I'd say, 'I really want to have them, but not yet.' Once, after I'd said the 'not yet,' Fred said, 'Well, you just let me know when you're ready.' He was six years older, which makes a difference, and he made it quite clear that he wasn't going to be hurt if it wasn't now, but he was also saying, 'When you're ready, it's okay with me. I'm ready when you're ready.'

"I was about twenty-five or twenty-six at that time, and one day we stumbled onto some little kittens. We called a vet, and he told me how to take care of them—bottle-feeding every four hours, wiping their bottoms—it was just like caring for a newborn baby who doesn't know how to take care of itself. I would go play a concert, and people would invite me to the reception later, but I'd have to say, 'Sorry, I can't; I have to go home and feed my kittens.' So when I went to my ob-gyn and he said, 'You're twenty-five—have you started to think about a family?' I said, 'You're asking at the wrong time. I know what it's all about now, and I don't have the time or patience for it.'

"At twenty-five," remembered Natalie, "I definitely was not ready to get up at night and deal with diapers. Then, as I turned twenty-eight, my sister and my brother were starting to have children. Pretty soon friends started. And I began to feel the jealousy. Somebody would have a baby, and I'd be thrilled, and the next thing I knew I'd be crying because I wanted to have a baby, too. I'd get over it and say, 'No, this still isn't right,' but more and more the baby news made me feel jealous. I became aware of a sense of emptiness in my life. That's when I realized a child was something I wanted very badly.

"Meantime, my career was going great. I was doing more and more playing. I was teaching on the college level—students, having decided that I might not be international glamour but I could really teach, were fighting to get into my classes. So things were going my way. I had survived the change of a department head. I was feeling good about things. My career was in place. I'd

really accomplished everything I needed to accomplish in terms
of both personal satisfaction and being able to command the
kind of part-time work I wanted. Also, at that point, a chamber
music group I was playing with had really taken off. We had gone
into some competitions and done well.

"Suddenly I had a lot of people telling me they would take
me on my terms. After I talked about having a child, the head of
the music department at the college said, 'You tell me what
hours you'll be available, and we'll try to work around that.'

"It may be that things worked so well because I'm not in a
cutthroat place. I know I'm very fortunate in that I work with
good people," Natalie said. "The personnel manager of the
symphony was appreciative of what it was to have a family and
knew I would be juggling both. The leader of the chamber music
group had two children herself, so she had been through the
logistics of having a baby and trying to keep her career going.
She was helpful in not making it hard for me. I've had many
people be nice and considerate at the right time.

"Nevertheless, one of my hardest times was that first two
months at home with the newborn baby," Natalie recalled. "I
knew Fred would help, but being the only one at home and away
from the rest of the world was scary. Things got better once I
started working again. I cut back rather sharply that year, teaching two mornings, three afternoons, and Saturday. And I played
rehearsals.

"Jennifer went along to the latter. The first violinist, who
was the leader, said that was fine. And Jennifer was a great baby.
She used to sleep in a closet kind of area in a little travel bed, and
when she'd wake up she'd sit in her baby seat. I played a concert
when she was three weeks old.

"Later, when she got bigger, I kept her in a little rocking
chair during rehearsals. When she'd start to fuss, I'd play the
concerto and rock her with my left foot—just pedal with my
right and push baby with the other! Later, when she was in a
walker, she'd toddle around behind the violinist. Everybody
loved her, and she went to rehearsals for the whole first year as
our mascot."

Natalie feels the transition from working woman to working

mother has been much easier for her than for some of her friends because she and Fred never expected to do anything other than share all the responsibilities that a child would bring. When Bradford was born, two years after Jennifer, the same held true.

"From the start Fred has done his part," said Natalie, "and we adapt when our schedules conflict. Right after Jennifer was born, if I was teaching and couldn't make it home before the lesson or class started, I had a student sitter come in. Now I have a full Saturday of teaching and Fred takes both children all day. And if I play in the evenings, he does full duties. He'll bathe the children, although when I'm home I usually bathe them. But if I'm not, he bathes them, feeds them, puts them to bed.

"Life is more complicated during the week, but Fred gets home as soon as he can. His schedule is important, too; he is a high school music professor and supervises a large department. But he can plan ahead, so if he's promised me that he'll be home at a certain hour, he usually is. Wednesday this year is a day that he gets to school just in the nick of time. He's arranged it so he doesn't have a rehearsal on Wednesday morning. That morning he'll stick around, get Jennifer onto a bus, take Bradford to nursery school, and then go on to school so that I can teach my one early morning class. Other mornings I get the kids off. We also trade off practicing with Jennifer before school, too. She plays the violin."

The ability to spend over half her teaching hours in her home makes a significant difference to Natalie. She is one of over twenty-five million Americans who work out of home-based offices, according to *American Demographics*. In her case, a Steinway grand and baby grand share a spacious ground-level room with access to an outside entrance so that her students do not enter and leave through her home.

"Even though we have two children now, my schedule is about the same," said Natalie. "Two, possibly three mornings, plus Wednesday afternoon and all of Saturday, I teach for the college. Our performing schedules vary. I am out half of the nights in November and two-thirds of the nights in December. So it depends on the month. September and October tend to be light for my schedule, heavy for Fred's.

"In March, when the opera is performing, Fred will be out every Friday and Saturday night. Generally, we've been very lucky—the playing flip-flops. If we have decided that it's important for us to both play the same job, we'll find a baby-sitter. We have a long list of sitters, and we have friends who share lists when necessary."

Even when one or both parents work part-time, they are still dependent on baby-sitters. As for all working parents, the problem is ever-present for the Marshalls.

"I used to feel guilty about the baby-sitters because we put them in a difficult position," said Natalie. "If we're both playing, and there's a problem with the children, it's not as if you can call us at a restaurant and we'll come home. If I'm onstage, the best I can do is give the sitter a backstage pay phone number. And if she calls, it had better be an emergency, which is a lot of pressure to put on a young sitter.

"And it can be bad. Once I'd had Jennifer throwing up all day—couldn't even keep water in her. Both of us were playing an evening rehearsal. I felt awful leaving the house, but it was a dress rehearsal—I had to go. Just as Fred and I were both about to go out the door, the poor sitter came downstairs and said, 'I think the other one's sick, too.' All we could do was check with the doctor once more before leaving. There was Bradford—throwing up all over! The baby-sitter never complained. I've always felt guilty over baby-sitters.

"And yet, I think the kids get more undivided attention from the baby-sitters," said Natalie. "They come in, play with the kids, take them on walks—I have been very impressed."

But sickness during the week, when she and Fred have daytime teaching responsibilities and student sitters are difficult to find, surprisingly isn't as much of a problem. "Fred has a few days he is actually allowed by contract to take for illness in the family," said Natalie. "I am under very few rules myself, which is usually true about college teaching. I'm supposed to be there for my classes, but nobody actually counts. I count—I try to be very fair to my students. But if I have to, I can cancel a class. I have done that on very rare occasions. I have one baby-sitter who will come in a pinch, if she's free, and take over sick kids, which she has done. When I have 'borderline' kids, where they're too sick to go to school because they may be contagious, but yet they aren't terribly sick, I have dragged them along. I take food and entertainment. They sit under a piano or empty my wallet in front of a class.

"Where we get into the most trouble is performance dates, which are very hard to break. You just don't call in sick. Even if you have a fever of 102 degrees, you do it. And rehearsals are critical, too. There have been times when I've even said to Fred in advance, 'This, this, or this date I can handle, but if the kids are sick *that* day, it's your problem.'"

Even with all the sitter problems, Natalie does not feel that the stress involved diminishes the pleasures of careers and kids. "I wouldn't do it any other way," she said. "And I think the kids find it interesting now, although they may be slightly jealous of the teaching in the home because I'm not spending the time with them. It's funny—when our kids play 'going to work,' they put on black clothes and play a concert!

"So they know what work means. I think that's important for them to see that. I think it's very good that they know that I don't sit around waiting for them to need me all the time, that I have other things in my life that are sometimes more important. It sounds cruel, but sometimes I come first, sometimes Fred comes first."

But like all couples, Natalie and Fred have the potential to clash. "Sometimes Natalie thinks I don't spend enough time kid caring," said Fred, who loves to spend time puttering in their garden and around the house. He is a master handyman and boasts a meticulously well-organized workshop.

"At times," said Natalie, nodding in agreement.

"When that happens," said Fred, his serious eyes twinkling a bit, "we usually blast at each other for a second or two."

"The real problem occurs not because someone won't do his or her share, really," said Natalie, "but because we're both at home and we both have the idea that 'Aha, it's Sunday, and I'm going to get a big list of things done,' and then there's baby-sitting too. That's where we've gotten into trouble. We're frustrated because neither one of us can finish our own agenda."

"Right," said Fred. "The problem is a false set of expectations. When we get a chance to talk about it, we can avoid the hassle. Like last Sunday we had to get the firewood stacked, and the only way we could do it was to divvy up responsibility. It worked. The stress was gone."

"We tend to be quite up front," said Natalie, "maybe to a fault. And, thank goodness, in most cases when one person is flying off the handle, the other is pretty calm. But occasionally we both let loose. Sort of an emotional catharsis—you just let go.

"Our decision making isn't where we are likely to fight. Even if we disagree on a purchase," said Natalie, "we discuss it, and one or the other will come around. For example, Fred wanted a computer, and I didn't care. Since I keep the books, he just asked, 'Is this something we can do? Do we have the money?' I said we did but it might be wise if we waited until we received another paycheck rather than buy it that day. So we waited. We rarely disagree on what we buy, even on how much we should spend."

"I did have to break her arm to get her to find someone to help with the cleaning," said Fred, "but she was driving us both crazy trying to keep the house clean, so this is working out very well."

And because Natalie and Fred love their music and their careers and try to spend as much time as possible around their home and their children, getting away is not on their agenda.

"We enjoy the kids. This is the time of our lives we said we'd do it," said Fred. "Maybe it's because we put it off. We've talked about this and neither of us has a real need to get away, like vacations away from the children or going out much. Usually they do everything with us; we all garden together. We are looking forward to the children being old enough so that we can get back into doing things we haven't done in years. We're both antsy to do cross-country skiing, to go back to the mountains for a vacation of hiking. That we miss, but not enough to do it without the kids."

"As far as time together goes," said Natalie, "we both love to talk about our work. Fred will come home and tell me about individual students, what they did or didn't do, what his groups, supervisors, and colleagues did. I understand how you can be having a great day, and your students are having rotten days, and your day turns from great to rotten because they're feeling rotten, not because you do. And the same way with the symphony. Fred knows the people I'm talking about, and he's very interested."

Because they spend their free time as a family, Natalie and Fred feel comfortable and satisfied with their time at home. Neither one feels that they need more time alone or more time with each other. They have a good balance in their personal life. But since life always changes for dynamic people like Natalie and Fred, the future is sure to bring more challenges.

"What we both want is more time to perform," said Fred. "I want more playing at night."

"As the kids get older, I'd like to pick up more day time for my music," said Natalie. "I'm not picky—if it turns out to be more college teaching, I'll take it. If the symphony takes more daytime hours, that's fine with me, too."

Thus independence and flexibility have become the keynotes scoring the daily rhythms of the Marshalls—in their professional lives and their personal lives.

## Ruth: Rethinking Options and Going Back to School

As the baby boomers give birth to fewer children, as colleges and universities see their enrollments dropping, a new kind of student is swelling the ranks: the part-time student mother. Typically she has logged five to ten years in the work force, often in a profession such as teaching, but chooses to take time out to care for her family and to bolster her existing career or develop a new one.

Too often, however, the family at a lower income level tends to think that this is not an option for the working mother. But as you will see, mothers in their early thirties can work out ways to return to school even when funds are tight—or nonexistent. If you want it badly enough, it can be done.

Ruth and Leo met when both were high school English teachers working at a summer camp. Both were seeing other people at the time, but they noticed each other. When Ruth returned from a year of teaching abroad, she again ran into Leo, who had already entered law school. One thing led to another, and eight years ago, just before their 30th birthdays, they were married.

Shortly after the wedding Ruth decided to pursue a law degree, too. But she chose to do it at a slower pace, during the years when their children were very young. When we spoke, she had just passed the bar exam and a new law firm had debuted: a two-partner office shared by Leo and Ruth, one full-time and one part-time partner respectively, specializing in family law and the rights of abused children.

Like many women who are uncertain of their goals or receive mixed messages about women's roles—both of which were true for Ruth—the decision to seek a law degree grew out of step-by-step "moves" rather than a long-term goal. A curious thing had happened to Ruth at the time of her marriage: she found herself caught between a halfhearted desire to be a traditional at-home wife (a role her mother urged on her even though her mother had never done it that way herself) and the urge to work even though her teaching career was no longer a challenge.

"I got very mixed messages from my mother," said Ruth, talking to me while seated on a chintz-covered sofa in their modest but comfortable southern New England home. "She implied that I should be a very traditional homemaker—help Leo become a lawyer who would earn enough money so that I could quit teaching, have kids, and stay home with them. Maybe deep down that's what my mother would have wanted for herself. But she's a complicated person—she'll say one thing and do another. She was a career woman with a fantastic job as one of the first women radio engineers. Magazine and newspaper articles were written about her because she was so unusual back then. When she got married, she was earning lots of money, but she gave it all up, moved to a small town to be with my father, and had babies right away. After she'd had three kids, she got bored and started working with my father in his camera store. She always said she was 'needed.' In reality I think it was too stifling for her to stay at home full-time."

Those mixed messages and her own career confusion hit

Ruth when she was teaching full-time but hoping to get pregnant. "Leo was also still teaching, but he was in law school at the time of our wedding," said Ruth. "When I had difficulty getting pregnant and continued to be disillusioned with teaching, I wondered, What am I going to do for the rest of my life if I can't have babies? It was Leo who brought up the notion of law school. So I took the boards, did very well, applied to our local state university law school, and got in. Ironically, almost the moment I was accepted into their four-year part-time program I got pregnant!"

Ruth opted for law school anyway. She quit teaching during her pregnancy and started at the university. I had Jamie three months after classes started, at the end of November, and it worked out well because I missed only two weeks of classes, thanks to Christmas vacation.

"My mother-in-law watched Jamie for short periods, so day care wasn't a burden," said Ruth. "I'd study during his naps, at night when I didn't have classes, and on weekends. Most of my classes were at night, and I'd leave right after dinner. It wasn't that law school was so hard, but the time apart was hard on our relationship. Either Leo was alone with Jamie or I was alone with Jamie — the three of us weren't together much. After dinner, I'd take off to study or go to school. So that part was hard.

"Yet, when our second baby was born during my third year of law school, the evening class schedule made completing my degree work a breeze. Again, I missed only two weeks of school. In fact, from the angle of fitting in studies with caring for toddlers, I loved having the kids during law school. I was able to be home every day and raise them and still accomplish something.

"Plus I loved school! It was a challenge to see if I could do it. As I got closer to the end of my four years, Leo and I were also able to plan further down the road, which was nice. We started to seriously consider being law partners."

But even with her exhilaration over her studies and the future, Ruth and Leo faced serious difficulties; both money and time were in short supply. "We had a lot of fights," said Ruth. "Here I was relaxed all day and looking forward to going out to class, and he'd be coming home after a strenuous day and have to take care of both babies. He felt like he had all the responsibility because we were desperately short of cash, too.

"We talked about the problem, especially the money, but we handled it very differently. He was more tense, while I didn't let it keep me up at night. My solution was to keep one eye on the want ads and just know if it all crashed that I'd quit law school and get a job. It was tough—month to month we never knew if it would work. It helped that, when Leo was in school, we had the income from both our teaching salaries, which was significant because teachers here make more than anywhere else in the country. We both attended a state school, too, so tuition was reasonable."

On a daily basis Ruth scrimped pennies for sitters so she and Leo could get out and have a few hours together at a movie or an inexpensive dinner. She knew that the time they could get one-on-one without children helped them cope with the stress. Leo, meanwhile, kept a tight rein on all their expenses. Even once he was practicing law instead of teaching, they still had to be careful with money because they'd lost Ruth's salary. But Leo felt that Ruth's law degree was critical to their future and did not hesitate to apply for more loans as they needed them. He could also see her emotional buoyancy, which was a result of her involvement in her studies and pride in her outstanding grades. She was happy at home with her children, so the little ones were doing nicely. Her good spirits and positive outlook also tempered his constant worrying. Together they managed to complement and balance each other's emotions during the two years that were the most difficult.

Finally the pressure broke. "Right after our daughter was born," said Ruth, "we could see the light at the end of the tunnel for my degree too. Better yet, it dawned on us that the kids would be just the right age for me to consider a part-time practice as soon as I passed the bar."

And that is exactly what has happened. "We have just opened our joint practice," said Ruth proudly. "We have new offices, and I'll be working three full days a week, from 8:30 to 5:00. During that time the children will be in a combined nursery school/day-care program that's located between our house and the office downtown.

"Two days a week I'll be home with the kids, although I usually fit in an hour or more of legal work at home those days. I hope to continue that for two or three years and then phase into a full-time schedule."

Ruth's increased participation in the law firm is a boon to Leo's growing practice. Billed hours are up and the financial pressures of the previous years are easing. With that ease has also come a lessening of the tensions between them. Now they have more time together—at work, at play, and with the children.

"I'm happy to say it's been over a year since I read the want ads," laughed Ruth.

## Is Part Time Right for You?

It is the dawning of a new era for the part-time working mother who has proven her worth to her employer or to others who will be happy to give her work. And for some lucky women the decision to go part-time is the result of a request by an employer. "I designed the accounting data base for the doctors' office where I worked before my daughter was born," said Melanie, who just turned twenty-four years old. "I made it clear that I wanted to take a longer maternity leave, but they begged me just to take the computer home and work when I could."

Melanie works in the evenings when the baby is sleeping, and the doctors are paying her regular salary prorated according to the hours she is able to put in. She doesn't even need to leave home when the work is done—she simply phones the information back to the office via her computer modem.

"Now I don't have to worry that our income is going to suffer because of the baby," said Melanie. "It's clear to me that the office needs me as much as I might want them—I'm calling the shots, and I think I'll be able to do this for as long as I want to."

Perhaps you're not sure you're in as good a position as Melanie was, or you're not sure part time can work for you. Even if your loving partner agrees with you that it might be right for you to work part-time, you may be having second thoughts. Are you wondering if you are about to sabotage everything you've achieved so far? Or is it simply an anxiety generated by the "myth of the perpetually propelled career?" You know the myth—the one that says "miss one step and you are out of your career pattern forever." Are you wary of trying to work from home?

I doubt you are making a mistake by considering going part-time. After all, not every lawyer wants to make $1 million annually by slaving around the clock and over weekends for a blue-ribbon firm; not every doctor plans to win the Nobel Prize. And not every woman who *does* want to make it big wants to forgo love and children.

If you find yourself daydreaming more than once a week about how it might feel to quit your job and stay home with your family, whether you have one child or more, you are likely to be a good candidate for the part-time career path. That recurring "quit fantasy" is more than a broad hint—it's a signal. Perhaps you should take time off (see the next chapter), or maybe part time is an option you should consider seriously. Take the following quiz and see how you feel.

## Quiz: Is Part Time for You?

Consider the following and circle your answers:

1. If you were (or are) currently employed full-time, your reason for working would be:
   a. the money only.
   b. the career potential and the money, but you're beginning to wonder if either is worth it, because you are feeling overly stressed trying to manage both job and home.
   c. the terrific boost of self-esteem you get from doing a job you love and that you are very good at.

2. When you're around the house, you most enjoy:
   a. getting your home all straightened up, having a new recipe bubbling in the oven, and putting the last tacks in the new curtains you've just sewn.

   b. spending time with the kids, clearing out your winter
      closet, and finding an open space for your new
      computer so you can work at home more often.
   c. escaping with a good book on new investment strategies.
3. Imagine yourself working part-time. You have two children
   under age five, and you:
   a. are feeling financially strained.
   b. have never been happier.
   c. are worried you're losing your place in the office
      hierarchy and feeling that keeping up the house is
      getting to be a drag.

4. Assume your mother never worked outside the home.
   Would you:
   a. be envious of her?
   b. be glad she was there for you but afraid she's given
      something up?
   c. feel sorry for her?

5. Your ideal day would be spent:
   a. taking care of the family, perhaps preparing a special
      meal.
   b. working on an engrossing project.
   c. doing both of the above.

*Scoring*
Give yourself 5 points for every (c) answer, 3 points for every
(b) answer, 1 point for every (a) answer.
*Totals*
5—You are an old-fashioned girl, aren't you? Why don't you take
the next quiz and see if you would be happier at home full-time?
6-15—Traditional at heart, you're wavering and worried. Part
time is likely to be perfect for you; see if you can find some good
part-time ideas in this book.
16-24—You are truly torn between your split ambitions. Keep
trying new options, and you'll find the right balance. Consider
job sharing and flextime options, ones that will allow you
slightly more time at work than at home.
25—Forget part time. Just be sure to take time out for you—just
you—because you probably have a tendency to do too much.

## If You've Decided to Give Part Time a Try

Having read the stories of other women, I'm sure you've got a good idea of how this all works by now. *Most* bosses are not going to offer you a part-time opportunity out of the clear blue. You have to make it yourself. You must dream, plan, design, and promote your own part-time position into being, wholly on your own. You can't afford to sit around waiting for directions. Face it: you have to push and shove if you want this.

Unfortunately, too many women are afraid that they can't have what they want, or they're afraid to try. And if you are convinced, before the battle, that you can't win, you won't win. On the other hand, maybe you are misinformed and the odds against you aren't so awful after all. That appears to be the case for many full-time working mothers who are contemplating— with great hesitation—asking for a part-time career option.

Recently published in the *Wall Street Journal* were the results of a survey showing that the biggest hurdle to sexual equality in the workplace may be "the vast perception barrier" between men and women. The survey of 134 male and female middle managers and executives at Fortune 500 companies, as well as some small businesses, showed that while both sexes agree that companies won't be able to attract and retain talented women without changes in corporate attitude and behavior, the sexes were deeply divided as to how companies will meet this challenge:

- Fifty-eight percent of men think companies will meet the challenge while only 34 percent of women think so.
- Fifty-six percent of men think women can reach the top levels of corporate achievement—i.e., become a CEO—on performance alone (as opposed to playing politics or having an advanced degree, for example) while only 23 percent of women think so.
- Fifty percent of men think men and women work well together while only 34 percent of women think so.
- More than 50 percent of men believe men accept women as their equals while only 33 percent of women think so.

Clearly, women may be doing themselves a disservice with negative thinking. It may be that your boss, male or female, is anticipating your request for some form of part-time work. Why not be very well prepared, stoked with confidence, and ready to make your boss an offer he or she can't refuse—one that will work for you too?

If you want to work part-time for your present employer, make a good, solid case for your part-time option. And if it's turned down, wait a few weeks before you ask again—or let your boss know you will seek out a work environment that will be happy to have you on better terms. Plan carefully:

First, set down your accomplishments to date and your goals for the future in a way that any executive, particularly one not familiar with your everyday work, can instantly see your value to your organization.

Second, while working on the first step, share your thoughts with your immediate supervisor to determine whether or not that person is likely to be supportive of the plan you are going to develop. Will he or she do so actively or stand by with quiet encouragement? If so, show your boss rough drafts as you sort through the options, in case he or she sees some parts working better than others.

Don't share your plans with people who take a negative approach or say "They'll never let you do it."

Third, write up a proposal for your organization that lays out specifics, including time, responsibilities, and salary. Be sure to include the hours to be worked as well as the length of time you wish to be a part-timer or "test" the option. Some women find it easier to initiate a plan if they and their employer agree to a three-month or six-month trial, which allows time to fine-tune details.

Fourth, select those sections of your proposal that you consider negotiable and those you do not. Write down, for yourself, what those are and how far you will compromise.

As you think about your position, be realistic about your company's policies and priorities. Be aware that your organization—whether a law firm, hospital, or government institution—is likely to have no idea what options might work. Your company may never have tried it before, or perhaps it has never been tried by your department. Each employee and each job is different. Even if your company has a history of turning down other employees' similar requests, remember that these employees might have approached the company with unrealistic or poorly prepared, vague plans. After all, most organizations are not "offering" the part-time option to their workers. Instead they wait for the employee to broach the subject. Perhaps they've never been offered a reasonable plan before.

Be aware, too, that what matters most when you bring up the idea of part-time work is how important you are to your immediate boss. How much faith does your boss have in how hard you will work or in your reliability in working when you say you will? How committed does your boss feel you are to your career, and to your organization, in the long run? If you two have a long and healthy investment in each other, you are more likely to be able to work this out easily.

Fifth, be willing to change jobs if you cannot get what you need. Discuss this with your husband so you are both fully aware of the risk and willing to take it together.

One option many choose is freelance status, which allows you to do projects for different companies or departments. Often this option eventually leads to a more entrepreneurial step such as starting your own business.

If you want to consider freelancing, follow these guidelines:

- Price yourself competitively within your field. Don't ask for so much money that you won't be hired, and don't undercut your peers who might send you jobs they are too busy to handle.
- Become active in local professional groups in order to expand your contacts and allow you to spend a minimum of time scouting for new clients.
- Most important, don't let your freelance schedule become more than full time. Often, companies are happy to use freelancers more often when quality work is assured, because the net cost is lower than paying salary and benefits.

If you find yourself doing more and more work for one group, try to negotiate an on-going relationship with a regular monthly fee that allows you to keep your schedule free for them yet relieves the pressure on you to earn a certain amount monthly.

*Note:* It doesn't hurt to start negotiations for a part-time position with a freelance option already in hand.

- Realize that you may need some help with child care if you have young children at home and your work requires long stretches of quiet. It's not fair to ask an active two-year-old to squelch his or her inquisitive, playful nature and need for stimulation!

"You must be willing to quit if you can't get what you want," said two different women executives. That's what they did. One had to; the other found her firm willing to negotiate. Both are now in work situations that fit their needs on a personal as well as professional level. When your employer knows you mean business, he or she will sit up and pay attention. If you are fully prepared to find a position elsewhere, chances are excellent you will get what you want.

Be aware that your needs will change. This year you may seek the part-time position that provides needed dollars but more time to be at home. Next year you may want part-time work that will boost your career goals, give you time at home, but be low-paying. Each of us finds ourselves with different goals at different times.

Cecilia is a good example. At age thirty-six she has three children, the youngest age three. She works six hours a week as an editor for a newspaper syndicate. The pay is terrible—$5 an hour. "The money pays for child care only," said Cecilia with a smile. "The job keeps me in the game. I love seeing the people at the office, and five years from now, when I want a full-time career again, that $5 an hour will be worth thousands. I'll be able to say my work has been nationally syndicated all these years. That gives me instant entrée to jobs in newspapers, magazines, publishing, or public relations. Not a bad trade-off, huh?"

Some women also find that they take the highest-paying job

they can find (such as word processing) to make ends meet, whether or not the job is in their chosen field. Others prefer to take work that is flexible, such as substitute teaching or working as a "temp," to maximize their hours with their families. It's important to remember that none of these decisions is irrevocable and that these positions can be ideal temporary solutions to a money or time crunch.

Whether you are working part-time to make ends meet, to keep your foot in the door, or for personal satisfaction (or all three!), be sure you review your decision periodically *but not every day*; if you find yourself reevaluating your part-time situation too often, it's probably a signal that you're overready for a change. And while you *are* working part-time, make a real effort to focus on your job when you're working and your family when you're at home. That way you may, indeed, find that you have the best of both worlds.

# 6

# One Full-Time Career Plus One Full-Time Mother: Is It Really an Equal Balance?

I s it possible to be a traditional wife and mother without losing self-esteem and jeopardizing your future?

Yes—if you and your husband truly consider yourselves to be equal partners in the relationship.

Many women today, even women who secretly yearn for this kind of lifestyle, feel that traditional couples are a throwback to the fifties, Ozzie and Harriet has-beens. After all, what woman can hope to be an equal partner if she isn't working, doing her fair share?

To begin with, today's full-time wife and mother who considers herself an equal partner in her marriage is a far cry from the gal that married dear old Dad. She is likely to differ from her mother in three ways: she is educated, she has already logged several (often six to ten) years in the work force full-time, and she has every intention of returning to work someday.

And contrary to what some may think, this full-time mom is not a woman who uses pregnancy as an excuse to quit a strenuous career; she's not lazy or insecure in work abilities. (While such women do exist—a minuscule population, to be sure—this book is not for or about them.) After all, it's one thing to believe honestly that you can raise your kids best this way, or to take real joy in doing it, and another to use motherhood as a reason to drop out of life or go on a permanent career vacation. While no one denies that full-time mothering is hard work, it rarely involves the same kind of stress or self-confidence that working outside the home requires, and it's clear that today's mother is well equipped to deal with both. So if she decides to stay home for a while, it's for good reasons.

Therein lies the key to her happiness as a full-time at-home mother and the secret to the couple's success at being coupled but equal: it is fully recognized to be a temporary choice. In fact, the average length of time most full-time mothers spend at home is just five years. I must admit that the statistic is true among those full-time mothers whom I could find; not only are they in short supply, hidden somewhere in the ranks of a meager 10 percent of American women under fifty who don't work full- or part-time, but they tend to go along very quietly—feeling ever so slightly embarrassed at their position.

Full-time at-home moms know others think their situation is the ultimate luxury, a testament to the earning power of their husbands, as well as a questionable badge of dependency. Meanwhile, in their own hearts, they consider it less a luxury than a high-risk choice—one that keeps them teetering at the edge of maintaining a strong sense of self-esteem, one that could too easily compromise their hopes for a future career if they are not careful in how they handle their time and their freedom.

The everyday reality is this: these "full-time mothers" are very busy women. Usually they do the work of several people—baby-sitter, teacher, cook, chauffeur, housekeeper, launderer. While it is true these women concentrate first and foremost on their children and their households, they are also involved outside the home. What sets them apart from the part-time working mothers discussed in the previous chapter is the limited number of hours spent on activities not directly related to home and family—no more than fifteen hours per week, generally closer to ten.

Many women consider the full-time mother option but pull

back, either because it seems too risky in terms of their career potential or because they fear losing control over their lives if they have to become totally reliant economically on their husbands. I think you will find this is not the case for the full-time mothers I interviewed. But these are special women.

Like women who work full-time or part-time, these women:

- work very hard and enjoy being busy.
- have a strong sense of self; they do not see themselves as extensions of their husbands or children.
- feel that their most rewarding career years are still ahead of them.
- have cooperative husbands.

In addition, they:

- have husbands who make a high salary and/or do not make enough money themselves after taxes to make hiring help worthwhile financially (this can be the case for a woman in a low-paying field—even glamour jobs in television and publishing leave many women just breaking even after paying for day or home care—or a couple in a very high tax bracket or living in a high-tax state).
- have little desire to be part of a traditional career track (such as law or medicine); these women tend to have free-floating careers and nonspecific—though usually high—goals.
- have a strong sense of themselves as productive and interesting people, not tied to title or salary.
- really *want* to be at home with their children.
- have a better-than-average ability to take risks of a personal and professional nature; not only do they put careers temporarily on hold, but they also risk losing independence.
- did not begin motherhood with the idea that they would quit work forever.
- have flexible husbands who are comfortable with both the "traditional" male-female roles and with having a strong, independent, wage-earning wife.

# The Making of Full-Time Moms Who Are Also Equal Partners

Most happy full-time mothers appear to get there through a combination of independence, flexibility, and a good deal of full-time work before their first babies are born. There is no denying that having the wife stay home takes a certain amount of money. But in these marriages the money is considered a product of mutual good fortune and mutual hard work. Each wife sees herself as having contributed to the making of that fortune, either through working before giving birth or by freeing up her husband to work as hard as he needs to. Given the slightest hint of financial strain, each would be back at work full-time. Unlike old-fashioned full-time mothers and homemakers who may never have held a job, never completed school, and weren't likely to consider themselves the career and intellectual equals of their husbands, these women have the experience, the education, and the drive to do whatever might be needed. Each is willing and more than able to help out. Not one feels locked into her situation.

As you read about Audrey, Jessie, and Heather, it will become clear that each woman has a strong, established sense of self-esteem that draws naturally from her early experiences in the work world. Each expressed an enduring pride in her work history, whether she was a teacher, a secretary, or a publicist. And each one plans to swing back into the world of full-time work when her children are launched. Rather than give up their career connections, they simply set them aside for a number of years and allow their family life to take temporary precedence in their world.

Audrey is the youngest of the full-time mothers I interviewed. A round-faced, pretty woman whose demeanor is sunny and full of energy, she is thirty-eight years old, has been married to a man the same age for thirteen years, and has two children, ages three and five. She has been home full-time since her first child was born—although her definition of "full-time mother" is one that will surprise you.

Audrey met her husband, Bob, when they were both twenty-five. They fell in love instantly. At their wedding she gave him the diary page on which she had written the day they met: "This is the man I will marry." She worked full-time until she married Bob but quit her job to follow her husband when he changed companies.

"This became a pattern for us," she said, "Bob was a career officer, an electrical engineer with the armed forces, so we moved frequently. Until our first child was born, I worked full-time at a variety of jobs. I have always expected to have an interesting life, so I've gone out of my way to try many different things. Sometimes I had clerical-level positions; several times I was a department manager. I am very good at public relations work, so that was what I tended to do, working for hotels and convention centers. I also completed most of the course work for a master's in English.

"Bob would be gone as long as seven months at a time," she said, "but I was very much a self-starter and happy just to do my thing, whatever job it was—sometimes it was a big job, and I would have my own secretary and a heavy work load; other times I was a temporary secretary myself."

Even though her husband was absent often during their first eight years together, Audrey's independent ways made it easy: "I always took care of myself and had a terrific time. I was never miserable. I missed Bob, but I had been out of college for two or three years when we got married, so I was used to being on my own. It was never a hardship. He knew when he married me, too, that I wasn't into a 'one big career' kind of life, so he didn't worry that I was resentful about the kinds of jobs I had.

"I don't think we've ever valued each other by the work we do. He's done a lot of different things. He was in graduate school when I met him, and then he was always in government schools. I just feel like I value him because of the type of person he is, and he values me because of the type of person I am. And having a big job doesn't define us. So that's why my being home is not a problem for me."

They may not have had "big jobs," but it is clear that both Audrey and Bob have high energy levels, like to work hard, and share an ability to focus on detailed projects. After her husband left the service, his expertise in a highly specialized area of scientific development was in great demand in private industry.

His income shot up quickly, work pressures increased, and their first year as civilians saw Bob tackling a very heavy travel schedule just as Audrey gave birth to their first child.

Initially she was content to take care of the baby and settle into their first home, not only the first they had ever purchased but the first where they knew they would be staying for a long, less indefinite period of time.

"I had been doing a lot of writing as a result of my work on my master's in English," said Audrey, "but I found that giving birth just took away my creativity and my desire to write. I felt like I was drained of that ambition for a while, until my second child was about two—then it felt like I could put some creative energy into something besides having children."

One day she discovered that she and a casual acquaintance shared a common interest in developing a newsletter for mothers of young children. One thousand dollars and a computer later, they had started their own business.

Today, after a year of part-time efforts that they strive to keep to fifteen hours a week or less, they have had to hire two more people to help with the publication of the monthly newsletter, which now goes to nearly 50,000 subscribers.

"The hours got to be too much," said Audrey. "I want to be a full-time mother first—my business partner and I both do. We work on computers because we don't even have to meet that way; we can edit and change things via our modems. Rather than make more money, we've hired more people in order to keep our own time open. Motherhood first, then business."

She laughs when I ask if she's surprised at the success of her joint enterprise. "As I said, I always knew that I would have an interesting life of my own," she replied. "I'm very hardworking and very production-oriented. So I never saw myself as just baking cookies and keeping a house. I knew that I would always have a big project that I'd be working on in my life, because I've always been like that. At the same time, the thought of having children is not a scary thing to me. A lot of women have said to me, 'I'm so afraid to have kids because I'm afraid I'll just lose everything—my identity.' But that never occurred to me because I knew I had lots of things I wanted to try."

Audrey's independent nature is mirrored in the lives of Jessie, age forty, and Heather, age forty-five. They too married men with strong ambitions who travel constantly for their work. One husband started his own company; the other took over a small family firm and transformed it into a major corporation. Just as it had been for Audrey and Bob, the early years for these couples were times when pennies were pinched and both wives worked in order to make ends meet.

Jessie was a schoolteacher when she and Phil were wed at the age of twenty-two. Her first child was born when they were both thirty-four, a second two years later, and at forty she has just given birth to their third.

"I held down a paying job for ten years and then went to graduate school for six," said Jessie. Slender and blond, she has a thoughtful, steady way about her. "My work years were absolutely needed because that's right when Phil was in the midst of rebuilding his uncle's company. Although it is thriving today, and I don't have to work, we were very much equal partners financially during our early years together. It was also a time when we traded off different roles, too. That's how I found out I hate to do the bookkeeping and he learned how much he hates to cook.

"Although I resigned my job when I got pregnant, I went into a doctoral program right after I had my first child. I still had that drive to prove myself. It wasn't until my second child came along that I could let go and just stay home for a while.

"After my first baby I discovered two things," Jessie continued. "I found out it was fun to be with my children a lot. I had loved my work as a teacher because of all the people I could meet and all the different things I could do—what I always called 'my adventures.' I thought I would lose that. Instead, I discovered I could have those adventures with my children—and enjoy them more. It's as if my talents in my career can really be put to work for my own little ones, and I get so much more satisfaction out of it, especially as they are getting older and we can talk more.

"I also became aware of how fast the time flies by. My oldest child was three before I knew it. Now I have a six-year-old, a three-year-old, and the baby. I feel very comfortable being home for about five years or so. Also, we have a new house that takes a lot of my attention."

Later she would mention another major activity in her life: she is the president of a large arts organization in their metropolitan Ohio community. Committee meetings and related activities demand between ten and fifteen hours a week of her time. It is less a social activity than one close to her professional interests. Awarded an NEA grant eight years ago, Jessie had worked full-time in community arts development, which is what motivates her involvement. She also serves as a consultant to several national children's television development groups—again an outgrowth of her early years as an educator, as well as her doctoral studies.

"But I am really a mom right now," she says with a chuckle, "and I have to say I love it."

Heather also is the mother of three, but she has two teenage daughters, ages eighteen and fourteen, and a six-year-old. "I had a glamour job when I met Joe," she said, brushing back a shock of the naturally curly blond hair that tumbles over her eyebrows and makes her look a good ten years younger than her forty-five years. She has an open, easy air that reflects her casual southwestern lifestyle. Her husband is also forty-five and is as healthy and refreshing to be with as his wife.

"I was a staff writer for one of the big women's magazines back in the late sixties. Right after we were married, Joe got his MBA, then he enlisted. We ski-bummed our first year out of the service, and then he and a friend started up a small company, which has been very successful these last five years."

It wasn't easy. "I worked full-time after our first two children were born," she said. "We had absolutely no money, and I had to. It was difficult, because Joe's work requires a lot of travel. He is gone, has always been gone, several days every week. That means I've done a lot by myself. But it's okay, because he works so darn hard for us, too."

Shortly before their third baby was born, when Heather and Joe were in their late thirties, the business really took off. Heather took advantage of the economic boost to stay home full-time the first year after her youngest child was born. "That was as much as I could handle," she said. "I love domesticity—I quilt,

I belong to a book club, I garden, I chauffeur kids." But she also keeps working—"just to keep my hand in," she said. At first, having built a reputation as one of the Midwest's top publicists during her years while Joe's business was growing, she helped out a friend who had launched a public relations firm. Then a magazine asked her to write a crafts column.

"Until my youngest turned five, I worked no more than ten hours a week," she said. "I wanted to be home as much as possible, to really enjoy those years with my daughters. Now I feel very good getting back into the work groove, but doing only about fifteen hours a week or so."

## The Traditional Work/Housework Split—but with a Twist

Couples in which the wife doesn't work outside the house generally make no pretense at shared household duties. The given is this: he brings home the money (usually more than the average husband), and she is responsible for most of the house-hold load. Though this sounds eerily traditional, remember that because Heather and Jessie and Audrey have each spent nearly ten years working full-time before having "time off" at home, they seem very content to do the housewifely kinds of things and see it as a period to be enjoyed in a relaxed fashion.

"I feel I'm lucky in that he makes the kind of money that means we have a choice," said Jessie. "Because of his hard work, I am able to hire a sitter to go do something on my own, or even take a trip for a couple of days if I need it. While Phil's gone during the day every day, I'm still able to hire someone so I can do my things too. It's not that I choose to do that very often, but knowing that it's there makes me very comfortable. So if the trade-off is that I have to be sure that everything is done around the house—fine."

In fact, it is only in the household where the wife's work pressures do have a tendency to stack up once in a while that you see a husband pitching in house-wise.

"Oh, he's great," said Audrey of Bob's willingness to help out. "He'll do anything—for the newsletter, for the kids, for the house. Usually there isn't much needed. For one thing, I'm good at keeping a house, and I like keeping a nice house. I'm just naturally superorganized. I don't run out of food and soap. I can grocery shop in twenty minutes, so maintaining a house is not a problem.

"Bob is gone so much that I'm used to doing all the gardening and a lot of house maintenance things. So I do everything— walk the dog twice a day, all the laundry. But it's even—he works very hard, long hours and travels a lot.

"But when he's home—and I feel really strongly about this for at-home mothers—I feel like when the man comes home it's got to be fifty-fifty on everything. That means after dinner, in our house, one person puts the kids to bed and one does the dishes. When he's here, he puts the kids to bed almost every night. He'll vacuum on Saturday if the rug needs it. He'll do anything and everything. He can clean the kitchen better than I can."

The husbands also contribute heavy doses of appreciation. Heather basks in the pleasure her husband takes in his family and she maintains the balance that suits her, with ease.

"Joe is a great father to our daughters," she said. "Very big on their athletic development. He's an excellent athlete himself, and he gets right in and participates in the different sports with each of them. Next week, they're going to run in a local 10K race—Joe and both our older girls.

"Ideally, Joe would like me to be home all the time, washing his socks, baking pies, keeping the house clean. I have mixed feelings about that attitude. At times I find it endearing because he's so honest about it and he appreciates and notices everything I do around the house so much. He raves about the cooking. If I make a pan of brownies, you'd think it was a gift from the gods. And other times it makes me chafe a little bit that he wants me there barefoot and pregnant.

"He'd like for me to quit writing my crafts column and be home all the time. But what person wouldn't want a geisha at home? That far I won't go. I'm happy at home, but I'm not *that* happy. And he's also very supportive when I do go out and work. He knows it's important to me. I don't make a lot of money, and we don't need the money, but he knows I need to do it just for myself.

"And for one other reason," Heather paused. "You never know what's going to happen. If you've been sitting in the suburbs all those years, you're going to be in a terrible spot if your husband loses all his money or some accident happens. I feel like I could always get a job somewhere, which provides a real sense of security for me. I've never made a glorious career. I'll never be a doctor or lawyer or a high-flown business executive, because I've never had the time or the desire to put what it takes into that. Sometimes I feel bad that I'll never have a full-blown, successful career, but—" an easy grin spreads across Heather's sunny features—"our family has never had room for two overachievers."

Heather's concern about financial security is a very real one and one that must be confronted by all full-time mothers who want to retain an equal partnership and self-esteem. On money issues, I found today's full-time mothers to be much better informed than the full-time homemaker of the past. In these three families, all the husbands are in charge of the finances, from bill paying to mortgages and insurance, but—unlike traditional households—not one wife "asks" for money. Instead each husband provides an agreed-upon amount on a regular basis and checks back to see if it's adequate. Not one wife felt that money was ever a problem between them, that their purchases were criticized or that they were considered heavy spenders. All three thought this was a result of having been joint wage earners in their early years together so that spending patterns were mutually understood and agreed upon long before funds became more plentiful.

In addition, the wives are fully versed in every detail of financial contingency plans in the event of an emergency. They know how much money there is, where it is, and how to manage it if they have to.

"We talk about the investments," said Jessie, "and follow them together, make the decisions together. We've invested in some apartment complexes recently, and I've gotten involved in

helping him decorate them. I would say our financial planning is
very much a joint effort, with Phil handling the actual transac-
tions."

Money is control, of course—a fact of life that does not go
unnoticed by any of the three women—and it's one of the reasons they do "keep their hand in" career ventures, even if
minimally. Jessie in particular is struggling with the issue of
control.

"One of my last big fears surfaced after I had my second
child," said Jessie. "I remember lying in the hospital thinking,
This must be my last child, because if I'm on my own sometime
in the future, I can only take care of two children by myself. I can
take them places with me, and I think I can financially support
them on my own.

"I have never been able to let myself depend totally on
another person," she said. "That's why it took me a long time to
say I was ready to have this third child. While I love my children
and I enjoy seeing them grow, I need to feel that I still have
control over the future—that I can pick up this little world of
mine all by myself and know that I'll be okay, that my children
will be all right. That I can be in control.

"It made a big difference to me that my doctoral work paid
off with several consultantships. This has been a professional
boost that made me comfortable with the time out for this third
baby. I see a whole new area of work for myself five to ten years
from now—so I'm able to relax and take it easy right now."

## Crises in Paradise

Are these relationships as perfect as they appear? How are these
women able to manage when things go wrong—if they don't
have a steady salary to reinforce them when life goes awry?

No, the relationships aren't perfect. So how these women
cope with peril is by being up front about their problems and
expecting exactly the same from their husbands. Unlike their
mothers, Audrey, Jessie, and Heather do not see themselves as
the emotional housekeepers of their marriages; they do not
consider themselves responsible for keeping everyone happy at

the cost of their own feelings and sense of self-esteem. Their husbands know they have to meet them at least halfway. More importantly, they place as great a value on family life as they do on their work—and they make sure to be there for their wives and children.

Each of these marriages—Heather and Joe, Jessie and Phil, Audrey and Bob—weathered a severe crisis that pushed the couple to the brink of divorce. It was there they discovered whether or not they would make it. Each couple *did* make it, because they were willing to confront the problems and work hard to sort out all the confusion and bad feelings. If they had to, they were willing to seek professional help in order to do it. Nor did they assume the crisis could be handled overnight. Instead, putting the same effort into their personal lives as they had into their professional ones, they were willing to listen to one another and to invest in each other their most valuable asset: time.

"It was the low point of our marriage," said Heather, remembering back to ten years ago, when she and Joe nearly spun out of their marriage. "We had two small children, which is stressful already, and Joe's business was still getting off the ground, so he was never home. It was a deadly combination: he was a workaholic, then you know how busy small children keep you, and I was working full-time, too. We really grew apart. We were truly in two different worlds. I think that went on for about three years from start to finish—a real rough time.

"It came to a head one night when we were discussing a friend's marriage that had just ended, and Joe told me he was thinking about divorce. What made it so terrible was the fact that I wasn't surprised. It was a feeling I'd had in my gut. Boy, what a turning point! In a way it was a healthy thing, because we got a lot out in the open, and from then on it's been great. But that was a definite shake-up in our lives. It took us a year to work back into ourselves.

"We decided to pay more attention to the marriage. Because we were both so busy, we weren't talking together; we weren't seeing each other. We had both been so young and dumb. We'd never given our marriage much thought until that point. Sud-

denly we realized that, if you don't work at it constantly, if you
don't pay attention to your marriage just like you pay attention to
your business and your kids, you're going to lose it. Even your
car gets a checkup every six months!

"We changed our ways immediately," Heather explained.
"From that point on, Joe has really taken the initiative in our
having time together without the children. To this day—and the
kids are older now, so it's easier—every Saturday morning without fail we go out for breakfast to the neighborhood deli where
we take about two hours to catch up on the week without any
interruptions.

"And on one of the two weekend nights, Friday or Saturday,
we go out alone to dinner. It's away from the children, the
telephone, the TV, and we just talk. I think that's the secret of
our marriage. We talk about everything, from the mundane to
the philosophical to plans for the future. Finances, gossip.

"You know," Heather went on, "we fell in love because we
had so much to talk about when we met, but then it sort of faded
during those three awful years when the combination of children and career put such a strain on it. And now it's not just me
who keeps us in line. Lots of time Joe will say, 'I feel like I haven't
been spending enough time with you lately. We really need to
get together this weekend and spend some time; just the two of
us.' A lot of husbands don't do that. Joe has been very faithful in
tending to that part of the marriage. And I am too."

A similar crisis hit Jessie and Phil before they had children.
"We were in our late twenties," said Jessie, "and Phil was working so hard at that time. He worked late a lot of nights, so I
pursued other interests with women friends. Pretty soon I would
just get really involved with something—maybe I'd take a trip
with a woman friend. I'd turn all my thoughts inward and go
someplace else with my energy. I'd go for an adventure with
friends rather than with Phil. More and more my energy was
directed away from us.

"But I didn't know how to change that; I didn't have the
skills," said Jessie, her voice soft and her eyes serious with the
memory of pain. "Nor did he. Although he's sensitive, Phil's not

real affectionate. So we were at opposites—I wanted more affection, I needed to just go off with him and hold hands, while he needed me to show more interest in what he was doing. We really had different ideas of what it meant to be in love and together and still feel a passion for each other.

"Finally," she said, "we got a little bit of marriage counseling, and that was the beginning of understanding each other's differences. Just enough of a beginning to be sensitive to the other person. I have always felt we were fortunate that nothing came along when we were in our late twenties and didn't know how to communicate—that might have ripped our marriage apart. It was an incredibly vulnerable time.

"And so we slowly, slowly worked our way back toward each other. I learned to open up more and tell him what I need. He actually does it better than I do now. For example, he's envious of the time I have with the children, so he's always pushing for more family time.

"To me, too, time with the kids is entertainment. The time when they're small and really like being with you doesn't last very long. I'm really enjoying it right now, and I know he misses it a lot when he's not here. I think knowing that gives me a lot more patience with his schedule. Knowing he would rather be home and really trusting in that is important for me.

"We've worked it out so that we usually have the weekends together as family times," said Jessie. "We don't want to miss out on each other's time as well!

"Before this new baby, we used to be very good about going out by ourselves on Wednesday nights, but that's been hard lately. Then we take a trip together about every two months— just the two of us. It may only be two or three days. We always know when we need it again. Like right now," Jessie added with a laugh, "we need one real soon!"

For Audrey and Bob the identical problem hit when Bob got out of the service and "he was really consumed with his job."

Audrey understood . . . kind of: "He was thirty-two and had been in the service since he was eighteen years old, so he really wanted to prove himself," she said. "He's very ambitious and hardworking, and he just worked too much. I was trying to remodel a house and have a baby—he was gone so much, and I felt he could have been gone less.

"And the only reason that was a problem was because of the kids. He had worked more than that before, but there were no kids, so I could do my thing. But I got stuck in the house, which was pretty bad. We took about two years to work our way out of this. Over months and months we talked and talked.

"We did two things," explained Audrey. "First, we decided that both of us are very committed to our marriage—committed to it being a nice, good marriage, not just any old marriage. And then my husband really put the effort in to change his work life and to balance a little better. He realized he had been trying to prove himself at his new job and went overboard doing it.

"I told him I really admired him, but when you're married to someone who's a workaholic it's like being married to an alcoholic. It's a serious problem. So I said, 'Do you want me to have a life of my own apart from you? I can still build a life by myself. But is that what we want? Look how young we are. Do we want to go another thirty years with you having your life and me having mine?' "

Like Heather and Jessie, Audrey confronted the dilemma. But it took her time to get to the crucial problems, because she was confused about them. She really didn't know what was wrong at first.

"Part of my problem is I'm not good at fighting," said Audrey. "I can't storm around and say, 'You said you'd be home at five and you didn't get home till seven.' I've had to work on being up front, which has been hard. I grew up in a household where no one really fought—and that's not good."

But she recognized the problem, even if it was difficult, and worked on it—with help from Bob. "The great thing about my husband is he just wants to have a nice time all the time. He wants life to be a pleasure for everyone, and he is willing to hear about the problems so we can fix things up. That taught me that I could have just as easily said, 'Gee, Bob, this is really a drag.' Or 'Why don't we just get some plane tickets and I'll go see my mom for a week?' Instead, no, I dragged around until our marriage was just a big mess.

"Now it's much better. Bob never realized all the things that were bothering me, because I didn't tell him. We had had such a happy ten years together—we were used to that; that was our normal life. So we knew we wanted that back, and we knew we could have it back. But it took about a year to bring it up and about a year to fix it. So I'm talking a long period when I was pretty unhappy."

"Now we both bring stuff up right away. We realized we both came from families where anger was hidden. Like his mom is still bringing up things that make her mad from years ago. We don't do that anymore. We're both totally up front about any hassles we have. But it made a huge difference to me that when we were having our problems Bob was the one who said, 'I'll go to a marriage counselor, whatever you want to do.' To me," said Audrey, "that shows supreme manhood—and Bob's just naturally that way.

"I used to think that, if you had a problem in a marriage, you'd probably never get over it and stay with the person. Now that I'm older and more mature, I see what a beautiful thing even our problem time was, because I feel like Bob and I can get through anything now. I feel like we had our test and we both wanted it to work and we did it, and now I'm not afraid of the future. I feel like, if we had a financial disaster or something happened to our kids, we know we can get through things.

"I have this quote on my refrigerator that goes something like 'Love is what you've been through with somebody'—and that's what I think it is!"

Communication is no longer a problem between them, and their lives are humming along. Bob's career is flourishing, Audrey's newsletter is going like gangbusters, and the children are happy.

"I think we have a very close marriage today," said Audrey. "I know that we love spending time together. My husband has always been very interested in my projects, whatever they are. He's keenly interested in anything I do. And I am in him. I think

that's why we got married—because we both get such different
kinds of things going. So he's always keen to know what's going
on with me and what I'm thinking about things—and I'm just as
fascinated with his world. The kids' ages make it hard to talk,
though, so we go out a lot.

"It's the only way we can really do our talking. He travels
quite a bit, and when he's gone we talk on the phone every night.
But I think we go out alone more than a lot of couples. At least
once a week we go out for dinner or we get a baby-sitter during
the day and go shopping or driving. Once we took off for the
afternoon and rented a bicycle built for two.

"When I go out with Bob, I do want to talk. That's why we
don't like to go to movies. Tomorrow we're going to a wedding
reception in the afternoon. Since we have a baby-sitter till 6:00,
we'll stay at the reception a little bit, and then we'll go out alone.
We love to go out by ourselves—not expensively but routinely."

As with the couples in the previous chapters, "full-time
mom" couples are able to work things out only if they communicate honestly and often. Clearly, two self-confident individuals
with a deep, mutual respect for each other *can* make a "traditional" marriage work.

"You know," said Heather, "sometimes I feel like ours is the
only traditional marriage that does work. There are so few
around. What am I—a vestige from the past? I think we have sort
of an 'Ozzie and Harriet marriage for the eighties,' which is so
odd, but it seems to be working for us. I just wonder why. But
I'm real happy. And what is it that makes ours succeed when so
many traditional marriages have failed?"

In the next breath Heather answers her own question—and
in doing so makes quite clear the difference between these
equal partners and the old order of married life: "There is this
couple in our neighborhood," she said. "They're a lot younger
than we are. She stays home with the children; he's an attorney.
She's an extremely dependent woman.

"I don't know how this man has stayed married to her. I
think he must be losing his mind, because she whines constantly. She's never happy with anything. She's never working.
Her children are ten and five, and she stays home all day and

cleans. She's very boring. I don't get the impression he's very happy," said Heather, "although he adores his children.

"You wouldn't believe it—if the slightest thing goes wrong at home, she'll call him at work and tell him to come home and fix it. She locked herself out of the house and called him at work to come home and let her in. The little girl hurt her hand in the car door, and she called him at work to come home and take her to the doctor. Now that's a very, very traditional marriage, and I wonder if it's going to work."

## Life After Motherhood

Early indications are that the success rate (in terms of accomplishing what they want to in their business and personal lives) for women who opt out for "family years" and opt back in again, is going to be far higher than anyone's expectations. Since we are the first generation of working women to experience this phenomenon, I'm afraid that the experts are not going to allow us to make definitive conclusions. But the future looks very, very bright.

For one thing, the statistics on what the career environment is likely to be for the older woman are quite surprising. Not only are two-thirds of the people entering the work force over the next twelve years going to be female, but four out of every ten women at work will be over the age of fifty-five. In fact, 20 percent of American women over age fifty-five are already earning regular salaries. Not only are their numbers increasing, but they are actively sought after by many employers.

Many are entering the job market for the first time after their children are grown as traditional full-time mothers who are now interested in making money and becoming involved in satisfying careers. Some have returned to school for undergraduate degrees; others have received specialized training, such as nursing certificates and computer skills. Already the number of women over age forty who are returning to school for degrees in law, business, medicine, public administration, the creative arts, and engineering is climbing. Indeed, some experts are calling this "the incandescent age of the older woman." And rightly so.

It is dawning on more than one American woman that she just may be "coming of age at fifty."

One impetus for this phenomenon was described eloquently by Carolyn G. Heilbrun, who wrote these inspiring words in a recent *New York Times* piece: "We women have lived too much with closure: 'If he notices me, if I marry him, if I get into college, if I get this work accepted, if I get that job'—there always seems to loom the possibility of something being over, settled, sweeping clear the way for contentment. This is the delusion of a passive life. When the hope for closure is abandoned, when there is an end to fantasy, adventure for women will begin."

## Lillian: Taking Things as They Come

Palmer Wright knew he had a bead on the right gal when he first laid eyes on Lillian thirty-nine years ago. For a brief time he was her supervisor in the Iowa bank where he would spend the rest of his career.

"This woman is extremely modest, and she underestimates her worth," said the sixty-six-year-old retired banker, his brilliant blue eyes snapping as he glanced with undisguised affection at his fifty-eight-year-old wife. "She is efficient. Real efficient. I met her when she was nineteen, right when she started at the bank. She was one of the folks we had an expression for because they worked so darn hard: 'We get our dollar's worth out of her' we'd say."

Lillian "thought he was real cute. I told my mother after my first week at the bank that I had met the man I wanted to marry. Of course, he had other women friends at the time, so I also told my mother there might be some problems, and she said, 'Don't let them get in your way.' "

So Lillian set her cap for Palmer, and things worked out her way. "We had a ball. We kidded each other," said Palmer in describing how they fell in love. Their ease with each other, the ability to say the positive in the same breath as the negative, is a trait that's true only of couples who are comfortable with each one's personal power in the relationship. And Lillian and Palmer know exactly how the beam is balanced in their house.

"Palmer has always been very understanding," said Lillian, a stocky, strong woman with a warm, round face. Her crisp blue eyes match her husband's. "He realizes that I'm real independent, and he doesn't try to dominate me. Of course, he's always said he realized it would be fruitless."

"I learned early," said Palmer. "She was young and not very tall and weighed about 105 pounds. So one afternoon after I came home from work I decided we should have a wrestling match. Well, I tried and I tried to pin that little girl—but I couldn't do it unless I hurt her, so the wrestling match ended up being a draw. I just figured out that day that there was no use alienating her, because that could be dangerous."

Their years together started off in a very traditional mode. Three children were born, and Lillian stayed home full-time until the oldest turned twelve. "Palmer was always sensitive to the fact that I was kind of tied down in the house with three little children and without the ability to get out and have a break. He was a real help—I'd say, 'Talk to me about anything as long it's above the two-year-old-level. Tell me what's happening in the world.' So he'd tell me about the bank while I'd do dinner, and a lot of times he'd clean up the kitchen and give the kids their baths and get them ready for bed."

Meanwhile, Lillian turned out to be a woman with a high energy level and a knack for the kind of problem solving that made it possible for her to get what she wanted. And when the children were small, she wanted out. Since money for baby-sitters was in short supply, she found another solution.

"Lillian really wanted to start playing golf," said Palmer, "so she did—at five in the morning with some of the neighborhood women. She was always home before I had to leave for the office." It was a hint of things to come.

Just as the children entered adolescence, the family felt a financial pinch that gave Lillian the urge to get back to work herself. At first she took in typing and ironing, then she took a job as a secretary in a major corporation that was located close to their home.

"I just walked in one day and asked, 'Are you hiring?' " said Lillian. "Palmer and I had been talking about putting the kids through school and how we were going to have to take a second mortgage, and I didn't want to do that, so I decided I'd rather go to work. The twins were twelve, and our eldest was thirteen. It was an adjustment for me, of course, because I hadn't done anything but part-time work since they were babies, and to go to work full-time with three preteens who were very active was difficult. But we lived close to my work, so I could run home on my lunch hour and be sure they weren't having orgies."

The family pitched in to help each other once Mom was at work full-time. "We became famous for leaving notes about the chores. They got a list every day, and they helped a lot in the afternoons. There was no distinction between chores, either; the boys had to do the same things as their sister. At first they resented that terribly, but we told them we didn't have any hay to pitch or cows to milk, so they had to help this way. So the kids took care of their rooms, they did the dishes, they helped in lots of ways.

"I still did the housework, the grocery buying, the cooking, and the laundry," said Lillian. "I taught all three kids to do some pressing and sew on buttons. They also did a little cooking—the boys more than their sister because she had a heavier academic load. Both boys have turned out to be very good cooks.

"The kids also worked. One threw papers and got up at 3:30 in the morning, while the twins sold popcorn at the neighborhood theater and didn't get home till midnight. Palmer was working real hard at the bank, too, and especially since the kids were all taking care of their own things, he got totally out of the habit of doing much around the house."

This went on for six years. As it did, something else happened. Lillian's energy level, now that she'd been freed from daily child care, and the confidence of extra income spurred her on to more activities. She and Palmer became avid bowlers, and she became an expert bridge player, playing with three different clubs and regularly winning prizes. She also signed up for a variety of courses, organized an exercise group for herself and some of her friends from the office, and started to travel—alone.

Travel was an interest they never shared. Palmer hated to travel, and she loved to be on the go. And so Lillian took some of her earnings and bought a camper. Every summer she and the kids and other friends or relatives would take off to the country. Palmer stayed home. It's a practice that's endured; two or three times a year Lillian will fly off to see old friends, take a brief vacation, or explore a city where one of her children has settled—without Palmer.

However, that's one of the few things they do separately. Even though he was not a part of the housework contingent when Lillian first went to work, that soon changed.

"What really got him back to helping me was a course on memory that I took right after I started work," said Lillian. "Each week they had you strive for something, and one week it was to get someone to help you with an idea of yours by showing appreciation. So I started to work on Palmer, trying to get him to help me chaperon at a music bar for eighteen-year-olds, which was something the kids had asked me to do. I didn't especially enjoy doing it, and one night Palmer offered to go. I let him— and then I went out of my way to let him know how much I appreciated it. After that, he did it every week!

"I learned to apply the principle of appreciation to most things," said Lillian. "Pretty soon Palmer was helping a lot more, although the kids still did most of the house stuff. Then they left for school, and I quit working. Since I was home all day, there was no reason for him to help."

Lillian served as a full-time homemaker for another six years, then something unexpected occurred—Palmer decided to take early retirement.

"He made this decision kind of quickly, so we really hadn't prepared mentally for retirement—or at least I hadn't," said Lillian. "As it turned out, he retired on November 1, we enjoyed the holidays together, and I went to work in January."

Lillian took a position as executive secretary to the chief executive officer of a large investment firm. In her previous position Lillian had done some accounting work. "I love financial management," she said, "so I started out as his executive secretary, but I've taken over as the financial manager of his private accounts. I'm his right-hand person and manage all his stock and bond market activity, including the family investments.

"I didn't think it would work out for us to be together on a twenty-four-hour-a-day basis," Lillian said frankly. "I know more people our age where the husband has retired—and they're splitting up. It's a big group of people. And part of the reason, I think, is that the man is home, he doesn't have any hobbies, and he's sitting around telling the little woman how she should do this and that. Well, she's done it for thirty-five years, and she resents his advice. So they start having troubles."

The sheer pleasure in working at something she enjoys, with a hubbub of activity around her, is also one of the reasons Lillian decided to return to work. But she had another reason too: money.

"I plan to work at least until I'm sixty-five," she said, "and I'm fifty-eight right now. Part of that is enjoyment, part is I need the money, and part of it is just plain old hospitalization costs, which are astronomical now. I've got seven years before I qualify for Medicare. And part of it's just having extras—being able to take a trip when you want to."

Palmer appreciates Lillian's efforts and takes real pride in her working. "She handles the big-ticket items—our new car, major improvements around the house. My retirement income pretty well covers the cost of everyday life such as groceries and taxes."

In return, Palmer has become a new man, a house husband—the full-time homemaker. "We just gradually worked into it," said Lillian. "I'd come home on the weekend and start scrubbing and cleaning, and one day he said, 'This doesn't seem fair—I'll clean my room and the bathroom.' And this just gradually grew to where he took over all the light housekeeping. He doesn't do floors or windows. Or curtains. Or laundry. And I do buy the groceries."

"Fine with me," said Palmer. "Early on in my retirement I said I'd spend a couple of days on the yard and a couple of days in the house doing housework, then I'd play golf two days and I'd take the other day off.

"Boy," he snorted, "I found out again what a chore housework is. She calls it 'light'—it isn't light, especially the bathrooms. Believe me, I got an appreciation for the common housewife!"

And so it goes. She leaves every morning at 7:30 and returns at 5:30. He keeps the home fires burning. She travels by herself on occasion because he still hates to leave home.

And when things go wrong between them, this very loquacious couple has a solution: "If one of us is out of line, he or she gets the silent treatment and door slamming," said Lillian. "That hasn't changed in thirty-nine years."

"Our problems aren't major," said Palmer with an affectionate glance at his wife. "They aren't going to change the shape of the world. It's just little things that are irritating to one or the other of us. But when one person is having a tantrum, the other one has been smart enough just to let the other blow off steam."

What they don't say—and probably don't realize—is that the easy banter between them touches on all the details of their life, skipping over the hassles with humor, keeping everything on the table. Even money is not a problem. "We maintain two joint accounts, one for each of us." said Palmer. "She amasses her fortune, and I just handle the budget items, and she lets me write checks on that account."

"We've had it this way since I went to work when the kids were still home," said Lillian. "At that time I said, 'I'd like to have my own account. I'm so tired of asking for $5 here and there.' So since then we've had the separate accounts, and I have things I pay for and so does he."

## A Tough Test: Can You Afford to Stay Home Full-Time?

On a scale of 1 to 5, measure how comfortable you are with each of these statements:

1. My husband earns enough money that we can afford to have me home.

2. I feel good about myself. The extra boost of approval that I get from work is less important to me right now than being able to manage my home and family more easily.
3. My desire to be home full-time is strictly a temporary choice—ten years from now I'd love to be working.
4. I feel "a woman's place" is where she feels she most needs to be in order to be happy with herself.
5. The best mother is the one who is happy with her work, whether that is inside or outside the home.

*Scoring*
The perfect score is 25 if you are trying to convince yourself that traditional homemaking will be okay for you for a while. This means you have made up your own mind and have the "bonus" benefit of a strong sense of self-esteem. A score of 15 to 24 indicates part-time might suit you better. Research your options and give yourself plenty of time to decide. If you score 6 to 15, you are feeling the pull between work and family so strongly that work should remain a priority in your life.
*Red Flag:* If you instinctively found yourself saying "no" to question 3, you are either too traditional for words or you need a vacation from work *very badly*!

# How to Make It Work

Don't decide to stay at home full-time without your partner's agreement. He must not only be comfortable with your being home full-time for a while but be willing to commit in writing to temporary, full financial responsibility for you and your children should your marital status for any reason change.

Then take care to monitor your own feelings of independence and self-esteem. If you discover within a year or two that you are happier when your life is balanced with part-time or full-time work, don't be surprised.

A recent survey of *Working Mother* magazine readers found that "women who took a year or more off work after the births of their children are more likely to be happy about working than

women who took off two months or less." It's also important to
realize that, no matter what your career status, you're likely to
have doubts about your parenting abilities—we all do. One
woman I interviewed said she worried, when she was working,
that she was not a good enough mother. Once she had decided
to stay home full-time, she thought her worries would subside,
but she *still* wonders if she's doing a good enough job!

Last, but critically important to succeeding at this: keep in
*very* close touch with your partner. After all, isn't this one big
reason you want to stay home?

# 7
# The New Balance: Husbands on the Home Front

**D**espite what you may think, more and more fathers are taking over at least half the responsibility for child care and homemaking. And many are happy to be doing more than that. Not only are 20 percent of married fathers in America now proud to be primarily responsible for the daytime care of their children, but millions more younger dads are happy to share *at least* half of the burden of kids, cooking, and cleanup. What used to be exclusively a working mother's dilemma is recognized at last to be a "family" dilemma. A dilemma, moreover, that ceases to exist in many families the moment the burdens are shared.

Men are learning that careers and kids do not combine easily. Thus it is that coincident with the talk of a "Mommy Track" for career women who want more time with their families comes news of an identical "Daddy Track." The *Wall Street Journal* reported "there's a new generation coming into management . . . as working fathers are finding new ways to fill their two roles by making a deliberate effort to cut back work hours and extend family time."

253

Robert J. Samuelson eloquently expressed a man's feeling about a "Daddy Track" when he recently pointed out in his *Newsweek* column that more younger fathers are making child-care benefits an employment issue, refusing jobs that require frequent travel and doing much more work at home. "My children are exasperating, exhausting, and exhilarating," said Samuelson. "They are the best part of me, and I won't miss their growing up."

At first, even though women were making their way up the road of equal opportunity and into the workplace, some still held tight to their power base at home, exhausted but reluctant to give up their one sure base of control: the house and children. While they may have begun to share their partners' ambitions for career and financial success, they weren't yet aware that their partners might be growing interested in an equal share of involvement in the home and family. Now we know, however, the men can be torn, too—finding that they prefer family activities over career. Now we know that neither men nor women can be sure in the early stages of their relationships and careers, to what degree they may want to be committed to career *or* family. For some people the degree of commitment can vary from year to year.

Nor is it always an easy adjustment to make. Some women struggle within themselves upon discovering they have a partner who wants to do more with the children, take over more decisions about the house. Yes, they appreciate the help—but does he really get to do all the decorating? Plan all the menus? Other women, meanwhile, continue to wring their hands in fatigue and frustration because they have discovered, too late, that they are yoked to men who enjoy the financial benefits of a working wife but see no reason to ease their wife's double load by taking up some of the slack around the house. The traditional male still views that as "her" problem. He wasn't raised to do any of that, and her work outside the home was, after all, her choice—"If it's too much, honey, stay home." But these guys are a vanishing breed.

It has taken us only a decade or two to figure out that the more flexibility there is for women—to work or not to work or to work part-time—the more flexibility there is for men too. By clearing the obstacles from the paths of women who want to have choices in terms of career advancement or home involvement, we have created environments in which men can make broader choices as well: in short, both partners win.

But it isn't just that the opportunities broadened; men changed, too. It is something you can observe if you look closely at the attitudes of men born before and after 1945. In doing surveys of numerous couples and individuals over the past six years, I have discovered that that year marks a turning point. Men born since then tend to be less traditional in their attitudes, more understanding of why we all have split ambitions. And it has everything to do with their mothers. These men were raised by women who had, in all likelihood, worked outside the home during World War II when the men were overseas; by women who, during the fifties, worked or went to school at least until they were married; or by women who, consciously or unconsciously, plucked the fruits of social change generated by the women's movement of the sixties and seventies and assimilated those changes into their lives.

Many of these mothers taught their children, male and female, to accept new roles for each other beyond the traditions of marriage, motherhood, and fatherhood; they taught them the value of openly expressing their feelings, whether those feelings are happiness, fear, or discontent; and they taught them the warmth and comfort to be gained by staying in close touch with family members. Above all, they taught them the exquisite power and satisfaction of intimacy as it can be found between individuals who can easily talk and laugh together, whether they are friends or lovers. They raised men and women who may finally understand what it means to be equals. While I am not saying that all men over the age of forty-five are incapable of being equal partners, those who prove that "age is a state of mind" are found in smaller numbers among that group. Obviously there are always going to be twenty-year-old men who have difficulty relating to women and seventy-year-old men who are young at heart and can make wonderful, sharing partners.

The social revolution of the sixties was responsible for amazing changes in the roles we allow, even expect, men to play.

Men are expected to be "sensitive," to cry, to express their feelings without fear of ridicule. Though there has been debate as to the mixed messages men get ("be strong"; "be sensitive"), and the "male" role is far from completely defined, there's no denying that today's man is different from yesterday's. We see evidence of this remarkable social change daily, most often in the ads and television series, not to mention movies, that shape our awareness of the world around us. The young and sensitive guys who became heroes of "Thirtysomething," *Moonstruck*, and *Three Men and a Baby* are just a few examples. Even Rocky had a soft side. All reflect what is happening and fuel the expectations of their mass audiences.

It's exciting that men have been given permission by society to be caring individuals, just as women have been allowed to express their rational, intelligent, less emotional sides. Just how drastic a difference these changes have made is shown in the results of several studies reported in recent years. "The Report on the Changing Life Course of Women," commissioned by *Cosmopolitan* magazine, found that as late as 1970, 18 percent of college women were in college to find a husband—but by 1980, just ten years later, the number of women seeking a "Mrs." degree had plummeted to 1 percent! I doubt that anyone would even bother to ask the question today.

The same study reported another significant change in young men's and women's attitudes toward family life: in 1952, almost 90 percent of college women said family life was more important than career, but by 1974 just 57 percent of women would place family before career. Also in 1974, 48 percent of men placed family before career. By 1987 even that percentage had risen, as *American Demographics* reported that 58 percent of married or formerly married men believe that "the most satisfying accomplishment for a man is to be a father." Thus the values of men and women have grown remarkably alike.

And that is just the beginning. Here are more signs of major change:

• *Newsweek* magazine reported in late 1988 that 74 percent of fathers surveyed in a Boston University study of men living and working in the northeastern United States believed "they should share child-care chores with the mother."

- The *Wall Street Journal* reported in early 1989 that the same Boston University study showed that almost as many fathers as mothers—36 percent versus 37 percent—reported feeling "a lot of stress" in balancing their work and family lives. In the same article the *WSJ* also reported a survey of 1,200 employees at a Minneapolis company that found "more than 70 percent of the fathers under age 35 had serious concerns about problems they were having managing work and family conflicts with their spouses . . . noting they were often not seeking promotions and transfers because they need to spend more time with their families."

- And, finally, a study done by the DuPont Company of 6,600 workers showed a doubling of men's interest in flexible work schedules from 1985 to 1988—*in order to have more time at home with their children!*

It should come as no surprise that some experts see the phenomenal increase in diaper-happy dads as the most significant change in relations between men and women in recent decades. The "active father" is no longer unique in family life; he's fast becoming the norm. No wonder, then, that we continue to hear more and more about dads who hurry home to baby-sit while Mom works overtime, about the Los Angeles Fire Department allowing firemen fathers to bring their babies to the fire station, and about numerous states having or enacting laws that require employers to give both men and women time off to care for new babies or sick children.

The payoff for this change in attitude goes far beyond the personal enrichment afforded the couples themselves. Those who profit most are likely to be their children. "The superbaby syndrome, special after-school activities, all of those . . . pushing symptoms are not really the keynotes to success," said *Family Circle*'s Susan Ungaro after the magazine commissioned a study, conducted by the Gallup Organization, of what helps a child succeed. "Investing time and personal interest in your child is the most important gift you can give," she said. The study was based on interviews with extremely successful people in business, entertainment, sports, politics, the arts, and sciences, and it included interviews with their parents. Among the findings reported were:

- Fifty percent of dads of achievers (versus 37 percent of other dads) said they devoted a great deal of time to furthering their child's interests.
- Seventy percent of the achievers' moms said they had frequent conversations with their kids (versus 61 percent of other moms), and 67 percent of the achievers' fathers (versus 56 percent of other dads) talked to their kids a lot. Thus fathers as well as mothers made time to talk to and share with the kids. And what did both parents value most in their children? "Independence."

## The Dads Who Make Home Their First Priority

Just as a bare minimum of American housewives (11 percent) call themselves "traditional full-time homemakers," so is the number of full-time at-home dads pretty limited. However, that is not to be confused with the number of fathers who take on the full responsibility of child care even though they may be working full- or part-time. That number—as I mentioned earlier—is at least 20 percent of all married fathers, or one out of every five dads.

That statistic is dated, however, and the actual number is likely to be much higher. A more recent study reported by the Catalyst organization produced the startling statistic that only 54 percent of married women who work full-time said child care was their exclusive responsibility. What does that mean? *That an additional 46 percent of married fathers are sharing the load.* That is an astounding change.

But it isn't something they do alone. Before we go any further, I think it is important to underscore that the home and child-care chores can't be shared unless the mother is willing to give up some control over her traditional domain—something surprisingly difficult for some working mothers.

In the families you are about to meet, you will see how mothers must learn to let go and allow the dads to flourish as caregivers and playmates. You will see how fathers take over these duties with great expectations and fine results—they truly love what they do.

## Mike: A Dad Who Does More Than His Share

While dads who do it all are rare, dads who take over at least half the homemaking and child care are becoming more and more common these days.

Mike, thirty-nine, who has a sixteen-year-old son from a short-lived first marriage, has been that child's custodial parent since his early twenties. He is 6'4" and strikingly handsome, with dark eyes and hair. An excellent athlete who subsidizes his annual income as a high school teacher with a summer job as the tennis pro for a local country club, Mike also plays basketball as often as possible and stays in shape with a variety of other physical activities, debunking any theory that only nonmacho guys do more than their share at home!

His equally attractive wife of seven years, Trish, thirty-one, is a kindergarten teacher. The two met when both were supplementing their teaching salaries with part-time jobs at a restaurant.

Since their earliest days, the young Kansas couple have evenly divided most house and child-care tasks, although Mike has continued to take primary responsibility for his son, Jim, and has always pitched in since the arrival of their daughter, Sara, two years ago.

"During the workweek we have a pretty set schedule," said Trish, a lithe woman with a dancer's figure and long, straight black hair. "I get Sara up, fed, dressed, and to the baby-sitter's. Then I go to work. Mike will pick her up and bring her home because he gets out of work sooner than I do, whereas I don't have to be at work as early as he does.

"Once we're home, it's pretty equal. Usually Mike will say,

'What's for dinner?' but that doesn't mean I necessarily cook it. A lot of times I might come home and Mike will have some chicken on the grill, so I'll add rice or baked potatoes."

"Meals are really a joint effort," said Mike. "In the morning we'll say, 'What do you want to have?' and get it out of the freezer. If we don't know, there's always cold cuts or hot dogs or we can order out. But it's very rare that one of us does all the cooking and cleaning up. We just help each other.

"The same is true for doing the laundry and cleaning house," he added. Their home is a picture-book scene of country-style furniture with warm wood paneling, beamed ceilings, and cheery chintz fabrics throughout the open, old-fashioned rooms. It is spotless and very attractively decorated.

"I think everyone is very surprised when they learn that Mike has helped decorate this house," said Trish. "We've picked out all the furniture together, and he painted the end tables.

"We clean together," she added, "but Mike always vacuums, and I dust and do the bathrooms. And I always say, 'How come you get to vacuum? I hate dusting!' "

"Every once in a while one of us will feel unappreciated, and we'll start listing everything that we've done that day," said Mike, grinning at his wife's good-humored chagrin over the dusting. "But we really do share the load—I hate paying the bills and balancing my checkbook. I just hate it. So Trish pays the bills and pays them early. She does some things because she knows I hate doing them. But I'll take the garbage to the dump, which she has never done. And I bring wood in. If I don't start the fire, it doesn't get started. That's a big deal since we have two fireplaces and a wood-burning stove.

"We just fall into work patterns, I guess. One day we'll recognize that one or the other of us has taken responsibility for something, and that's that."

Not surprisingly, given how much they share the other areas of their life, Mike and Trish also pool their income and place equal value on their individual careers. "Mike makes a lot more than I do because of his two jobs," said Trish, "but if I were to stop working, we'd have a real hard time."

"And by the same token, I don't expect her to take care of the baby all the time," said Mike. "When it came to changing diapers and stuff, I did whatever needed to be done. If the baby cried in the middle of the night, we'd both lie there and pretend we didn't hear it. But eventually one of us would get up. It's not like 'Trish, your baby's crying.'"

"In the beginning, I did more with Sara because I was home on three months' maternity leave," said Trish, "but once I started back to work, I realized I couldn't do it all. Yet even then we never sat down and decided who would do what; it just evolved.

"There are times when I feel that Sara is more my responsibility than Mike's," added Trish, "particularly if there's a period when I'm buying her clothes, or I'm keeping track of her medical visits. Then that will be offset by Mike's becoming more involved for a time. For example, she was sick a lot last winter, and Mike took her to the doctor a lot when I couldn't get away to do it. On the days that she was sick, when I couldn't miss a day of school because I had started a new job and it was very important to be there, Mike stayed home with the baby."

"But it did get to the point," said Mike, "that I had to tell Trish, 'If she gets sick one more time, you're going to have to stay home with her. I just can't do it.' Which she did. And that was the only day Trish had to stay out of school all year."

What makes the difference among men? Why does one father resist much involvement with his children, but a guy like Mike come through doing at least half the parenting?

"I think it's partly from what he went through with Jim," said Trish. "I don't know that he would have taken this active a role otherwise. He didn't have a choice with Jim—he had custody, and he had to be there for all their meals, everything. I think that really helped when Sara came along. He had already done it, so he stepped right in. That's how I knew he'd be a good father when I first met him."

It also helps that Mike came from a family where work was shared equally. "There were no male and female jobs in our house," recalled Mike, "just work to be done, and we all did it.

My father did everything from cutting grass to doing the laundry to washing dishes. Actually, my son does less than I did. Mother was always the decision maker.

"Also, she worked crazy hours at times. Before she became a head nurse, she worked the delivery room—three different shifts. Because of her schedule, my father would do the washing. We would iron our own clothes, so I iron very well," said Mike with pride.

But even with their truly egalitarian relationship, Trish and Mike, like every couple, must face the challenges that come with change.

"It isn't like it doesn't get hectic," said Mike. "We had a tough year because of Trish's move from one position where she had a lot of leeway to a new position where she had a lot of demands made on her. I didn't feel neglected, but we did talk about it often, and I'm hoping that next year is going to be different.

"I was very upset at times, because it cut into our time together. Trish had to spend so much time in the evening preparing for the next day while I was just sitting around because I don't need to work in the evenings. Sometimes it felt like the most time we had together was right after dinner. Jim would leave the table, and Sara gave us maybe ten minutes to just talk.

"It wasn't all bad," said Mike, "because we would be in the family room, which becomes our central place during the winter. I'd be reading the paper, and Trish would be working on something. So we were together in that sense. We're such good friends that if we're sitting in the same room it feels like we're doing something together. That helped."

Still, Trish agreed, it had been a difficult year. "With my old job I could stay up until midnight and it wouldn't bother me," she said, "but last year if I wasn't in bed by ten, I'd really have a hard time. So weekends became more important to both of us."

They concentrated on using that time to be together doing something they enjoyed in order to counter the pressures of the weekday routines. "We love to entertain and see friends," said Mike, "so we'd either go out or visit friends or stay home and do something special here. With a little baby you get tired of trying to find a sitter, so we'd feed Sara, put her to bed by 8:00, sit down, watch a movie on HBO, cook a nice little feast for the two of us, have a bottle of wine, and really enjoy the night. That way, if we couldn't go out, we'd make our Friday and Saturday night at home a real splurge."

"Even then," Trish added with a laugh, "we'd both fall asleep about 10:30. Then on Sundays we'd sit around, read the paper, and have a late breakfast. Nevertheless, some weeks it was terrible." Trish's new job and the stress she felt from trying to prove herself were taking their toll. Because he is also a teacher, Mike understood what was happening.

"I know how hard teaching can be," he said, "especially if you're a compulsive person. She's been trying to do the best job she can. She won't say 'In two years I'll be as good as a teacher who has taught ten years'—instead Trish says 'I want to be as good as a ten-year teacher *this year*.'"

Trish was aware of the family strain she was causing. "I told Mike that the thing that bothered me the most was coming home and having no patience with anyone. Finally, I said, 'I'll go back for one more year, and if this year's like last year I won't do it. I just don't want to come home and be that way.'"

"But a change came over her the day summer vacation started," said Mike. "She was a nice person again. In fact, in a few years I'd like to see both of us in rocking chairs, taking the summer off. So my plan is that if Trish does decide to keep teaching, I'll go back and get my master's, then she'll get her master's. Holding those degrees would make up the difference in salary between what we both make now and what I make as a tennis pro in the summer. When you teach, you can take your salary in ten months or spread it over the year, which is what we would do. That would make it financially feasible for both of us to take the summer off.

"It's funny how I've changed since my early twenties," said Mike. "I used to come home from work and want to go out and shoot baskets or play tennis. Now I find myself wanting to come home and sit down and see the baby. I want to be in my house. I

think the baby is so special. Ideally, we'd work part-time. I think
if we could do whatever we wanted," he said, laughing, "Trish
and I would opt to stay home all the time!"

## Playing Mr. Mom

The most extraordinary of the men who take on at least half of
the home and child-care responsibilities are those who choose
to do so full-time. Paul and Bruce are two fathers who devote
their days first to children and home, in that order, and second
to their outside pursuits. Both have struck a comfortable balance
that allows their wives to pursue their careers full-time. But
unlike the traditional homemakers of the past, men like Paul and
Bruce do not plan to remain full-time homemakers permanently.
Theirs is strictly a temporary solution, much like the arrangements decided on by the "full-time mothers" in Chapter Six.

Like those "full-timers," these dads are definitely pursuing
nonparenting, nonhousehold activities during the years while
they are at home full-time. Bruce is continuing to generate a
healthy income even though he works at his career as a literary
agent in the evenings and on weekends only. Paul is involved in
carpentry, computer accounting, and rental property investments that also contribute significantly to the financial well-
being of his household.

### Paul: "I'm June and She's Ward"
### (Except that June's a Whiz at Investing)

The spacious old Victorian home, painted forest green and
midnight blue with a bright yellow stripe racing along its patri-
cian trim, sits in the shade of the cottonwood trees on a quiet
old-fashioned street. White curtains move in a gentle, clean
breeze; a chatter of children's voices is heard as they step off the
front porch and head toward the school playground two blocks
away; a mouth-watering aroma of baking linzer torte fills the
kitchen with its handmade cherry cupboards.

It's a calm and typical summer morning in this little corner
of Utah. Paul spent the hour after breakfast helping eight-year-
old Beth with her spelling words while feeding four-year-old

Robby. Now the forty-three-year-old father sits in the rocking chair on the back porch that he screened in last year, his arms around his son, the two of them quiet, rocking gently. It's almost time to carpool, and, following delivery of Robby and two friends to nursery school, Paul must make ten phone calls to finalize a project for the PTA—of which he is president this year.

"Is my lunch ready?" calls Michelle, Paul's forty-three-year-old wife, as she pulls her station wagon into the drive, stopping between early morning rounds at the hospital and a full day of appointments at her office on the other side of town, ten minutes away.

"Yes," says Paul. "I wasn't sure if you wanted tuna salad or a sandwich, so I put both in. Don't forget the preschool picnic tonight—we have to be there by 6:15—and I volunteered you to grill."

"Okay," says Michelle, turning up a tanned, serious face for a quick kiss as he hands her the paper sack holding her lunch. Then off they go in their separate directions: she to her patients, he to their children and the house.

"She's Ward Cleaver and I'm June," said Paul with a wink, referring to the all-too-perfect television family in "Leave It to Beaver," as we started to discuss their daily routine.

"I'm an internist, an adult specialist," said Michelle. "I have a main office out in the community with about 2,000 patients, and I also head up one of our state institutes for the mentally retarded on a part-time basis. I have a six-person staff in my office, which I share with another physician. At the institute I directly supervise five other doctors and two nurses.

"What I sometimes find hilarious about my life with Paul," she added with a laugh, "is that I'm the one who won the 'Betty Crocker Homemaker of Tomorrow' award in my high school. But the only cooking I do is the charcoal grilling, because it's the only way I can be sure my meat will be as rare as I like it." But if she is scientifically minded, so, once upon a time, was Paul, the full-time dad, who attended one of the nation's top colleges as a science major and a National Merit Scholar.

Both Michelle and Paul have taken very different routes than might have been predicted for them in high school or college, which shows how the best decisions for the future are those that evolve from education, experience, and intuition. It also reminds us of how little we know from the beginning about what will be of greatest importance to us at later stages in life.

Michelle spent a decade, from her early teens to her early twenties, thinking she wanted to grow up and become a mother and a housewife—only to enroll in medical school at age twenty-four. Paul, in turn, was a gifted student in the sciences and math who realized late in his twenties that he hated the pressures and stress of work in an office environment. He worked as a carpenter and was part owner in a mini-storage business when they met. How these two people found each other and successfully fit together the puzzle pieces of their varied needs and goals shows the wisdom and courage it took to put their faith in spontaneity and in their own willingness to try the unknown.

Though they had attended the same college at the same time as undergraduates, they didn't really know each other well. Instead they both kept in touch with mutual friends over the years. So when these friends told Michelle, then an intern, that Paul had been in a car accident that put him in the hospital, she called him up to see if she might be of help to "a friend of a friend" from out of town.

"She called and we talked and we hit it off," said Paul. That was at Thanksgiving. I drove back to Michigan to see her at Christmas, then she came out to visit me in Utah during the winter, and we went on from there.

"I've always associated with fairly strong-willed women who have their ideas about what they want to do," said Paul, whose mother was the primary wage earner in their family when he was growing up, "so I was very comfortable with her plans to become a physician."

"At first, I thought of getting together with Paul as something just for fun," said Michelle. "I was in the midst of my residency. Also, I had already decided that if I were to have a relationship with anyone it would probably have to be a surgeon, because people who love medicine and want to work hard at it, like me, are pretty powerful personalities. It's hard to find someone who isn't threatened by that unless it's another doctor.

"That's why I figured that being with Paul would be very temporary. So I was relaxed about us from the very beginning because it seemed unlikely we'd ever want to be together. He lived in another part of the country, and he worked at something that was totally incompatible with my work. Immediately I'd thought, No future—just fun, and let myself fall in love, even though I thought it was only temporary.

"Then I found out he had just been in a relationship that had bombed out, and so had I. We got to talking about how we both wanted kids and wondering how that could ever happen since neither of us was remotely involved with anyone. That was the discussion one night.

"The next day Paul said, 'This is going to sound weird, but what if we thought seriously about being together—you be the doctor and I'll take care of the kids. I don't know if I can hack it. I think I can, and I wouldn't leave you if I couldn't and we had kids; we just have to agree that we might have to work out some other child-care arrangements if I can't do well taking care of them.'"

"I was cruising high at that point," recalled Paul. "I was handling my life well. I had a lot of confidence, and I thought, I can do any job. Sure, I'll stay home and take care of kids—the novelty appealed to me. But it wasn't carved in stone. We agreed I would try, and if it didn't work out we'd slip into more traditional ways. So I wasn't irreversibly committed.

"What we did know was that we definitely wanted kids, and this was a way that she could do it. What were her alternatives? The traditional thing for a female doctor to do is to marry another doctor, and then traditionally the female is subservient to the male's career ambitions. This left her a lot more free career-wise."

"It's true," said Michelle, "when you're a resident in internal medicine, you're so immersed in it that you can't imagine being anything other than a doctor. You eat, sleep, think medicine. And you can't imagine your practice being controllable. If I were less of a workaholic, I would have gone into residency for a field of work like dermatology, but I love being this kind of a doctor. I never imagined I'd enjoy anything so much."

Over the next year Paul made more than his usual trips to Michigan as Michelle completed her residency. Then they decided to take a road trip and seriously think over Paul's proposal.

Along the way, they made a prenuptial pact—this one to accommodate Paul.

"I definitely wanted an agreement as to where we would live," said Paul. "She had already signed a contract to work for a medical group in a suburb of Detroit, and she didn't want too many changes in her life at the same time. Michelle made the point that she was just starting to practice plus getting married, so she thought it would be wise to stay in one place. I agreed I would come back from Utah and spend one winter in Michigan, which I abhorred, and then we would move someplace in the American West. So I did my year—and then we moved."

The compromise was agreeable to Michelle, who understood the reasons for it. "Paul told me that living in Michigan would put all kinds of stresses on us because if he ever wanted to do anything other than raise kids it wasn't a great place to be doing the kind of building he does," said Michelle. "Not only is the building season limited in Michigan, but his knowledge of the building trade is here in Utah. He also felt it was important for him to have the option of being able to work more months of the year. So one of the conditions of our giving the child-care plan a try was to balance out the exchange by living where he wanted to live.

"We hashed all this out in August of 1978 while we were on that road trip," she said. "When we got back from our month together and were still speaking to each other, we decided we could handle anything and got married a week after our return." Their daughter, Beth, was born in 1980, shortly after the move west. Four years later they adopted a son, Robby. So far, Paul's plan seems to be working well.

Although Paul rarely does outside work on new projects, he and Michelle make it a practice to buy an older home every few years, completely redo the interior and exterior, then sell it at a significant profit and move. Paul is the designer as well as the contractor, if not the craftsman, for all the carpentry, plumbing, and wiring. This he does during the odd hours of his free time, which varies according to the ages and stages of the kids. They also own three other houses, which they rent out as investment properties and on which Paul does all the repairs.

Paul's day begins and ends like any full-time mother's—in semipredictable fashion: "My day breaks up constantly," said Paul, his exasperated but pleasant expression making it clear he is quite content. "First, I have the morning dance of getting everyone up, cooking breakfast, and fixing Michelle's lunch. That usually goes fairly smoothly. Robby's gone three mornings a week, and then he usually wants to have friends over or to be at a friend's house, so I either have other kids playing here or, if he's at someone's house, I feel that I should be on call in case the kids have a falling-out.

"During the day I'll run errands and try to get some work done on houses, although that gets shoved aside by the kids' schedules or book work since I take care of all our financial matters and pay all the bills.

"Around five o'clock Michelle calls from the office to give me an ETA—estimated time of arrival. The kids might have a snack around six, but we try to wait so we can all eat together. Dinner is generally six to six-thirty."

Their routine has varied only slightly since Beth's birth eight years ago, when Michelle took a six-week maternity leave and then returned to work full-time. "Sometimes I would take the baby out to the clinic to see Michelle," said Paul, "and it was a very easy way to go. When kids are little, they just eat and sleep and need to be changed, so I would work like crazy while Beth napped, and then I'd just have her along with me. I did all the cooking and grocery shopping, which was also easy since I'd been cooking for myself all my bachelor years up to the age of thirty-three—that was nothing new.

"Those first four years were a breeze, and the summer before we had Robby I got a lot of work done on our current house. Our kitchen is brand-new, and I made all the cherry cabinets. But when Robby arrived, work on the house slowed to a crawl because he's a very active kid who has needed a lot more attention than Beth. Or maybe it's having two kids, but it's been a lot more work."

Paul does most of the laundry, but the area of clothes management is where he and Michelle have an interesting arrangement. "Michelle takes care of her own wardrobe," he said.

"She does all her own wash and ironing, she buys her own clothes, and she's wardrobe mistress for the kids. That's how she keeps in touch with them. As hand-me-downs come to us from around the neighborhood, Michelle sorts them, patches any that need it, and puts them in the kids' drawers."

"Beth and I talk over what she wants to wear," said Michelle, who takes time every night to carefully lay out what the children will put on the next morning. Michelle, who has very specific ideas of where she wants what, is also in charge of cleaning the bedroom she and Paul share. That is the only housecleaning either one of them does in depth, as it turned out to be an area where they disagreed on "standards." Consequently, a compromise had to be negotiated.

"We have someone come in to clean." said Michelle. "That's because there is a difference in opinion—between his mother's ghost and my mother's ghost—on how clean things have to be. We found we were having these tremendous fights on Sunday afternoons because I would get into this 'I have to get some of this cleaned up' routine, which had to do with vacuuming the carpet and cleaning the top of the stove and getting the refrigerator straightened out—things I felt weren't getting done.

"Now we have a much better system, where Paul doesn't have to be concerned about those things. We have Debbie to help out. She is a wonderful, steady single mother who is going to college and comes at odd hours and cleans. This week she was here Tuesday, put in three hours, and I'm satisfied."

There are other concerns, of course. Michelle, for example, has had to relinquish the traditional role of mothering to Paul. "He is much more nurturing than I am, and I admit that," said Michelle. "Lots of times I'm not at home, or I may be there physically but I'm tense from work, and I'm just not a very verbal person. Paul gives a lot more that way."

"Yeah, I'm a lot more likely to cuddle the kids," agreed Paul with a gentle smile. He is a loquacious, witty man, extremely well read, whose busy manner and sharp attention to detail complements his wife's sometimes absentminded presence around the house.

Michelle has had a few pangs of loss as she has turned the care and nurturing of the children over to Paul. "I've had fewer guilt feelings than I thought I would," she said. "It's true I've missed some of the special moments in the kids' lives, but I've been around a lot of them, too, especially because we're to- gether full-time every weekend. But it's true, I'm not the one to go to school conferences and I'm not the one that they go to when they skin their knees. That's hard. They don't think to come to me to cuddle because they've always gone to their dad to be cuddled.

"It's not as bad as I thought it would be, because Paul really does a good job at that while I do other things for them. But Beth knows how to get me by saying 'You weren't here' when some- thing important happens. Or yesterday Paul asked me, 'You still think you'll be home by 6:30?' and when I said yes Beth chal- lenged me, saying, 'That's what you say!' She knew I'd run late, and she wanted me to know she resented that. She told her daddy to expect me at 7:00 because she had looked at my stack of telephone calls and dictation. She was right.

"There are times when Beth has told me, 'Sometimes I'm really mad at you for not being here,'" said Michelle. "I say, 'Okay, what should I do about that?' And then she'll say, 'Most of the time you're just fine and it's okay.' So I'll say, 'If you weren't mad at me for that, you'd probably be mad at me for something else, right?' She says, 'Yeah. I just choose that.' So we have an understanding, and my guilt level is pretty low," said Michelle.

"If I were a full-time mother, I might be as hard and de- manding as my own mother was—although she's mellowed and is a wonderful grandmother now. But I sincerely believe I'm doing the right thing and that my kids are better off with a softer father."

Of more serious impact on their relationship is the conflict that arises as a result of different energy levels and expectations between the two adults in the house. Yet they recognize their differences and approach them with dedicated efforts to under- stand each other and a strong commitment to work out the problems.

"My gripe is that nobody gives you any strokes," said Paul. "Payday is a stroke—not just to have the money to do things with; it's a sure sign that somebody considers you worthwhile. I don't have a payday. The kids aren't going to tell me, 'Gosh, Dad, you're doing a great job.' My wife will occasionally. She tries, but it doesn't occur to her very often.

"And she doesn't see me as doing very much, because often there doesn't seem to be much done at the end of the day," said Paul. "Michelle's a very energetic person. She does a tremendous amount of work. And I don't do as much as she does, but I do as much as most people do. Because I'm not as energetic as she, she sees me as a person who's not working as hard as he could. It's a constant source of disagreement."

However, it's one they do not ignore. "I tell her I keep plugging and get things done," said Paul. "I also point out that the children have not turned into monsters yet, that the house is in reasonable order, and so on. But this is in direct proportion to how haggard she is at the end of the day.

"Rather than get too excited about her complaints, we'll talk about it," said Paul. "We're on pretty equal terms because we're both strong-willed people. I see it as an advantage that she is not somebody I am going to beat down verbally, which I tend to do with other people. I'm never going to do that to her, and she's not going to do that to me. So we're well matched."

Michelle agrees wholeheartedly. She also sees the hazard of her profession in some of her behavior patterns around the house. "The kind of work that I do demands keeping ten balls in the air constantly, and on a bad day I am very likely to feel like three other things could have been accomplished," she said. "So if I still have three more things on my list to get done that evening, I'm rather intolerant of my partner sitting down and relaxing.

"It's interesting that it wasn't a problem until I went back to work after our first baby. That's when I started coming home and demanding 'x, y, and z,' and Paul would be overwhelmed by taking care of a new baby. I was awful. I'd be sitting there nursing—because that was my next job—and delegating from the chair. That's when we both recognized that, like a lot of men doctors out there, I had a tendency to bring my work habits home. All I need," Michelle grimaced, "are constant reminders.

"What has helped is that both of us were in long-term relationships before we got together, so we know we have to put a lot of effort into making our marriage work. Early on we agreed to no backbiting, no running to somebody else. Just work it out—so we talk. We just talk.

"Our only other problem that ever results from our less-than-traditional arrangement is a somewhat expected one," said Michelle. "It has to do with outsiders' attitudes toward Paul.

"Most people who deal with me as the go-out-of-the-house female don't see me as any kind of anomaly—it's Paul they think is odd. And so I feel like I have to protect him, which is something I'll do by steering the conversation into what some people might think are his 'real accomplishments,' like our investments or renovating the house, rather than talking about how wonderful our kids are because of him.

"Meanwhile, he isn't affected by that at all and much prefers to assertively state—when some doctor at a medical dinner asks what he does—'I stay home.' Then he'll expand on it, but he doesn't mind if they look sort of blank at first and then say, 'What else do you do?' That doesn't happen often and usually only around some of the men with whom I practice.

"Lots of families in our neighborhood have unusual balances between the parents," she said. "There are some where the dads are home quite a bit, although most of them are still rather apologetic about that and insist it's very temporary."

"One thing that's been interesting for me is my acceptance among my peers," said Paul. "I'm not really 'one of the girls,' but I think I'm accepted and I'm very grateful to the people in my neighborhood for how well they've accepted me. I joined a baby-sitting co-op about five years ago, and I'm obviously the first male member, yet it's been no big deal. That's great, because a lot of my daily activity revolves around the co-op. Then, too, I was elected president of the PTA, but that's a little different because several committee members are other fathers, so it's quite a natural combination of men and women working together for their kids. But that's different from how it used to be.

"I think—" Paul paused—"I've got an advantage over most wives. We do very few things in the medical community, but we do go to medical dinners, and I'm sure there are people who wonder just what I am—but I think I'm given a little more leeway than the average wife just because I'm male. In other words, they talk *to* me, not past me. Also, most people are discreet, and only occasionally will they say something, which is along the lines of 'That sounds like a pretty good deal—sometimes I wish I could do that.' But I can't imagine very many people actually doing it.

"On the other hand," said Paul, "it was interesting what happened last summer when we took a vacation trip with the children. First, I had a family reunion in Arkansas where we met a lot of people I expected to be very traditional and not very accepting of my arrangement. Then, a couple of weeks later, I had my college reunion, where I thought 'These are all liberal arts graduates that know that I'm a fellow of this college, and everything will be fine.' It was just the other way around!

"My family was quite supportive, while a lot of the males in my college class basically dismissed me when they found out what was happening. Women were interested—I had good conversations with women, and some of the men were fine, but a few of the men, especially the real successful ones, the ones who were into megabucks and high positions, could not relate. As soon as they found out that I was staying home, the ground opened up and I disappeared."

Fortunately, both Paul and Michelle feel confident about their lifestyle and find that their problems are vastly outweighed by the things that work right for them—including things that are problems for other couples.

One area where they have had no problem has been the management of the money Michelle brings in. Paul has taken over management of the bookkeeping for her medical practice as well as their personal finances—doing both with the assistance of a computer, which he has set up in their dining room.

"Basically I manage everything and check with Michelle from time to time to see if she agrees," said Paul. "We have no budgets and no guidelines. We work out of one checking account. Michelle writes a few checks in her check register, and from time to time I enter them into my check register, but I write 90 percent of the checks. She just writes a couple a month for spending money. One lucky part of our trade-off is that we're able to live in a house that's very cheap, since the mortgage payments come out of my business. Also, we agree that we want to retire early, so our long-range planning points that way. That was also something we discussed on the road trip we took before we got married."

"Frankly, there's so much money coming in now, especially because of the investments that Paul makes—more than I ever thought I was capable of making—that talking money with him is a source of pleasure," said Michelle, "never a matter of stress. Even with the local economy going bad, we're in terrific shape, and I can't tell you how many physicians lost heavily in the stock market crash. Paul has really done well steering us. For example, during that fatal October in '87 we were already out of the market. Paul had been reading the danger signals in August and pulled nearly everything out before it started down."

Indeed, it's Paul's work with their finances that has changed his ideas of what he wants to do in the future. "I'm envisioning that after the kids are both in school full-time, I'm going to want part-time work outside the home. Right now I'm thinking it may be something to do with accounting and computer programming. Robby will be starting kindergarten in another year, so it's going to be another two years before I'm ready to do it, however." By that time he's likely to have a million-dollar investment portfolio to show for a résumé—not bad for a house husband running the "home show" in a sleepy little Utah town. In the meantime, Paul's plan is working smoothly. It even allows the family to get away most weekends. They plan the weekend camping trips so that both the children can hike easily through the beautiful canyons and mesas that surround the region where they live.

"Almost every Friday, I take a half-day to pack everything and get food ready for the weekend," said Paul. "We think it's the glory of the one-income family that we can get away dozens of weekends a year, whereas our friends who are both working would have to pack Wednesday and Thursday nights, and just getting ready for the trip becomes too stressful. Nobody gets away as much as we do.

"Robby loves it when we can all sleep in the same space

under the stars. I think he and Beth may be the only kids who play house under the trees and the open sky. We plan to just backpack longer and deeper as the kids get older, because they love it, too.

"But we do it for more than just the kids," he said. "Michelle has a high-stress occupation, and she really relaxes when we go away. When we go camping for the weekend, we try to leave around eight on Friday. Michelle comes home from work, we have a leisurely supper, and then we put everybody in the car at eight and start driving. The kids are in their pajamas, and they fall asleep in the car.

"Along the way we talk—usually she's winding down. Generally we discuss the politics of her work more than the day-to-day care of patients. Government regulations or something happening in the hospital or among the other doctors. Or we'll talk about the house, the kids, our plans, the world, politics."

And when they get where they're going, not only is it a break for Michelle, but since most of the food is likely to be grilled, Paul gets a break from the cooking. And, of course, they share the time with the children.

"I'm pretty content," said Paul. "I've got somebody I respect intellectually and she respects me, and we have a lot to talk about, a lot in common."

"I lucked out here," said Michelle. "This is really great. I am very satisfied."

It's a typical scene in the new kitchen with the handmade cherry cupboards: Robby has no clothes on as he practices tying his shoes; Beth and her dad are searching madly for her shorts in a basket of laundry; and Michelle is on the phone giving orders for the treatment of a man who has a blood clot in his left leg after heart surgery.

Through the open window you can see the green cotton-wood trees, the roses in bloom, and wash hanging on the line next door. It's almost six o'clock, nearly time for the preschool picnic.

## Bruce: A Full-Time Dad with a Part-Time Career, Earning More Each Year

The spacious Georgetown apartment is quiet. The children are tucked in and the supper dishes put away. As the hum of late-night Washington, D.C., lulls the little ones to sleep, Sheila and Bruce complete the details of the day's work.

For thirty-four-year-old Sheila, it's time for a final look through edited copy. She is a senior editor on one of the nation's major newspapers. For thirty-four-year-old Bruce, it's a few precious moments at last to work on one of the literary properties he is developing as a book packager—a moment stolen from his busy day as a full-time father to five-year-old Brittany and three-year-old Tim.

Like Paul, Bruce combines his active at-home fathering and homemaking role with the career he had pursued before the children were born. Unlike Paul, who found that his work pace—and income—slowed during the children's early years, Bruce's income has continued to increase even though his work pace is definitely slower. The efforts of the early years have paid off. In fact, Bruce's annual income is greater than his wife's, although it is always difficult to predict what it will be and when it will arrive.

Sheila, whose career is the source of their regular, reliable paycheck, is torn between the demands of her work and her children, and she confessed that deep in her heart she wished the economics of life would make it possible for her to be home with the children, too. Yet she is quick to say she loves her job!

With the exception of Sheila's fluctuating urge to be a full-time mother, Bruce and Sheila's current arrangement has turned out to be a solution that is very comfortable for both of them. It was entered with almost unspoken agreement from both.

"Just before our marriage, I got a job as a writer for a national magazine, which is where I worked for ten years before I came to the paper," said Sheila. "After I went to the magazine, Bruce, who had been interested in literature, began to write for the magazine, too. Soon he quit his job at the bookstore and continued his writing from an office in our home. Then he began to agent and package books, also from home. That is how it's been since we got married.

"I think that the generation of women that I'm a member of went to college assuming we would have careers—not just jobs," said Sheila. "I was geared toward journalism from the time

I was in high school, and it was just a matter of getting a subject of expertise. I just assumed that I would work full-time, that I would grow in the job, which is exactly what I did.

"That first year or two, while we were getting to know each other, Bruce and I both felt intuitively that we should grow into our marriage a bit before we had a child. So we were married about two-and-a-half years, during which he was always at home writing or developing a book. By the third year of our marriage the timing just seemed right to try to have a family—and I got pregnant right away!

"Bruce was just finishing up his first book at that time, so we talked, and he said he would enjoy being at home with the baby," said Sheila. "That worked well for me because I was in a career where I was hoping to continue to move up. You do have fears that, if you stop, it's not going to be that easy to reenter. Meanwhile, he was in a very different situation because he was a committed freelancer at that point without a guaranteed, regular income. We had no health insurance except mine."

Certainly critical to Bruce's interest in being a nurturing at-home father is the fact that his parents made it clear to their children that they took great pleasure in raising them—while Dad worked days, and Mom worked nights. At the same time, his parents helped each other out in many ways, without regard for the "traditional" roles of mothers and fathers.

"My father always pitched in with the cooking and child care," said Bruce. "He even helped to care for my mother's mother, who was an invalid, as well as for my grandfather, who was not an invalid but eventually had to be put into a nursing home.

"Even today, my mother, who is sixty-seven and still working, will get down on the floor to play with our kids or take them on nature walks. Dad too is very active and takes great pleasure in having his grandchildren around."

And so it all fell into place that Bruce would be the parent at home. "It was very natural to us," said Sheila. "First, we shared the same strong sentiment that we would raise our own children. Then, it was just always understood that because Bruce worked at home he would raise our children. This means I have been able to stay in the marketplace where I really want to be, and he's at home where he feels very comfortable. We've never had any help at all."

Like many couples with well-developed equal partnerships, Bruce and Sheila have been willing to scale back their financial goals in order to have a more relaxed family life. In keeping with that mutual goal, they also pool their income.

"To me the idea of separate accounts is preposterous," said Sheila. "It speaks of some kink in the relationship. We don't feel that we need to have separate control. We have no problem mutually agreeing on what to do with our money. I think you need to have control only when you anticipate some sort of disagreement. We have none of those fears and never have."

But even if it is all "very natural" to them, neither takes their unique solution for granted. As you will see, both feel strongly that it works because they value each other as true and equal partners.

"I think that the ease of working out any unconventional relationship is in direct proportion to the strength of the relationship," said Sheila. "I don't think that people who have a very strong relationship even think about some of these things, because you know you'll find a solution—you have confidence in your ability to give and take as a couple. And you have the ability to let your feelings be known to your partner.

"I think when you have similar values everything works itself out. The two of you make it happen because you're united in your goals. Bruce and I have the same priorities in life—so it all works.

"I'd say that the only thing that we sometimes miss is sleep," added Sheila. "We were like any two people raising a child for the first time—we didn't know what was involved. It was more difficult than we expected."

"We had a couple of big surprises," said Bruce, who felt the impact even more than his wife. "The first was how little our daughter slept. We were expecting that newborns sleep twenty hours a day and take long naps. But Brittany's idea of a nap when she was an infant was half an hour!

"The other thing—and this may be a reflection on our

attitudes about parenting more than children in general—but I think that the totality of it, the all-inclusive twenty-four hours a day, with no break, is a surprise that you can't understand until it happens.

"We both felt it," said Bruce, "right after we got home from the hospital. Our first months of new parenthood were incredibly stressful—plus I was trying to finish up a book."

Sheila recalls the time vividly: "We'd read all these books that said that they slept eighteen hours, which they don't. You think that you'll have a lot of time, which you don't. Bruce had assumed that he'd work a little more part-time when our daughter was very new than was actually possible." They survived the big change, although not without some qualms. Sheila recognized the pressures Bruce was under, and she also admitted her own unhappiness with some parts of their plan even if the solution overall was the best.

"It became clear right away that the person who is at home makes a lot more immediate career sacrifices in the sense that you have to postpone what you're doing," she said. "For us it still made more sense for Bruce to stay home, because he wasn't stepping out of an office job where you must stay in the groove if you want to keep moving.

"On the other hand, I think it's sad we have to make an 'either/or' choice, because if you have the chance to stay home with your children, it's an incredible experience and it's something that I miss—it's just not practical for us both to do it. We simply couldn't afford it.

"Right now, if I feel a little bit deprived, it's because, if I had my druthers, I'd really like to stay home," said Sheila. "The question of having a third child is a tough one now that we know the work and time that's involved—as rewarding as it is. I feel like I don't have as much time as I'd like to spend with these first little ones, and that's what keeps me from having a third.

"If I knew that I could stay home and we could be comfortable financially, I think the idea would be much more appealing than it is right now. We haven't ruled it out, but we have kind of left it open," she said. "Right now our daily life is a strain. Bruce and I work hard to keep everything balanced. We have to put a lot of energy into it.

"I miss the children often," said Sheila. "Fortunately, I'm in a very flexible company, so if there's something important happening in school, I can take the time to go. But kids grow up so quickly, and every day there's so much development. I think the whole concept of quality time is a total fraud. I think that children want you to be with them for the very ordinary miracles that occur all the time. And they like the mundane parts of existence. They like going to supermarkets and playgrounds. They like incidental conversation. They're not always 'on' when you're there for them.

"When I get home at night, everybody's had a full day and they're sort of tired. They're not as fresh as they are in the morning or afternoon. So I miss a lot of their most energetic times.

"I compensate for that by feeling good that Bruce is with them, and he's the best possible other person to be there. He shares what's going on with them in a way that no one else could. He certainly observes and reports better than anyone because everything that happens with Brittany and Tim is much more meaningful to him than it would be to anybody else except maybe our mothers."

Bruce echoes his wife's words. He too feels that pull between family and career, although for him the role as daddy is still his paramount concern.

"I'm eager for the time when I'll be able to work more," he said, "but I see that as something that will come naturally. In September Tim will start nursery school and be gone from nine to noon five days a week. That's free time that I haven't had in five years!

"Yet I have never been a career-driven person, and I found my work as a writer and an agent later than some people do. I didn't really think of it as something one could do as a career until Sheila encouraged me—and eventually things worked out. I've struggled just as every other freelancer has, because it's very difficult, financially and otherwise, when you're first starting out.

"At this point in my life, in our lives, the children absolutely come first. We hold that value in an extreme—more than most people we know. I really love being with them all day, as crazy as it may make me, when everything has gone awry."

Bruce makes it clear that for him the satisfactions are enormous. "I have a relationship with my two children that I think is pretty unique," he said, his voice pleasant and direct. "First, because none of their little friends have fathers who are around all day; and second, I think I really devote myself to them. I may sound a little presumptuous, but I probably would find it more important to make sure that they're doing something that they're enjoying rather than my doing some errand that needs to get done. I often put off the practical stuff if we're at the playground and they're having a good time. Why spoil it? It's fun for me too. I get to get in the sandbox and dig!

"In some ways, that fun is what makes it difficult to consider having another child right now. All of the decisions that Sheila and I have ever reached have been mutually agreed upon, but they were decisions that were almost organic and unspoken. We knew when we first decided to live together that it was a mutual thing—we said so at the time.

"Then, getting married and having Brittany and deciding to do things the way we did was a very smoothly reached and internal kind of decision that was arrived at without a lot of debate or analysis. We felt that the time was right, and everything worked out. Similarly, when we felt it was time to have a second child—almost to the day we both said, 'Let's start thinking about it, and let's do it.' It was definitely planned and thought out, but we arrived at it mutually and at the same time. I think that a decision to do anything else, whether it's having another child or making a major move in terms of our lifestyle, will happen that way."

Meanwhile, their daily life has its comfortable, steady routines. "The morning is spent getting the kids up and out of bed, dressed and fed, and off to school," said Bruce. "Brittany gets to school by nine, and then Tim and I are on our own for a while. We usually put in a few hours at the local playground or do the errands that have to be done.

"That may include some grocery shopping, although like most city folk we are 'take out and eat out' people more than most Americans. I do all the weekday cooking while Sheila takes over on the weekends. So some days I may take Tim to the fruit market and the bread store and the other shops. Then we come home late in the morning and have some lunch. After that we hang around the house for a while, which means doing some kind of playing here—anything from arts and crafts to reading books to wrestling on the floor or fighting monsters with swords. Then, mid-afternoon, we head out to pick Brittany up.

"You see," said Bruce with a sigh, "Tim does not nap. He may be only three years old, but even last year his naps were only in the stroller on the way to pick up his sister—and now they are entirely gone. After we get Brittany, she might have a ballet class or something like that. Often I take the two of them to the playground or to the library. Brittany has a couple of friends with whom she has 'play days,' so sometimes she'll go off and I won't have her in the afternoon, or conversely, I'll have a third child over here.

"Although I take the children to lessons and play groups, Sheila tries to go along on doctor visits and teacher conferences, especially the latter, because I see the teachers more often than she does and it gives her a chance to touch base and ask questions.

"One of our luxuries is that we do have someone come in once a week to do the major housekeeping," he added. "As far as basic picking up or cleaning up goes, we share most of that. I do the laundry; Sheila organizes the closets."

He does set aside time for himself: "I really have to squeeze in time at night after the kids are in bed in order to get some work done," said Bruce, "and I do a lot of work on the weekends when Sheila is around. If I'm involved in a project, it isn't unusual for her to take the kids out for the entire day. Or, if I need to get something done on a weekday, I'll drive them to a relative's house, and they'll spend the day so I can concentrate on whatever projects I'm handling. Once in a while I'll have a sitter come in in the morning for a few hours, but that's rare—generally the weekdays are exclusively kid time."

Sheila's turn is at night. "Because I'm home at night, I usually take care of the bathing and getting the children into bed," she said. "If we have a choice between cleaning up after

dinner and handling the baths, I usually take over the baths. I
think Bruce prefers the dishes because he's talked to the kids all
day. I'm sensitive to how he's feeling. I know on the one hand the
level of his conversation during the day has been joyful because
it's so simple and wondrous and unpredictable, but, on the other
hand, it's not exactly intellectually stimulating. His day has a lot
of playground time, a lot of mothers, and the conversations are
focused on children.

"On Saturdays I do things with the children while Bruce
works. In the last couple of years he has tried to adjust his work
so that he can still be productive and creative and yet continue
to be responsible for the children. He shifted from writing,
which was keeping him out of the house too much doing research, into literary agenting and packaging.

"That has worked out extremely well, as he's sold about
twenty books. This is work you can do pretty much by mail, and
Bruce has been quite successful. He doesn't solicit writers—
instead, he creates books, then finds the people to write and
publish them, so his job is putting the two together. I think you
can say," said Sheila with obvious pride, "that we've deliberately
adapted the contour of our lives the past couple of years to the
children—and it is working out beautifully in terms of our
careers."

All in all, Bruce and his family are very happy. The kids are
thriving, Sheila's career is thriving, and Bruce, whose career is
also thriving, clearly enjoys his role as an at-home dad. "I get a
lot of people who ask, 'Are you baby-sitting today?'" said Bruce.
"I take pleasure in saying, 'No, this is what I do—every day.' It's a
simple mistake for someone to make, but it still shows that most
people think if a man is with the children it's because the
mother is doing something else at that moment. So it's still an
unusual thing. But I'd certainly not say it's freakish or taboo.

"Women, in particular, have been very supportive," he said,
"which reminds me of a funny incident that happened when
Brittany was young. We were going to the pediatrician on the
bus—she was about three months old—and there was another
father with a small child nearby. We started to share some
anecdotes about our babies. This woman was listening and

laughing, and finally she said, 'I really enjoyed this—I haven't seen two men talk about babies in my whole life, and it was fun.'"

## Quiz: Can Your Man Really Make It as a House Husband?

The *idea* of staying home with the kids is often more appealing than the reality (as many women know). Take this quiz to see if your husband really could take primary responsibility for the home.

1. The man in your life loves to:
   a. go big-game hunting, drive a Corvette, and read old Henry Miller novels for the grace of the language.
   b. grill chicken, coach your son's basketball team, and meet the challenge of a tough business deal.
   c. spend three hours on a favorite recipe, watch Mr. Rogers with the kids, and give you a back rub.

2. If you and your sweetheart both work, but had to take a severe financial loss because his company was sold and his position eliminated, he might:
   a. need counseling to cope with feelings of failure.
   b. be willing to take over the homemaking and baby-sitting temporarily in order to save money while looking for a new job.
   c. consider staying home full-time to take care of the kids and the house, even if you had to scale back your lifestyle to accommodate the loss of one income.

3. It's a Sunday night and the barbecue you had been invited to has just been canceled. Your husband says he would like to:
   a. watch the baseball game on TV in the family room while you feed the kids.
   b. get caught up on the bills, brush the dog, and help you put the kids to bed.
   c. curl up with you, a glass of white wine, a new CD—and just chat for a couple of hours.

4. Your husband works full-time, but you know he's unhappy at work. When you receive a big raise and promotion, he:
   a. gets furious and says men are discriminated against in the workplace today.
   b. sends you a big bouquet of flowers, then signs on to work overtime all month.
   c. resigns his position, plugs in the Cuisinart, and sends you off to work with his delicious tarragon chicken salad in your "lunch pail."

5. The man you love:
   a. finds his mother a tedious woman to be around.
   b. goes fishing with his dad once a month; every once in a while they invite you or his mother to go along.
   c. makes sure to call his mother once a week for an update on what's new in her life.

6. The man you are married to understands that:
   a. you are in charge of the children—he resents it when you ask him to help out.
   b. the woman is the primary caretaker of children, although he will pitch in on the weekends.
   c. you aren't cut out to be a Cub Scout den mother, so he spends more time with the kids, and even organized a play group for the youngest.

7. The man you are living with:
   a. makes it clear that Thursday night is his night out with the guys from the office.
   b. tries his best to let you know when he has to work late and can't get home in time for dinner.
   c. sits down with you every Sunday night to be sure the household expenses have been paid and to schedule the weekly dinner menus. He also makes a list of the groceries he needs to buy this week and double-checks to be sure you know you are doing the laundry.

8. During the last year the man you love was more likely to:
   a. buy himself a new fishing rod.

b. sweep you and the kids off to a long weekend at the lake, even though you found it hard to relax because you had a major project due at work Monday.

c. select and purchase, after checking your opinion, two new pieces of furniture for your home.

*Scoring*

Give yourself 5 points for every (c) answer, 3 points for every (b) answer, 1 point for every (a) answer.

*Totals*

8-12—You've got yourself a traditional kind of guy. My condolences.

13-23—This man is pretty good at sharing, and you have a good chance of becoming truly equal partners, but I doubt he'd be happy at home full-time. You may both be going through changes and unsure what your roles should be. Stay in close touch with each other.

24-35—This man could be happy at home, but you might want to explore work he can do from home as well.

36-40—Congratulations—this guy is Mr. Mom! I hope you're emotionally strong enough to let him take over the home front while you pursue your career. If you'd *both* rather be home, try switching off every few years.

# How to Make It Work

Set up a weekly conference time when you are both likely to be rested and free of regular responsibilities. Review the week and how it went for both of you. He should listen to your office exploits, and you should pay close attention to what happened at home. Review your finances and update each other on new sources of income as well as current bills.

Consider whether you need to reassign tasks. Does either of you need more time alone? Does either of you need more ready cash?

Finally, go do something together, just the two of you. And when you get home . . . if I have to tell you what's next, you and your spouse need a long vacation.

# 8
# How to Fit Your
# Puzzle Pieces Together

I t has been said that one gains nothing if one risks nothing, and clearly this is true: elderly people interviewed at the end of their lives rarely regret anything they did but have considerable regret for what they did not do.

It's easy to be intimidated by change. But as you've seen in reading the stories of the women in this book, change and the personal growth that it generates are well worth the effort—and sometimes even the pain required. No one ever said that putting together the life you want would be easy! It does help, however, to consider this challenge the greatest adventure of your life. It's not a storybook adventure, of course, but a real adventure, with risks you'll be surprised to find you can live with and rewards far greater than you ever imagined. It's an adventure well grounded in reality. By this I mean there are two kinds of people in this world: those who believe in happy endings and those who do not. Only those who do not believe in happy endings have a chance at balancing their split ambitions.

The others are deluded. The woman who thinks all will fall into place once she has married the right man is as misguided as the woman who thinks that once she has been promoted to senior management with its high salary and fabulous perks all her problems will ease. These are women who mistakenly think that life reaches one happy resolution and just stops there. How wonderful if it did, but it doesn't. All the difficulties of life that lie in wait for each of us—realities that occur independent of our education, our personality, our good spirits and good intentions—underscore the basic fact that life is a continuum with only one certainty: change.

The wise person understands there is no comfortable cushion of closure to be counted on—ever. How we handle that reality reflects not only the kind of person we are but the kind of person we will become. The woman who believes in happy endings only to find herself divorced and on her own someday (and quite surprised at how quickly and cruelly it seemed to happen to her) is all too likely to become a bitter, unhappy person, wondering why life treated her so badly. She doesn't realize that she made the choice to close her eyes to the fact that nothing in life is permanent—no spouse, no career, no lifestyle.

The woman who doesn't take anything for granted, on the other hand, meets the exact same challenge with energy and the drive to tackle the problem, to turn bad news into good, to push beyond a divorce, for example, to a new and better kind of life. She is the kind of woman who views the future not as a magic place where you land after a big wedding and settle in one comfortable spot while the heavens rain down presents and babies and happiness forever, but as a stage with a never-ending series of acts—happy, sad, serious, funny, frantic, slow, easy, difficult—through which you evolve, sometimes with one partner, sometimes with a new partner, sometimes alone. She is the kind of woman you want to be. She is a survivor and an optimist.

She sees a rough experience in life as simply that—something to be expected and not a reflection on her own value. She also views it as a temporary situation and one sure to change for the better. She knows that there will be days when everything seems right and life moves ahead with giant steps and that there will be other days when everything seems to backslide and all progress seems blocked. She doesn't look at the backsliding as failure but as one stage, an anticipated stage, in working toward an ideal balance. This is the kind of person who believes that life—and love—lies in the *process* of living and doing.

## The Ultimate Risk

To be a serious player in the adventure we call life, you have to be willing to go to almost any length to get what you want. You compromise only in the ways in which you get what you need, not in whether or not those needs are met.

Claire, thirty-eight, is an example of a woman who knows what she wants and is sure to get it. A prominent real estate investment analyst in Chicago, she is married to an architect her age who, for years, has taken care of their child and supervised the house while she far outearned him. For years they had a "perfect" life, but now she wants more.

Claire wants to pull back on their lifestyle. She wants more time with her child and less time at work. She wants more say in how decisions are made regarding the house and spending. She'd like to relocate and is willing to cut her salary in half in order to gain more autonomy. Her husband was at first resistant to change in their routines. He had been the nurturing parent and the primary homemaker. But he listened to her needs. Her request for "more room" at home came as his firm's project schedule meant more demands on his time. Slowly they moved toward a new balance of responsibility and power between them.

Claire and Alec have made some changes. They've traded off, after a decade, and she's handling their finances for a change, while he's taken over the cooking. That's helped some. But Claire still feels she has a lot to work out and has begun to get counseling. She told Alec that divorce is highly likely when one member of a couple goes for counseling and gave him the option of joining her. To her surprise, he did.

Claire is still not sure where her life will take her, but she knows she won't settle for anything but the *right thing for her*. "I highly suspect that I'm going to join the statistics of women who are dropping out of male-run corporations like mine," she says. "And I'm not sad. I feel like I've learned a lot from my job. And I have people who are begging me to stay in because it's been such a long struggle to get women to the top at this company. But I have to ask myself, 'Why?'

"Even though one reward is helping other women, that isn't at the core of what drives me to work and what I want out of life. I don't want to sacrifice my life just to have influence! I'm more interested in taking the next step to see if I can find a more personal balance. I want richer rewards for me as a person. I've been giving my body and mind and soul to a corporation for years. And I want to take back control. I've given over so much of the control of our family life to Alec that I felt adrift emotionally. Now that is changing."

As she has proven once in her career and now in her personal life, Claire is willing to live the questions. And so she says, quietly, decisively—to her colleagues and to Alec—"Can we work this out? Because if we can't . . . I'm willing to walk."

Two months after we talked, she did walk—out of her company and into her own consultancy, to which she will devote three days each week. To her great surprise, her earnings will remain the same. Meanwhile, her relationships with Alec and their young son have grown deeper and more emotionally involved. You can see it in her face and hear it in her voice— Claire is a happy, excited woman.

# Partnering

We've already looked at the many ways in which couples have worked out complex work and personal issues. But the fact remains that you can't have the equal partnership that makes it all possible unless your spouse or lover is willing to play the game too.

## *What If My Partner Won't Cooperate?*

Not all of us are fortunate to have a partner who shares our goal of an equal partnership. Some husbands—and wives—don't want a new balance. They don't want to change the way things are. What do you do then?

Please recognize that you are likely to "push" your relationship no matter how little or how much you do. But you wouldn't have read this far in this particular book if you were not anxious for some change.

Before I present your options, let me remind you of your basic rights, which are necessary for everyone's happiness:

*You have the right to tell your partner what you need and why.*
In my first marriage I needed the self-esteem that I gain from my work. The man I was married to did not see our marriage as one that could include my career, and so we separated and divorced. Today I look back at that marriage not as a failure, but as one in which we both grew to become better people with other partners. And I was right—I still need my work as my main source of feeling good about myself. The man I am now married to admires my accomplishments and has a vested interest in my continuing to work: we need both our incomes to maintain a moderate, middle-class lifestyle.

*You have the right not to give in to unreasonable demands.*
If you are in a relationship that allows for one partner's future to be enhanced at the sacrifice of the other's, that is not fair. In today's world, with all the opportunities for women and working families, it is highly unrealistic as well. Your future deserves the same opportunity and protection as your partner's.

Meredith, whose story you read earlier, was concerned with her husband's heavy drinking. "I will leave if you don't stop," she finally said. He agreed to attend AA meetings for a while, then he came home one night and told her, "I like drinking. I plan to keep drinking." He never thought she would do it, but within a month their divorce was granted. She arranged for joint custody of their children, rented a much smaller home, started back to school full-time, and was able to find a sitter to come in. She never thought she could do it, but she did. She feels good about herself, and her children are thriving. She is also engaged to be married—to a man who doesn't drink.

*You have the right to mutual respect and love.*
If your partner will not listen to your needs and consider working toward a compromise between the two of you, then you are not being shown the same respect that you are offering. You must have respect from your partner so you can offer the same and feel right about it.

Each of us has the right to be loved as much as we love. If love is caring about someone else as much as you care about yourself, then the partner who balks at recognizing your needs and refuses to help you achieve what you want in life may not love you. You must ask yourself why you would stay with a person who doesn't love you.

I know some of the "whys." Many of us are afraid we can't make it on our own. Some of us worry about what our families and friends will say. And certainly we worry about the effect a separation or divorce may have on our children. I encourage you to go back and reread the stories of people like you in this book—women who did not seem to have enough money to make it through a divorce, like Meredith; women who worried about the effect it would have on their children, like Laura; women who worried that they just couldn't make it on their own, like me.

You can do it. The first year is difficult because of all the uncertainty, but five years later you will look back with confidence and pride at finding your own way. The key to surviving a divorce is to stop worrying about what will go wrong and concentrate on how to handle the problems at hand. Go step by step, thinking of each not as a final solution but as "evolving" toward a better way. Month by month, things get easier. Chances are quite good that along the way you will meet another person who is willing to be your equal partner.

But before you take such a big step, consider the following: Have you been clear about your needs? Have you tried choosing the easiest of the changes you would like to make in your relationship and given the two of you at least three months to test that change? If your relationship is shaky, give yourself six months or a year to test the new balance. Remember, as a couple you are unique, with an individual set of concerns. What works for others may not work for you. Do it your way, on your own schedule.

Have you been firm about your intentions by following through with what you think you need? Have you said, "I will do such-and-such if you will do such-and-such?" Have you followed through? When you stop doing more than your fair share, for example, your partner may wise up quickly. (Note: This works well with children, which means it ought to be even more effective with adults. However, you must be careful to avoid saying "I told you so" or making any other belittling remarks. Simply point out that the exchange will work when you both do it.)

Have you shown appreciation for the little things that do go well between you? If your partner makes some caring gestures, even if it isn't what you want, do you see them, recognize them, and tell your partner that it makes a difference?

Have you tried marital counseling? Many, many couples find that a marriage counselor or a therapist who specializes in family therapy can help them begin talking to each other again, can help them find better ways to negotiate the changes that each may want to make. Also, many companies pay half or more of the cost of such services. Please check this out, as it could make a tremendous difference for you.

Remember, the best relationships happen over years, not overnight. Time heals many bad feelings. My guiding rule is this: If you can get your partner to make one small change, you may be able to win more eventually. Give yourself plenty of time and keep trying. I know it's tough, but it's worth it.

Remember the story of Lillian and Palmer, who did not enter a true egalitarian relationship until Palmer's retirement and Lillian's return to work? You may decide that the right time to make a major effort to balance your split ambitions will be in the years ahead and that now is only the time to start—slowly. If you give your partner a year in which you try together to make some changes, you may be pleasantly surprised. At least you will know you gave your relationship a chance.

## *When Nothing Works*

For some of you, nothing may work. You may have to face the fact that you married the wrong person. Well, lots of us did. Divorce is difficult, but it isn't the end of the world.

To counter the feelings of fear and anxiety that such a major change can precipitate, I suggest you make a list of the worst things that can happen if you choose to consider a divorce. Opposite each "worst," write a response. For example, if one "worst" is that you will be very low on money, is the response "get a job"? If the worst is needing to move to another house, is the response "rent for a time"?

As you look over your list of "worsts" and your responses, you may find the prospect not quite so frightening. Most people do. Just facing what you feel frightened by is often eased by naming the terror. The very fact that you can put your finger on what you fear reduces its power to harm you.

If you are going to consider divorce, you must plan. Think hard about every part of your life and write down a plan for your daily routines, which should include how you will pay for food and housing and care for your children. Think about your financial resources. Will you need to find a job or look for a better job? Start now. Think about your emotional resources. Will your family and friends help? Talk with those you trust and share your feelings about the future. You may be quite surprised by the people who will help out.

Most important, if you are considering divorce, seek out professional help from a lawyer and a therapist. This is a time when you need to be strong. Strength comes from knowing your rights, feeling in control of your legal matters, and having someone to help you when your self-esteem is battered, which usually happens during a divorce.

## *When Even Divorce Is Out of the Question*

A few of us are bound into relationships that are enormously difficult, and yet, for personal reasons, divorce is out of the question. If that is your situation, I respect your ability to recognize it. I hope there are some changes you can make that will help you feel better about the situation. I encourage you to review all possible options, however, and keep looking for new ones. Very often the best options come disguised as unusual choices or opportunities—you have to try them before you know exactly how right they are for you. Keep your eyes open and remember that you do have choices. If you choose to remain in your relationship, you need to know why. Even if it is impossible to escape a difficult situation today, remind yourself that life may change things for you—and your prospects tomorrow may be quite different. Stay aware and be ready to make the changes and take control of your life when the time is right.

## *When You Think You've Got the Right Guy but Are Not Sure About the Details*

By now it should be pretty clear to you that you can't balance love, work, and motherhood by yourself. Fortunately, if your lover is consciously willing to be your equal partner in love and life, or you think the two of you can work out some reasonable compromises, you're more than halfway there. Following the seven steps that come next should start you on your way.

### *Step One: Commit to breaking the rules*
Once you decide that you want to be the kind of person who recognizes that life has some curves to throw at you, you aren't likely to be surprised by much. That immediately enhances your everyday feelings of security. You are prepared for surprise; therefore, you are prepared to find ways to control change. Your pride and satisfaction come from meeting the challenge, not from avoiding it.

Making it all work in your relationship is a bit more complicated, whether you are single or married, with or without children, working part-time, full-time, or currently at home. In order to do it, you need to take time with your partner, or future partner, to establish the basic attitude you must share.

Start by thinking of yourselves as experimenters, as people who are choosing to step beyond the old rules. Agree on a willingness to try new ways of doing things—between the two of you, with your families, and in the workplace. This will open your thinking to new options. In fact, if you become bogged down at times, it may help to remind one another that you have only one rule to follow, and that is *to break the rules*.

Give yourself permission to do this by degrees. As you begin, you may feel most comfortable testing small changes, new balances between just the two of you. As you gain confidence in each other's flexibility, you can make greater changes and extend them beyond yourselves—into your job situation or for longer periods of time. A good example is the husband who takes over the cooking and grocery shopping for a month while his wife completes a work project, only to find he really likes it and would be happy cooking all the time if she will take over handling the bills.

*Step Two: Try new options*
Reread your notebook, if you've been keeping one as you read, and try jotting down the options that appeal to you. Put those that seem comfortable and most likely in one column, those that are provocative but unusual in another. What may seem to be an unusual option today may fit well next year. Keeping it in your notebook ensures against losing any of your good ideas. Now, on a page close to your options, list your assets. Break them out into three columns: things you already balance well together, things you do best, things your partner excels at. These should range from your income-producing abilities to your domestic and child-care skills. When you have completed that, add two more columns: things you each want to do better.

Review these columns and mix and match your options and your assets until you are both happy with the possibilities. Don't forget the possibility of thinking of your options as temporary trade-offs: e.g., do it one way for six months, then reverse roles.

Consider this to be a permanent, ongoing activity for the rest of your life; now that you've started to look for new ideas, don't stop. You'll find this to be invigorating, anyway.

Now, review the options you have researched. Pick four. From those, choose two that you will implement this year, two for next year. Ideally, you will both participate in this selection. If not, make the choice on your own and see if you can begin to interest your partner in participating with you by following the next step, which should encourage his interest.

*Step Three: Seek out new ideas and resources*
The next step in expanding and opening up the boundaries of your daily life, both at home and at work, is to reach out to all sources for new ways to do this. You want information and insights about a changing world that is affecting your own life. This book is a starting point, and other books and stories in newspapers and on television may help as well. The best resources, however, are all around you: other people who are trying new balances may be found among your friends and colleagues at work or friends of friends.

Observe how others are doing it. If possible, ask for specifics: what's working, what isn't, what kind of child care they have, and how much it costs. What kind of approach did they take at work and what was the response? How long did it take them to make their balance work? You gain confidence in making your own changes when you know others are trying, too. Their solutions may not be right for you, but they will encourage you to think in ways that will help you find a better and unique balance.

Whatever you do, do not ignore or hesitate to investigate unusual solutions. You never know where you will find an idea or part of an idea that will work for you. These days especially, new opportunities come in many disguises. A turndown of a request for a shared job may lead to a better part-time position; a husband's reluctance to share child care may mean he's willing to take over housecleaning duties instead.

Whatever it is, the unusual option may be the best. Believe

me, no solution is too unusual as a starting point if you and your partner are willing to consider and compromise somewhere in between the usual and the unusual.

### Step Four: Be patient

Don't begin to try your new options without giving yourselves permission to fail. Success is not doing it right the first time. Success is allowing time for the two of you to evolve into the right balance. It may take two tries; it may take twenty tries—the satisfaction when it finally works is always greater the harder you've tried. Just as veteran athletes use one season's failures to spur the next season's victories, couples merging their split ambitions make every attempt at balance count by viewing their failures as equally or more important than their successes, because it is through our failures that we all learn the most. Those of us who experience these failures, while acknowledging that we're working for better solutions, also grow closer because of the hard times we experience together.

Another lesson to learn from sports enthusiasts is known as "learn to love the plateau." Developing a physical skill means working hard for long periods of time without seeming to get anywhere. This is true of anything in life. Life does not move from peak to peak; most of us spend most of our time on plateaus where things improve slowly. We may find we're doing something wrong, or we may be doing it perfectly right—it's just slow going. But knowing that we all have plateaus as we move cautiously forward is sure to soothe your anxieties and inspire your courage. Remember that sometimes we experience the greatest difficulty just before everything works out.

It may be a good idea not to start with your toughest balancing act. Begin with the easiest one. Give yourself time to work into the best balance. In fact, you may decide, as you initiate your first option, to establish a "three-month test plan." This means you will live with this option for a good three months unless it proves terribly difficult. During this time each of you will go through a series of adjustments. After three months you can incorporate your second option. Test that, too, for three months. Now use the remaining six months of the year to smooth out any difficulties you may encounter. This gives you plenty of time to reach a level of familiarity with new routines and responsibilities before adding another option to your family dynamic. Don't be surprised if this is as much as you can handle at this time.

Three months is a good experimental period for work options especially. One new mother, on returning to her job after a three-month maternity leave, told me she was hesitant to commit to a flexible-hours option at work because she wasn't sure it would work for her. "Ask them for a three-month trial," I suggested, knowing her supervisor was likely to be a little uncertain, too. "That way they will feel they have an opportunity to see how it works, and neither of you will feel permanently committed until you've worked out the kinks." The identical approach can be used by couples testing out new balances within or outside their relationship.

*Step Five: Learn how to listen to each other*
Partners in a healthy relationship listen to each other on matters great and small. Everything about each other counts. You have a greater need than ever to listen to each other if you are thinking about a change in how you share your life together.

I recommend you set aside fifteen minutes a day to check in and see how things are going with each other, then aim for at least an hour alone together each week in which you do nothing but go over finances, work schedules, children's activities, etc. If you can, make this a time away from home and when you are both feeling good. If you are stressed from overwork or a particular crisis, put off the discussion for when you are both rested and calm.

If you have just launched a major change, such as a new child-care situation or a new job, this will be a critical juncture at which to take time to be together one-on-one. Be sure to give each other time to say what is working and what is not working. The essential attitude to have during a time like this is not to worry about what can go wrong, but rather to focus on how difficulties can be handled. This means that when you try a new balance and it doesn't work, don't just drop it and move on, but talk it over and see if you can pinpoint what element didn't work. Remember that the seed of every new solution lies in the previous failure—gaining an insight into your shared experiences is just as important as the mutual willingness to break the rules. By "insight" I mean focus on the specifics of what happened, what didn't happen, how you each felt about it, and what you each think needs fine-tuning or complete reworking.

Don't try to rush each other or yourself. Instead, agree on a pace that is comfortable for both of you. If going full-steam, such as working full-time with a young child to care for, is just too much to handle, then cut back to part-time work and feel good when you have a mid-level balance. Again, if you acknowledge the value of doing it at your own pace, you won't penalize yourself for choosing a compromise that allows you to enjoy both work and family; you will see it as a choice you make for deeply personal reasons unaffected by outsiders' opinions.

If one of you finds some part of your balance isn't working, say only that. Don't feel as though you must defend or justify the failure; instead review the practical aspects tnat weren't right. The fact is that if a particular change doesn't work for one of you, it won't for the other. Try a new approach. The essential dynamic to keep in mind during this time is this: you are not solving a problem—you are *evolving* toward a better balance between you.

Appreciation is another key to succeeding here. This means that you should *each devote equal time* to listening to and discussing what is working well, in addition to addressing the problem areas. Plan ahead. Before your discussion, choose compliments for your partner that will be meaningful and relate directly to the changes you are both making. Share these in detail, then listen for compliments for yourself and your actions.

If you find you are listening too much to problems, then ask for time for the two of you to focus on the benefits and the fun side of what you're doing. You'll be surprised at the effect that has. I recently took a skiing lesson and told the instructor I was worried about ice. In fact, skiing had ceased to be fun for me because I spent all my time on the hill looking for the dangerous patches. "Stop looking for the ice," said the instructor. "The minute you point your nose at an icy spot, you'll end up there. Instead, watch for the good snow. Keep your eye on the good snow, and that's where your skis will take you." He was right. The same is true for personal problem solving. Look for the "good snow" between you, and you'll find feelings of warmth and happiness. So, end your listening sessions with the good news.

Stay alert to two warning signals as you listen. One is the masking of complaints about one thing with a complaint about another. If your partner is criticizing how you fold the morning paper, that may not be the real problem. The real problem may be that you aren't doing your share in the morning. Most of us can recognize such "masked problems." When you do, the best approach is to handle it directly—"I know you think this is the problem, but maybe there's something else to it. Let's talk about it. . . ." It may take several tries to get the real problem on the table, but keep after it.

The other danger area is listening to outsiders who may be affected by changes you're making and find them unsettling. These can be family members or good friends or just acquaintances. Do not listen to them. The very fact that people try new options can make others feel insecure, jealous, or threatened. Make up your mind not to listen to anyone who tells you "it can't be done." If it is your boss, just be patient and keep coming back with new options. He (or she) will have his (or her) guard down one day and be willing to reach the first compromise with you. You can keep from letting the "tyranny of expectations" sabotage your efforts if you remember that almost every couple in this book has had some negative comments made to them at some time—most often by their colleagues at work. Tough as it sounds, ignore them. You'll be glad you did.

How you handle the conflict that is sure to surface between you will also make a big difference. This is an important area for couples who wish to be equal partners and establish a good balance between them: they must be able to fight well. A good fight, by the way, is conducted the same way that a savvy salesperson convinces a tough customer to buy a product: "I understand you don't want to buy this," says the salesperson, "but can you tell me why?" Then, as the customer details every objection, the salesperson agrees with the validity of the points made and offers new information or compromises with a better price on the product. That is how a couple should fight.

You should both be able to express your anger freely, yet not let your angry feelings get out of control. The best way to do that is to decide first what is the best time for you to fight. Some couples feel better confronting the problem when it occurs, even if it means doing so when others are around. "Sure, our kids see us fight," said more than one father in this book. "They also see our fights resolved, which is very important." Other couples are more comfortable setting aside a later time when they can be alone to fight.

I hasten to point out, however, that there is not one couple in this book that doesn't fight at some time. They have, however, all arrived by different routes and over varying periods of time at the same ground rules:

• Both partners feel free to express their anger.
• Each one knows how to take the time to listen, question what isn't understood, acknowledge the validity of their partner's anger, and understand the reason for the anger.
• Both partners can resolve their anger by reaching a compromise.

If you and your spouse have consistently found it impossible to disagree without ending in unresolved screaming matches, you may need to consider marriage counseling. Sublimated or unspoken anger is the most difficult problem to straighten out between two people, especially if you have reached a point where one of you cannot listen to the other at all, does not hear what the other has to say but rather hears only what you "want" to hear, or erupts in uncontrolled anger.

Counseling is difficult but rewarding for many couples. You will note that several couples in this book sought counseling when they had reached an impasse in dealing with their problems. In choosing a counselor, I suggest you talk to friends who have had positive experiences with a therapist and ask for a reference from your family physician. If you live close to a college or a university, the student health office usually has a list of recommended therapists in your community, too.

Don't shy away from this kind of help if you need it. Fighting the good fight pays off in more ways than one. Not only does it help you continually clear the air during the more difficult times of establishing a new balance between love and work, but it immeasurably improves your level of intimacy, both personal and sexual. The person you can fight with is the one you will trust with your fears and your worries. That is the only person you can trust with your love.

Something else happens, too: you prove your independence in a nonthreatening way. What you are basically doing is taking responsibility for your own feelings, which sounds easy but is difficult for many of us. And because you are not going to "give in" to one another without a good and healthy reason, you won't take each other for granted.

### Step Six: Reward each other

The first reward you will experience from establishing a better balance between you is likely to be more time to have fun together, whether your best times are at home with the children or getting away for a while. You will also find that your regular discussions assessing how things are going will become easier, if not downright enjoyable.

Other rewards should be special ways that you show each other your appreciation. Think of some tangible, affordable demonstrations of love, such as surprise day trips, unexpected little gifts, a warm touch, or a hug. Whatever means the most to the two of you, do it often. Another possible reward is to allow each other the opportunity to enjoy the solitary pursuits that appeal to each of you, whether it's cooking or reading or painting. Peace and quiet are energizing for many people.

Above all, show your appreciation daily. Laugh together every day. That's love.

### Step Seven: Dismantle and reinvent your balances when necessary

Each stage of your life will bring new changes, new challenges.

Be aware that when something does work well, even that is only temporary. If you have young children or are still adding children to your family, you will have to realign your balance at least once a year. If your children are older and your careers are stable, you may be able to coast along at this level for three years or more. Other factors influencing your balance may be job changes, health problems, or a growing awareness that what was balanced is now out of kilter.

As you grow more experienced, the time it takes to rebalance things between you should shorten from several months to just a few weeks. You will learn to stay alert for new options, and you will have a greater store of trust and confidence from your previous success.

## Playing the Game

The payoff for working to balance everything you want out of life isn't always getting everything you want. But you will awaken every morning with a warm, secure sense of moving forward toward exciting personal goals. There will be days when you're exhausted from juggling your multiple roles, but the deep satisfaction gained from your successes and your fascination with what the future may hold mean that even the "downtimes" are easier to manage. Your life is never dead-ended, but overflowing with possibilities.

But that is only the beginning. Your enthusiasm for "trying it all" imbues you with a riveting aura of independence that attracts exactly the kind of people you most want as friends and, possibly, lovers. Independence attracts independence.

What can happen next is the richest reward of all: the opportunity to share life's most treasured moments—the thrill of a hard-earned promotion, the exquisite touch of a gentle breeze, the shared glimpse of a child's beaming face—with someone as dynamic as you. And ahead is a future that you can face independently *and* together, a future that is always open-ended and ready to be shaped into what you most want it to be.

# Bibliography

## Books

Beavers, W. Robert. *Successful Marriage: A Family Systems Approach to Couples Therapy*. New York, London: W. W. Norton & Company, 1985.
Although written for the professional therapist, this book provides a clear presentation of the basic tenets of systems theory. I found it to be extremely helpful in understanding why being "equal partners" works well for so many couples. I recommend it highly for readers wanting a clinical analysis of these relationships.

Gilligan, Carol. *In a Different Voice: Psychological Theory and Women's Development*. Cambridge, Mass., and London: Harvard University Press, 1982.

Rilke, Rainer Maria. *Letters to a Young Poet*. New York: Vintage Books, 1986.

Rohrlick, Jay B. *Work & Love: The Crucial Balance*. New York: Crown, Harmony Books, 1980.

## Other Sources

Peterson, Sally H. *The New Dyad: Older Women and Younger Men*. A dissertation submitted to The Fielding Institute, 1984.

The Woman's Workshop Newsletter. Issues: summer 1988, fall 1988, winter 1989. P.O. Box 843, Coronado, CA 92118.

## Articles

Abramson, Jill. "For Women Lawyers, An Uphill Struggle." *New York Times Magazine* (March 6, 1988).

Bennett, Amanda. "The Baby-Busters." *Wall Street Journal* (October 26, 1988).

Bloom, David E., and Todd P. Steen, "Why Child Care Is Good for Business." *American Demographics* (August 1988).

Cole, K. C. "Play, by Definition, Suspends the Rules." *New York Times* (November 30, 1988).

Collins, Gail. "The Mommy Track to Nowhere." *New York Woman* (September 1989).

Conant, Jennet. "Playing Doctor at Conde Nast." *Manhattan, Inc.* (November 1988).

"Corporate Women: A Question of Balance." *Hartford Courant* (March 21, 1988).

Goleman, Daniel. "Therapists Find Last Outpost of Adolescence in Adulthood." *New York Times* (November 8, 1988).

Goleman, Daniel. "Want a Happy Marriage? Learn to Fight a Good Fight." *New York Times* (February 21, 1989).

Healy, Michelle. "Attentive Dads, Freedom Spur Kids to Success." *USA Today* (March 14, 1988).

Jacoby, Susan. "What's Worrying Americans Most in 1988?" *Family Circle* (January 12, 1988).

Larcen, Donna. "The Remarriage Pool." *Hartford Courant* (September 23, 1988).

Passell, Peter. "Earnings Plight of Baby Boomers." *New York Times* (September 21, 1988).

Pogrebin, Letty Cottin. "It Still Takes a Bride and Groom." *New York Times Magazine* (July 2, 1989).

Reardon, Patrick. "Projected Eligible-Women Shortage May Drive More Men to Marriage." *Hartford Courant* (October 30, 1988).

"The Reluctant Father." *Newsweek* (December 19, 1988).

Richardson, Brenda Lane. "Professional Women Do Go Home Again." *New York Times* (April 20, 1988).

Riche, Martha Farnsworth. "The Postmarital Society." *American Demographics* (November 1988).

Rimer, Sara. "Women, Jobs and Children: A New Generation Worries." *New York Times* (November 27, 1988).

Robinson, John P. "Who's Doing the Housework?" *American Demographics* (December 1988).

Rosen, Jan M. "Finding the Right Levels of Risk." *New York Times* (November 12, 1988).

Russell, Cheryl. "The Sure Thing." *American Demographics* (July 1988).

Schwartz, Felice N. "Management Women and the New Facts of Life," *Harvard Business Review* (January-February 1989).

Schwartz, Joe. "Closing the Gap." *American Demographics* (January 1988).

Stipp, Horst H. "What Is a Working Woman?" *American Demographics* (July 1988).

Waldrop, Judith. "The Fashionable Family." *American Demographics* (March 1988).

Wilson, Barbara Foley, and Kathryn A. London, "Going to the Chapel." *American Demographics* (December 1987).